GUIDE TO INTELLECTU

D0947339

OTHER ECONOMIST BOOKS

Guide to Analysing Companies
Guide to Business Modelling
Guide to Business Planning
Guide to Cash Management
Guide to Commodities
Guide to Country Risk
Guide to Decision Making
Guide to Economic Indicators
Guide to Emerging Markets
Guide to the European Union
Guide to Financial Management
Guide to Financial Markets
Guide to Hedge Funds
Guide to Investment Strategy
Guide to Management Ideas and Gurus
Guide to Managing Growth
Guide to Organisation Design
Guide to Project Management
Guide to Supply Chain Management
Numbers Guide
Style Guide

Book of Business Quotations
Book of Isms
Brands and Branding
Business Consulting
Business Strategy
Buying Professional Services
The Chief Financial Officer
Economics
Frugal Innovation
The Great Disruption
Managing Talent
Managing Uncertainty
Marketing
Marketing for Growth
Megachange – the world in 2050
Modern Warfare, Intelligence and Deterrence
Organisation Culture
Successful Strategy Execution
Unhappy Union

Directors: an A–Z Guide
Economics: an A–Z Guide
Investment: an A–Z Guide
Negotiation: an A–Z Guide

Pocket World in Figures

GUIDE TO INTELLECTUAL PROPERTY

What it is, how to protect it, how to exploit it

Stephen Johnson

PUBLICAFFAIRS
New York

The Economist in Association with
Profile Books Ltd. and PublicAffairs

First published in 2015 by Profile Books Ltd. in Great Britain.
Published in 2015 in the United States by PublicAffairs™,
a Member of the Perseus Books Group

The greatest care has been taken in compiling this book. However, no responsibility
can be accepted by the publishers or compilers for the accuracy of the information
presented.

Where opinion is expressed it is that of the author and does not necessarily coincide
with the editorial views of The Economist Newspaper.

While every effort has been made to contact copyright-holders of material produced or
cited in this book, in the case of those it has not been possible to contact successfully,
the author and publishers will be glad to make amendments in further editions.

PublicAffairs books are available at special discounts for bulk purchases in the U.S.
by corporations, institutions, and other organizations. For more information, please
contact the Special Markets Department at the Perseus Books Group, 2300 Chestnut
Street, Suite 200, Philadelphia, PA 19103, call (800) 810-4145, ext. 5000, or e-mail
special.markets@perseusbooks.com.

Typeset in EcoType by MacGuru Ltd
info@macguru.org.uk

Library of Congress Control Number: 2015939618
ISBN 978-1-61039-461-1 (PB)
ISBN 978-1-61039-462-8 (EB)

First Edition

10 9 8 7 6 5 4 3 2 1

In memory of Glen Hess
A great business lawyer, and a great human being

Contents

Figures and tables

Figures

Tables

Preface

I HAVE WORKED IN INTELLECTUAL PROPERTY LAW for over 30 years, initially at Bird & Bird in London and then at Kirkland & Ellis LLP in Chicago, New York and San Francisco. I now work with a not-for-profit organisation focusing on IP's role as an incentive for research.

The idea behind this book was to write a guide for business people and investors explaining the strengths and weaknesses of patents as collateral (security) for loans. That was over six years ago and there was a huge lack of communication between the worlds of finance and IP. Today, patents are increasingly being used as collateral and a market for patents is developing. However, IP remains an opaque area for many business people. The scope of the book has expanded, but the idea is to try to shed some practical, business-focused light on IP.

After starting my career in London, I arrived in the US at the end of 1982, which marked the founding of a new specialist patent appeals court, the Court of Appeals for the Federal Circuit, and the beginning of a new appreciation of the economic importance of strong intellectual property rights, initially in the US, then in Europe and the rest of the world. As a result, patents emerged from an obscure backwater and now play a central role in many industries. During the same period, the rise of the personal computer and the expansion of international brands led to the growth of industries based on copyright and trademarks, and IP assumed huge business importance throughout the world.

Today, however, the function of patents in stimulating innovation has been called into question by the mass of patent litigation in the smartphone industry and the activities of businesses that acquire existing patents simply to enforce them. The trend towards strengthening patent rights in the US has started reversing.

Legal mechanisms have also failed to cope well with the rampant piracy enabled through technology and the internet, and the balance of rights between the owners of intellectual property such as films and television shows and users of the internet remains a national political and international diplomatic issue. The law remains in constant movement and fundamental questions remain to be answered, or if answered in the past, are subject to review and revision.

Despite this uncertainty, an international IP strategy can still be developed, largely thanks to the legal frameworks established comparatively early in the history of industrialisation by such treaties as the Berne Convention on copyright in 1886. These treaties set out an international order for patents, trademarks, designs and copyrights, resulting in a degree of uniformity of general principles. This process of convergence continued in the 20th century globally and notably within the European Union, where, for example, UK IP law now relies heavily on European concepts.

Although an international IP strategy can be developed, it has to be implemented locally in major markets throughout the world. Considerable differences in IP law remain at a national level, even within the EU, and thus there may be differing results in individual countries.

In attempting to cover what is now a huge field (and to keep it a manageable size), this book is painted in parts with a broad brush, with an emphasis on the US, followed by the UK and Europe. However, Asia and especially China have become much more important with regard to IP. China is often characterised as a haven for copyists, but the reality is that the Chinese government and Chinese businesses are highly focused on filing for IP rights. Western businesses that ignore China in their IP strategy may well regret that decision in the future. In 2014 the first patent case addressing important issues on patents on industry standards reached the European Court of Justice. Tellingly, that case was not between US or European companies but between two Chinese groups, Huawei and ZTE.

The book focuses on the issues and principles that matter in running a business, and for those seeking a quick guide, the main points to note and strategic considerations are listed chapter by chapter in an executive summary at the back of the book. There is also a section containing useful information and resources for readers who may wish to track future changes in the law, which is in a constant and rapid state of flux. Extensive further references can also be found at www.profilebooks.com/stephen-johnson. However, as well as the rapidly changing state of the law, each IP issue depends on the facts and the specific country in question. This book is not intended to offer legal advice as to any country and in all situations a lawyer should be consulted.

I owe thanks first to Christopher Rees, a long-time friend and a partner at Taylor Wessing in London, who generously reviewed my manuscript from a UK and European perspective; to David Tenenbaum of Global Economics Group, who reviewed and contributed to the chapter on valuing IP; to Stephen Brough and Penny Williams and the team at Profile Books for their editing; to Andrew Clark, who checked facts and citations and made useful suggestions; and to my research assistant, Megumi Yukie. More generally, I owe thanks to all my colleagues and clients, who over the years have provided such interesting work as well as their friendship. However, please note that the content of (and mistakes in) this book are entirely my own, and that the views expressed are mine and do not reflect those of my current or former clients, or my current or former colleagues or employers. Lastly, thanks to my wife, Kimberly, who so generously encouraged and enabled this effort and to my children, Graham and Violet, who have lived through its long gestation.

Stephen Johnson
April 2015

1 An introduction to intellectual property

INTELLECTUAL PROPERTY (IP) is worth an enormous amount of money. A crude calculation of the value of intangible assets, including IP, held by public companies can be made by subtracting the value of financial and tangible assets from their market capitalisation. According to a survey by Ocean Tomo, an IP merchant bank, the implied share of intangible assets as a percentage of the value of the S&P 500 was 80% in 2010.[1] Although a portion of the intangible assets of corporations comprises goodwill (an accounting entry which addresses, for example, the value of an acquired business not attributable to identifiable assets), a substantial amount is attributable to IP, such as patents, designs, trademarks, domain names, copyrights, databases, trade secrets and know-how.

By default, investors in most publicly quoted companies are investing in intellectual property. Each year BrandZ, a global brand equity database, determines the world's most valuable brands. The leader in 2014 was Google, with a calculated brand value of over $158 billion.[2] According to the *Wall Street Journal*[3] and other sources, an actual transaction transferring the IKEA brand from a parent to a subsidiary company in 2012 valued the IKEA brand at $11 billion. A year earlier $4.5 billion was paid for the portfolio of patents owned by Nortel Networks, a bankrupt Canadian telecommunications company.

IP affects countries' economies. In March 2013, the US Bureau of

For a quick summary of points to note and
strategic considerations, go to page 280

Economic Analysis announced that it was changing the calculation of gross domestic product (GDP) to capture output based on IP and to recognise a new group of "intellectual property products" by capitalising research and development (R&D) spending and treating it as a balance-sheet asset, rather than treating it as an expense on the income statement, and adding to GDP a category of creative works, such as long-lasting television programmes. These and other technical changes in GDP calculation had the effect of increasing US GDP by 3%.

The US and Canada lead the world in viewing intellectual property as an investment asset in itself. For example, Intellectual Ventures was established in Seattle in 2000 by Nathan Myhrvold, formerly of Microsoft, and later Peter Detkin, formerly of Intel, to assemble a portfolio of patents acquired from third parties to be licensed to corporations, as well as to develop new intellectual property. And it is in Canada and the US that private equity funds have been established to focus on the acquisition of royalties arising under pharmaceutical or biotechnology licences. The idea of investing in "pure-play" IP has now spread to Europe and can be seen in the success of companies such as IP Group.

Individuals and organisations in the US have made a point of acquiring patents with a view to profiting from their enforcement. The large sums awarded in damages for patent infringement in the US (according to Lex Machina, a company providing statistical analysis of US IP litigation, the median amount for such awards was approximately $1.26 million in 2013, but with a much higher average amount of over $34 million as a result of some large awards),[4] together with the costs and uncertainties of litigation, have fostered an industry of professional plaintiffs that purchase patents for enforcement. They are often referred to in derogatory terms as "patent trolls", or more recently "non-practising entities" or "patent assertion entities" (PAEs), and some of them are publicly quoted. This type of patent enforcement, where the sole purpose is to obtain a financial reward, has, because of the costs imposed on the technology industry, become a political issue; it has also spurred patent reform legislation in the US that targets PAE litigation practices but arguably may weaken patent rights in general. Barack Obama addressed these issues in February 2013 and subsequently has taken action aimed at trying to counter some of the perceived ills of PAEs:[5]

> *The folks that you're talking about are a classic example; they don't actually produce anything themselves. They're just trying to essentially leverage and hijack somebody else's idea and see if they can extort some money out of them.*

However, research by historians of the patent system shows that an active market in patents and the involvement of investors is nothing new. B. Zorina Khan, a professor at Bowdoin College in the US, points to the *Railway Times* of 1870, which reported that in the US railroad industry:[6]

> *[There is] a ring of patent speculators, who with plenty of capital, brains, legal talent and impudence, have already succeeded in levying heavy sums upon every considerable railway company in the land. This case is not an isolated one, there are hundreds of them, and the railway company that made up its mind to insist upon its rights had to keep a large legal force, a corps of mechanical experts, and other expensive accessories, in order to secure that end.*

IP may be property, and valuable property at that, but it is very different from a tangible asset in the way that it is valued and treated for accounting purposes. IP developed internally may be invisible on an organisation's balance sheet because it is not recognised under generally accepted accounting principles (as *The Economist* stated in August 2014, "if it's intangible, bean-counters won't touch it"[7]). Methods of valuing IP remain, if not in their infancy, certainly still in adolescence. The same applies to markets for buying and selling IP. Legal aspects are far from settled. For example, the remedies available to owners of patents used in critical technical standards in the telecoms industry are only in the process of being clarified.

The market impact of successful patent challenges in the pharmaceutical industry, where patents on blockbuster drugs may be invalidated and generic medicines allowed onto the market, reveals that IP is an asset class where legal challenges and the scope of legal protection can have a dramatic impact on the fortunes of a company reliant on intellectual property. In 2015, for example, an activist US hedge fund announced that it would challenge certain types of patents on pharmaceuticals as part of a strategy of shorting the stock of the owners of those patents.

Equally, digital technologies and the internet have destroyed value for the holders of copyright and to a lesser degree the owners of brands. Virtually any user of the internet can copy and distribute copyrighted material. The impact on the music industry of illegal copying and sharing was early and severe. As technology developed and bandwidth broadened, film and television started to suffer. Technological change has also resulted in the publishing industry facing greater levels of copyright infringement.

For trademark owners, especially in the fashion industry, the internet has become a worldwide marketplace for the sale of counterfeit goods. The regulation and control of piracy on the internet remain controversial, and there are concerns about the effect on free speech of stricter controls. Meanwhile, organised crime has not been slow to take advantage of the internet in profiting from copyright piracy and counterfeiting as well as fraud; thus the internet has become a vehicle for cybercrime and hacking, with such dramatic examples as the hack of Sony Pictures in 2014 which revealed reams of corporate information.

Intellectual property is an intangible creation of the law and intellectual property rights can be enforced only through legal process. To capitalise on the value of this asset class, business people and investors need to understand the legal strengths and weaknesses of IP, how it may be protected, its practical and legal limitations, and how transactions or strategies may enhance or destroy its value. This book aims to explore these legal issues from a business perspective.

International norms, national systems

As noted in the Preface, IP's international legal standing dates back to the 19th century. The current international era dates back to the conclusion of the World Trade Organisation's Agreement on Trade-Related Aspects of Intellectual Property Rights (TRIPS) negotiated as part of the 1986 to 1994 Uruguay Round of trade negotiations. TRIPS substantially raised the standards for the protection of intellectual property, and it requires minimum standards from all WTO members. TRIPS builds on two fundamental older treaties: the Paris Convention, which covers international patent, trademark and design rights in member states; and the Berne Convention, which covers copyright protection in member states. In addition, TRIPS legislates for the topography of integrated circuits and the protection of trade secrets.

Although treaties have led to a degree of harmonisation and simplified the process for applying for registrations of intellectual property internationally, the legal rights underlying intellectual property generally remain national in nature, and ownership and other legal rights may differ along national lines. Litigation in the phone industry also shows that differing legal systems may lead to differing results in related litigation in different countries.

Notwithstanding or possibly because of TRIPS, IP has become both a diplomatic and a business issue internationally. According to a 2012 article in the *Financial Times*, "Intellectual Property: A New World of Royalties", the US ("the imperial capital of intellectual property rights") now earns almost as much from royalty and licence fees from abroad as it does from farm exports.[8] It was felt that TRIPS pushed the agendas of technologically advanced countries as opposed to those of the developing world, particularly in the field of pharmaceuticals. This is still an issue with India and other developing countries (see below), but it is by no means always a developing-world issue. A dispute has begun to develop between the US and Canada over implementation of Canadian patent law leading to invalidation of Canadian patents owned by US companies.

Meanwhile, the US is seeking to protect its creative industries against infringement. For example, the intellectual property provisions of the pending Trans-Pacific Partnership (TPP) treaty – between the US, Canada, Mexico, Australia, Brunei, Chile, Peru, Japan, Malaysia, New Zealand, Singapore and Vietnam – expand on and go further than TRIPS, and seek to further protect the interests of copyright and other IP owners. In the process, the US is pitting not only the differing economic agendas of countries in different stages of economic development against each other, but also the interests of industries such as entertainment and software, which are dramatically affected by piracy, against those of large internet companies such as Google and Yahoo, which are wary of being required to police users who may be committing those acts of piracy, as well as against advocates of free speech.

By contrast, the interests of large internet companies seem to have influenced the agenda on issues such as protection of data privacy, where proposed changes in EU regulation have prompted a massive lobbying effort in Brussels to enable these companies to maintain their current business models of monetising data. More than 4,000 amendments – a record – were proposed for the latest draft of the EU Data Protection Regulation. As a result of Edward Snowden's intelligence revelations, data privacy has become a major diplomatic issue.

However, outside the area of data privacy, it is probably fair to say that in the US and Canada, the EU, Australia, New Zealand and Japan the similarities between approaches to IP outweigh the differences. For example, each of these regions has historically accounted for the majority of international patent filings under the Patent Cooperation Treaty (PCT), which is the primary international treaty allowing for multiple international patent filings in a streamlined manner.

The BRIC countries

In the BRIC countries (Brazil, Russia, India and China) attitudes to intellectual property vary enormously. China may have a poor record of prosecution of "knock-offs" in the fashion and entertainment industries and a history of software piracy, but according to OECD statistics between 1995 and 2005 its international patent filings grew by an annual average of 33%. China entered the top 15 patent filing countries in 2005 and now is among the top five filers of patents under the PCT. It is also developing rapidly in terms of the importance of IP, as Chinese companies and individuals become more innovative and benefit from IP protection. For example, in 2013 ZTE Corporation and Huawei were among the top filers of PCT patents, according to the World Intellectual Property Organisation (WIPO).

Patent filings have become a focus of Chinese government policy, with ambitious patent filing targets being set in the National Patent Development Strategy 2011–20. In the area of infringement, in 2010 the government launched a "special campaign" against IP infringement and counterfeiting, which led to judicial and administrative changes as well as increased enforcement activity. Subsequent moves by the government suggest a more determined commitment to dealing with issues such as piracy. Some observers, however, have highlighted policies aimed at encouraging indigenous innovation in China, which could be perceived as discriminating against other countries.

Between 1995 and 2005, India's patent filings grew by 26% per year on average. By contrast, Russia became a member of the WTO only in December 2011. Following new laws and commitments to improve its protection of intellectual property, there has been a significant increase in patent filings in Russia, but from a low base. Table 1.1 shows the balance of external royalty payments for the BRIC and selected other countries in 2013.

TABLE 1.1 **Intellectual property: balance of external royalty payments, $ million, 2013**

	Payments	Receipts	Net
US	39,016	129,178	90,162
Japan	17,831	31,587	13,756
Germany	8,399	12,908	4,509
UK	9,037	12,947	3,910
France	10,150	11,556	1,406
Brazil	3,669	597	−3,072
India	3,904	446	−3,458
Russia	8,389	738	−7,651
China	21,033	887	−20,146

Source: World Bank (http://data.worldbank.org)

Brazil and India may be grouped together superficially, in that each has the treaties and laws in place following TRIPS to protect intellectual property, but in practice IP rights remain problematic and inefficient. However, Brazil does appear to see IP protection as an economic driver, whereas India gave the impression of being more ambivalent.

However, in 2014, the administration of the new prime minister, Narendra Modi, has expressed an intent to draw up policies on IP.

Although the information technology (IT) sector in India may be regarded as being pro-intellectual property, and India has been a forum in the worldwide patent "phone wars", the country's pharmaceutical industry has historically been opposed to patent protection as restricting the production of generic drugs and thereby denying poor people access to medicine. India now provides patent protection to drugs following the TRIPS round, but litigation over the scope of rights continues. For example, one of many disputes over drug patentability led to a March 2012 headline in the *New York Times*, "Patent v. Patient".[9] However, in July 2013 the *Financial Times* reported that an Indian health-care company, Zydus Cadila, had brought to the market a new chemical entity – a treatment for diabetes – that was discovered and developed in India.[10] Thus over time, as India moves from being a low-cost producer of generic drugs to an innovator, attitudes may change.

What is intellectual property?

What does the term intellectual property mean? Put simply, it is a collective term for patents, trademarks, copyrights, design rights, trade secrets and other similar rights (a couple of decades ago patent lawyers woke up and found they were intellectual property lawyers, which sounded a lot better). According to the WIPO website, "intellectual property refers to creations of the mind".[11] Intellectual property is often distinguished from real property, meaning land and buildings and other structures attached to land, and personal property, which generally refers to items that you can pick up and touch and move around, such as a book or a laptop. Confusingly, however, in many systems IP is technically a form of personal property. As stated in the UK Patents Act of 1977: "Any patent or application for a patent is personal property."

IP law covers a set of rights in works, inventions, ideas and information and how they are expressed or used, and the ways in which the products of companies are recognised by consumers and in the marketplace. As a general rule, intellectual property laws prevent or set limits on copying or use of these types of rights. Furthermore, the rights of an owner of intellectual property to prevent such copying or use vary by geography and time depending on the rights obtained in a particular country and whether those rights are in force or have expired or have been lost.

For example, if you buy a hard copy of this book in England, you own that copy and the law that applies is the law of personal property. However, I as the author own the copyright in the text, and as copyright owner I have the right to determine who may make copies of this text. I have entered into a "licence" (a permission to use a patent, trademark, copyright, trade secret or other form of IP) with the publisher of the book, Profile Books, to allow it to publish the book. Profile in turn has a licence to use the Economist trademark from the owner, The Economist Newspaper Limited, which controls how that trademark is used and can prevent unauthorised use.

The ownership of the copyright, what rights it gives me, the ownership of the Economist brand and the rights to that brand are all governed by intellectual property law. If you are reading this book using a laptop or tablet, that device incorporates hundreds if not thousands of inventions, the inventors of which have been granted patents. A number of those patents no longer have legal effect or will have "expired" because of the passage of time since the patent was obtained. Some may be owned by the laptop or tablet manufacturer, and others by third parties. Some of the third-party patents may have been licensed in a cordial business negotiation, but others may have been asserted by third parties in expensive litigation resulting in the laptop or tablet manufacturer agreeing to pay for the right to use those patents. Patents are a form of intellectual property, and all the issues of patent ownership, duration and infringement are governed by intellectual property law.

From a business perspective, the single most important piece of intellectual property relating to the laptop or tablet may not necessarily be any one of the patents but rather the brand of the device itself, for example Dell, Apple or Lenovo. Others may argue that the most important intellectual property rights may be those of the developer of the operating system, for example Microsoft, which owns the copyright in the operating system programs used by Dell and Lenovo and also owns many thousands of patents on inventions relating to its software.

Rights to all these types of intellectual property are enforced through a legal process. The owner of a piece of land may build fences or walls to keep others out or otherwise practise self-help, but the owner of a piece of intellectual property must generally go through litigation to enforce his or her rights. An intellectual property right is in many ways just a right to use the judicial system to exclude others from copying or using the owner's creation. IP thus inevitably brings with it the cost of enforcement. Apart from the common features of the intangible nature of the right and its dependence on legal process, patents, trademarks, copyrights and other types of IP are quite different in their business and legal characteristics. Briefly, these forms of intellectual property are as follows.

Patents

At one end of the spectrum are patents, which protect inventions by preventing others from making or using the invention. The legal rights granted by patents may be powerful, but patents are legally complex, expensive to obtain from a government agency, expensive to enforce, of limited duration and subject to numerous legal attacks and technicalities that may destroy their value. Patents are covered in more detail in Chapter 2. A lesser form of patent known as a "utility model" is important in China.

Trademarks

Trademarks and brands primarily relate to the association of the mark or brand with a particular company or "source". A trademark identifies a trusted manufacturer of a product: for example, Cadbury or Hershey brands of chocolate, or Shell or BP brands of oil. However, trademark law also protects company names and many other forms of identifier. In many countries, registration is required for the protection of trademarks. Trademarks are covered in more detail in Chapter 3.

Domain names are related to trademark rights and are covered in more detail in Chapter 7, which deals with internet issues.

Copyrights

At the other extreme are copyrights, which protect literary, musical and other forms of creative expression, including software, from being copied. In most countries, works of authorship are protected once created (as I write this book, for example, copyright is being created word by word). Although considerable complexities and expenses surround copyright ownership and enforcement, the act of obtaining legal protection for copyrights is almost automatic and cost-free. Copyrights are covered in more detail in Chapter 4. In the EU a "database right" was introduced in 1995 to give protection to information arranged systematically in databases. This approach has not generally been followed outside Europe, but within the EU member states it remains an additional layer of protection for collections of data.

Design rights

Copyright protection is generally not available for utilitarian objects, although standards for copyrightability vary and protection may exist in some countries for works of applied art or for a utilitarian object that rises to the level of a piece of art. Thus, for example, copyright may protect an original design on a fabric, but it may not protect the design of a bag made from that fabric. Design rights are intended to fill this gap. In the US there is a special form of patent called a design patent that may be applied for from the US Patent and Trademark Office. In the EU, design rights are protected under the Community Design Regulation and at a national level. Design rights are covered in more detail in Chapter 5.

Trade secrets

Trade secrets are a form of property that exists in information of value that has been kept secret or, where disclosed, that disclosure is subject to agreement by the recipients to keep the information confidential. Trade secrets do not require any registration or other procedures, but physical and IT measures, as well as contractual protections, must be put in place to preserve the confidential nature of the information. Trade secrets are covered in more detail in Chapter 6.

Plants and native species

Plants may be protected by many forms of intellectual property. In the US, potential protection includes special plant patents, plant variety protection (also known as plant breeders' rights) and, if the invention requirements are satisfied, normal "utility" patents on the plant. Protection varies among countries, but under Article 27(3)(b) of TRIPS countries are required to provide for the protection of plant varieties "either by patents or by an effective *sui generis* system or by any combination thereof".

IP protection of plants is contentious both in the US, where restrictions on the use of genetically engineered traits have been challenged by farmers in the courts, and internationally, where IP politics among developed and less-developed countries are an issue. As a specialist area, it is beyond the scope of this book.

A related issue among developed and less-developed countries is local medical knowledge and the use of local genetic resources. For many years, natural substances and traditional medicines have been a source of drugs. Controversies have arisen from time to time where patents have been obtained in the West on traditional remedies (for example, the use of turmeric to promote wound healing, US Patent No. 5,401,504), and there have been IP issues relating to the anti-bacterial qualities of New Zealand manuka honey.

The Nagoya Protocol is a treaty that governs, among other matters, the sharing of benefits from the use of plant genetic resources. This is not a matter of intellectual property as such, but rather an intangible right (see www.cbd.int). The WIPO is also working on a text that may serve as a future treaty protecting genetic resources.

Forms of protection

A single item may be protected through various forms of intellectual property. For example, when I wrote the first draft of this chapter I was working on a plane, and wished that fluctuations in the power supply to my laptop from the aircraft power system did not affect screen brightness. Suppose that an entrepreneur had the same idea and roughed out a concept for a device that would connect to the USB port of a laptop and interact with its systems to optimise screen brightness and power use when travelling. Suppose also that the entrepreneur plans to work with an electrical engineer and a software writer to perfect the technology and then with a design engineer to develop the device itself.

At this stage, the entrepreneur has a novel idea that may be protectable. A number of forms of intellectual property may be applicable. By contrast, there may be a number of ways in which the entrepreneur may lose intellectual property rights or even transfer them to others:

- **Trade secrets.** Ideas must be kept confidential and others to whom they are disclosed must also keep them confidential.
- **Patents.** The entrepreneur may already have or may develop patentable inventions. Or the engineers with whom the entrepreneur works may make the inventions. The entrepreneur must make sure that he owns what the engineers invent and decide whether to file for a patent or patents.
- **Design protection.** If the entrepreneur comes up with a pleasing design for the plug-in device, that design may be protectable. Or the design may be developed by someone to whom the work has been contracted.
- **Copyrights.** The software that controls the device to be written by the engineers may be protectable through copyright. Again, the entrepreneur wants to own that copyright.
- **Trademark and brand protection.** The entrepreneur may seek a trademark for the product, for example "XYZlight".
- **Domain names.** In conjunction with choosing the brand name, the entrepreneur may wish to obtain rights to XYZlight.com.

In this simple example there are at least six different forms of intellectual property that may apply or be obtained. In brief, however, in order not to risk losing them, the entrepreneur will have to register or take other steps to protect the different rights, with the exception of copyright. And when working with someone else, the contract will need to specifically spell out whether the entrepreneur is to own the IP rights and assign those rights. The types of IP, the process of applying for IP rights and issues relating to ownership are described in subsequent chapters.

Other forms of intangible property

Rights of personality

The descriptions above cover some traditional categories of intellectual property. However, there is a blurred line between intellectual property and other intangible assets or legal rights. For example, in the US movie stars may have rights of personality or rights of publicity through which they can control commercial use of their image. Under English law, as confirmed in a 2015 case involving Rihanna, a singer and actor, no such equivalent right exists, but a celebrity may successfully rely on other theories.

Personal information

Although not intellectual property in the traditional sense, personal information about individuals obtained, for example, through their use of websites is subject to protection under the laws of many countries. Personal information is not the same as confidential information because the information may be known to a number of people but not broadly known. Information about consumers, although not strictly secret, is immensely valuable, and the tension between protection of personal information and its exploitation and misuse is one of the political and policy issues of the moment.

The law has yet to develop a coherent and consistent approach to aggregations of "mere information". This is an understated way of describing "big data". Data has been described by Neelie Kroes, the European Commission's former vice-president responsible for the Digital Agenda, as "new oil for the digital age".[12] Just as ownership and protection of oil interests became a paramount concern of the industrial economy, so it is inevitable that the ownership and protection of big data will attract the attention of lawyers and policymakers in the coming years.

Permits, government licences and contracts

Certain permits or governmental authorisations are immensely valuable and may serve as barriers to entry. One example would be an approved application to market a pharmaceutical product. Another would be the right to broadcast in a particular region. Contracts are not intellectual property rights, but they may also be valuable and provide a barrier to entry. For example, an exclusive dealership for a country may be the basis of an entire business.

Intellectual capital

Many would say that modern companies are especially reliant on intellectual property or knowledge in its broadest sense – what some have termed "intellectual capital". This book does not address all forms of intellectual capital, but it does examine the main components of IP in a business and investment context.

Building IP into a business strategy

This introduction presents a number of reasons for businesses to focus on IP as a strategic issue. First, IP can be valuable. Second, its value may be lost as a result of a failure to obtain ownership, through expensive legal challenges or through piracy. Third, there are a number of complementary available protections for IP domestically and internationally that can be used to establish ownership, reduce risk and support the wider business strategy. However, an IP strategy needs to take into account IP's legal strengths and weaknesses as well as its practical limitations. For example, experience shows that legal remedies are unlikely to plug the holes in a business model that encourages international piracy.

This book covers all major forms of IP. Chapter 16 discusses developing an overall IP strategy, but there are some priorities:

- All businesses should obtain ownership of or rights to IP developed for their business and ensure that their IP (such as confidential information) cannot simply be taken by employees or contractors. This is implemented through well-drafted contracts with employees, consultants and contractors that cover IP ownership.

- If ownership is handled correctly by contract, copyright protection should at a basic level take care of itself because of the lack of registration required. The same applies to unregistered design rights. The sensitivity of personal information held by many businesses and the prevalence of hacking should also drive good confidentiality and security practices in most situations.

■ Good IP management may mitigate many risks. Simple steps such as establishing ownership of IP, filing for registrations and patents, and systematically managing both the IP and licences to and from third parties may avoid unnecessary disputes.

■ At a more sophisticated level, the biggest IP asset of most businesses is their name and brand, and this should often be considered the primary asset for protection. Beyond that, it more or less comes down to the kind of business you are running. In a technology or life sciences field patents are paramount; many creative businesses, however, rely on copyright as a source of revenue; and for any business selling products to customers, branding and design rights are key.

Not all readers will need to study Chapter 2 on patents, but the other chapters are broadly applicable.

2   Patents

THIS CHAPTER ADDRESSES PATENTS – what they do, how to obtain them, what rights they give, and their strengths and weaknesses. Patents protect inventions from being copied. Strategically, patents protect product sales from competitors and level the playing field with patent-owning competitors (see Chapter 10), may be used to generate income from licences (see Chapter 11) and are considered important although not well understood by the financial community (see Chapters 14 and 15).

A patent is a statutory right granted as a reward for making a useful invention. The patent system is based on the belief that creativity will be fostered by granting a statutory right of exclusivity to inventors in return for them making their inventions public. As Abraham Lincoln, himself an inventor, said: "The patent system added the fuel of interest to the fire of genius."

The UK has the longest continuous tradition of patents. In 1449 Henry VI granted a patent to the Flemish-born John of Utynam, giving him a 20-year monopoly for a method of making stained glass used in the chapel at Eton College. In the US, patents are enshrined in the constitution, which includes the following paragraph giving authority to the legislature:

For a quick summary of points to note and
strategic considerations, go to page 282

To promote the Progress of Science and useful Arts, by securing for limited Times to Authors and Inventors the exclusive Right to their respective Writings and Discoveries.

The patent right enables the patent owner to exclude third parties (infringers) from practising a patented invention for a prescribed number of years, and in return patent owners must disclose their invention to the public.

The generally accepted rationale for patents is to provide an incentive for innovation. This incentive is seen most clearly in the pharmaceutical industry, where strong patent protection in developed countries is regarded as a pre-condition to incurring the expenses of product development. It is seen least clearly in the world of technology, where thousands of patents may cover a single device and many patented features may have been developed at little cost even in the absence of patent protection. Patents also enable inventions to be commercialised through providing a defined property right that can be sold, licensed or otherwise made the subject of a business transaction. Patents are the way in which much technology developed by universities is commercialised.

There are several essential truths about patents:

- **They must be sufficiently inventive.** Not just any development will qualify for patent protection. A patentable invention has to be new and not obvious in respect of the prior state of the technology in question. There must also be no statutory bars to obtaining a patent. In Europe, for example, an invention must be kept secret before the filing of a patent application. Patent applications are generally subject to examination by the patent office in the country (or region, in the case of an application for a European patent) in which the patent is sought to determine whether the invention merits the grant of a patent.

- **They are always open to challenge.** Even though a patent is examined by a patent office it is still vulnerable to challenge for being invalid (that is, failing to satisfy the statutory standards for patentability). The correct scope and interpretation of patents are also subject to legal debate. Thus the enforcement of patents often raises a large number of legal issues and arguments. A defendant accused of patent infringement will often seek to have the patent challenged as invalid and will carry out extensive searches for prior publications or prior uses to render the patented invention not novel or obvious, and hence invalid.

- **They vary hugely in value.** The commercial value of patents varies enormously. Studies show that many or most patents cover inventions that have no commercial value. However, some patents may be immensely valuable. This may be because one company is able to prevent others from making a single valuable product (for example, a blockbuster pharmaceutical product), or because many companies pay to use the patented invention. For example, in 2013, Microsoft earned $1 billion in patent royalties from Samsung alone on Android phone sales and has licences with many other phone manufacturers. However, even though a product may be a huge commercial success, the patent supposedly protecting that product may have fatal flaws; and, as sometimes seen in the pharmaceutical industry, the patent may be revoked, thus destroying the product's profitability. With patents, what you see is not necessarily what you get.

- **They are not automatically usable.** A patent does not give the owner the right to do anything. In many countries, for example, the developer of a new patented antibody for therapeutic purposes would have had to obtain rights from a number of companies owning prior patents that covered technologies necessary to manufacture the new antibody. Thus a patented invention may be dominated or blocked by prior patents that, unless licensed, may prevent commercialisation of the invention.

Note that this chapter addresses "invention" or "utility" patents – see Chapter 5 for design patents.

There are a number of steps to be considered when applying for a patent:

- Is the invention of a type that may be patented?
- Is the invention already public? Is there time to file for a patent given any prior public disclosures, uses or sales of the invention?

- Is the invention patentable in terms of being sufficiently inventive, new and not obvious?
- Who drafts the patent?
- In which patent office will it be filed?
- How will international protection be obtained and in which countries?

There are also the matters of whether the applicant has the right to file for the patent (this is a question of ownership and inventorship and is dealt with in Chapter 8), and how much the process will cost (which is covered in Chapter 9).

What kinds of invention can be patented?

The US patent statute (35 USC. 101) sets out what may be patented:

Whoever invents or discovers any new and useful process, machine, manufacture, or composition of matter ... may obtain a patent therefor.

In Europe, Article 52 of the European Patent Convention (also known as the Convention on the Grant of European Patents) states:

European patents shall be granted for any inventions, in all fields of technology, provided that they are new, involve an inventive step [broadly meaning not obvious] and are susceptible of industrial application.

The Japanese Patent Act is unusual in defining what is meant by an invention as "the highly advanced creation of technical ideas utilising the laws of nature". This follows German thinking, which underlies Japanese law. China has followed the basic concepts of these systems, and the requirements for novelty, inventiveness and industrial application are enshrined in the WTO's Agreement on Trade-Related Aspects of Intellectual Property Rights (TRIPS). Therefore they are found in most patent systems throughout the world.

Patents may be obtained for "things" and for processes or methods. Thus patents may be obtained for machines, chemical compositions, different types of structures and all kinds of processes, including chemical and biological. The products of patented processes may also be subject to protection.

However, over the past 30 years and continuing today, patents as a form of property have been subject to both political and ethical debate over the scope of what should be patentable. In the area of life sciences, the debate has ranged from fundamental questions of whether patents should be obtained on sequences of DNA, or living organisms from bacteria to plants to genetically modified animals, to the often economically driven extent to which medicines should be patented, which pitted Western governments against those of developing countries during the TRIPS negotiations.

In the US, the Supreme Court has outlawed patents on abstract ideas, laws of nature and natural principles, natural phenomena and natural products. In broad terms, the court has taken the line that to be patentable, an invention must amount to "significantly more" than an ineligible concept or something occurring in nature.

While in the US the scope of patentable subject matter has generally been decided by the courts by way of "judicial exceptions" to the categories of patentable processes, machines, manufactures, or compositions of matter set out in the patent statute, in Europe certain limits are set out in the European Patent Convention (Article 52). This excludes from patentability discoveries, scientific methods and mathematical models, aesthetic creations, schemes, rules and methods for performing mental acts, playing games or doing business, programs for computers, and presentations of information, but only to the extent that the European patent "relates to such subject matter or activities as such". This "as such" language has, however, been narrowly interpreted so as to allow, for example, inventions that use a computer program but are technical in nature. At least one senior US judge has said that the new US Supreme Court cases "for all intents and purposes, set out a technological arts test for patentability", so the differing international approaches may to some extent be converging.

Laws of nature, genes and diagnostic tests

In 2012 the US Supreme Court decided in *Mayo Collaborative Services v Prometheus Laboratories Inc.* that medical tests based on correlations between drug concentrations in the blood and treatment efficacy were not patentable. This was because they were merely an abstract idea based on a natural phenomenon. In 2013, in the case of *Myriad Genetics*, a molecular diagnostic company, the court decided that isolated and purified human DNA as contained in genetic tests for certain important breast cancer genes (BRCA) was not patentable because it was a product of nature. However, certain DNA sequences (cDNA) used in tests and allegedly not found in nature were held by the Supreme Court to be patentable.

Because a diagnosis of certain BRCA mutations may give an indication of a high likelihood of contracting breast cancer, and thus diagnostic tests are a genuine life-saver and a huge medical advance, the Myriad case generated considerable interest, highlighting the issue of whether patentability is necessary to encourage necessary innovation, or whether a patent raises the cost to end users – patients in this instance – or deters new research. The decision in the case was sufficiently specific not to address these fundamental issues because a number of patent claims covering the diagnostic test were not challenged in the litigation. However, Myriad continued to enforce its patents, and yet more of its patent claims to tests were invalidated in December 2014 on the basis that they used only conventional steps in addition to the abstract idea of comparing DNA sequences. It remains to be seen what is patentable in the area of DNA-based diagnostic kits in the US and the extent to which more specific patents will be upheld. This raises considerable uncertainty for investors in the type of diagnostics needed for personalised medicine as well as for patients hoping for better diagnostics generally.

Following the Prometheus and Myriad cases, in 2013, in *Ariosa Diagnostics Inc. v Sequenom*, at the trial court level, a patent covering a prenatal test for Downs syndrome and other conditions was declared invalid (US Patent No. 6,258,540). The invention was made at Oxford University and licensed to Sequenom, a US biotech company. It enables prenatal diagnosis of fetal conditions through the discovery that the DNA of a fetus (including DNA from the father) is actually present in the blood plasma of the mother and can be analysed. The invention is a huge advance because a simple blood sample may be taken from the mother as opposed to needing a sample from the fetus itself through the invasive process of amniocentesis, which is risky and stressful. However, the invention was found to be invalid, as it allegedly added nothing patentable to a naturally occurring phenomenon – and so the competitor charged with infringement was free to sell its test. In a dramatic example of the importance of patents in the medical field and the business impact of developments in patent law, the shares of the party seeking to enforce the patent, Sequenom, fell by over one-fifth following the court's decision. The case went to appeal. (The patent is discussed further below.)

Further US litigation related to the famous (or infamous) sheep Dolly. The court decided that an invention covering a sheep genetically identical to a natural sheep was not eligible for a patent, and that patentability would require something "markedly different" from that found in nature. This type of requirement for patentability of something significantly different from or more than something found in nature or a mere concept seems to be crucial to the approach of the US Supreme Court.

One interesting aspect of the Myriad litigation is that in some ways the issues are peculiarly American. This is for two reasons. First, the logic of the Supreme Court that naturally occurring compounds should not be patentable may not apply under the laws of other countries and has, for example, been specifically rejected in a subsequent Australian case involving Myriad. Second, diagnostic patents are not always enforced under government-run health-care systems. A report on gene patents and diagnostic testing in the UK has found that such patents have more or less been ignored by potential infringers and not enforced by patent owners.

Stem cells

In Europe, by contrast, there has been much controversy over the scope of permissible patenting of human embryonic stem-cell-related inventions, where the applicable Biotech Directive 98/44 prohibits in Article 6(2)(c) the patentability of "uses of human embryos for industrial or commercial purposes" as being contrary to "ordre public [public policy] or morality". In December 2014, the European Court of Justice decided that the prohibition applies only to cells that have the capacity to develop into a human being. No parallel law exists in the US to the same extent.

Software

There has been equally intense debate over the extent to which computer software should be the subject of patent protection as opposed to copyright protection for a program (see below). Different answers have been reached in the US, Europe and the rest of the world. Many (but not all) companies in the software industry feel that the perceived difficulty of defining the scope of software patents plays into the hands of patent assertion entities (PAEs). If a patent is uncertain in scope, a plaintiff can sue under such patents, relying on their ambiguity and on the large legal fees involved in obtaining clarity on scope to force a settlement (see Chapter 11). However, others feel equally strongly that the software industry needs strong software patents. In the case of *Alice Corp. v CLS Bank International*, the issue was how to identify whether a claim covers just an abstract idea (in this case relating to reducing risk in settlement of trades) and thus is not patentable, or whether it contains a patentable computer implementation.

Although not deciding exactly what an abstract idea is, the US Supreme Court found that mere generic computer implementation failed to make the idea in question patentable. Uncreative computer implementation of an idea was not enough to supply the innovative concept necessary for a patent. Subsequent to *Alice v CLS*, a number of issued patents which merely claimed general concepts implemented by known computer technology have been found invalid. As well as being closely watched from the perspective of the value and scope of software and business method patents, the case was significant in the banking world because CLS plays a significant role as an intermediary in foreign-exchange markets. The case brings US law more in line with the European approach.

Business methods

There has been a similar debate over the patentability of business methods and financial instruments. In the US, the Supreme Court decided in *Bilski v Kappos* in 2010 that methods of doing business may be patentable as a "process", even though the particular invention, a method of hedging risk in a commodity market, was not patentable because it was found to be simply an abstract idea and thus not a patentable process. The Supreme Court expressed the view that although an abstract idea, law of nature, or mathematical formula could not be patented, "an application of a law of nature or mathematical formula to a known structure or process may well be deserving of patent protection". This arrives at the same conclusion as the Japanese approach to a patentable invention mentioned above. In Europe, the prevailing view is that under the European Patent Convention a pure business method cannot be patented.

Theory and practice

Certain types of invention may be out of bounds, but patent agents and attorneys are expert at writing patents in ways that try to ensure that the invention as described and claimed falls within the statutory requirements. In addition, the US patent office publishes guidance on patent eligibility that takes into account decisions in recent cases. For example, as noted above, a patent may not be obtained in the US on a purified and naturally occurring DNA sequence, but DNA-based diagnostic products may well remain patentable. In such cases, however, the patent that can be obtained is likely to be narrow in scope. Unfortunately, whether narrower patents provide sufficient incentives for investment will take years to work out. However, standards vary between countries and regions, so whether an invention is patentable should not be decided based solely on local law. If a valuable patent may be obtained in the US, or Europe, or major Asian markets, it may be worthwhile applying for it, unless the process of patenting would reveal trade secrets that would protect sales in regions where patents could not be obtained.

Recent cases do cause problems in regard to issued patents that may have had claims drafted to comply with prior law and businesses relying on those patents. Here settled business expectations may be upset.

FIG 2.1 **Simplified patent filing sequence**

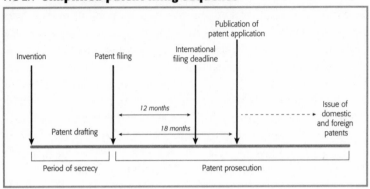

Source: Author

When should a patent be obtained?

Many countries (other than historically the US) have a doctrine of "absolute novelty" for patents. This means that the invention cannot have been disclosed publicly or sold before the filing of a patent. It is therefore essential if contemplating international patent protection to file for a patent before any commercialisation or other public disclosure. Prior publication that destroys patentability is a common occurrence in academia, and may amount to no more than a conference poster describing an invention. It is also best to file as soon as possible, given that priority goes to the first to file. Under the America Invents Act, the US in 2013 replaced its historical "first to invent" system by a "first to file" system that has a limited exception of one year for prior publication by the inventor. Once a patent application has been filed, there are time limits, usually of one year, for filing international applications based on the priority of that first filing. A simplified version of the patent filing sequence is shown in Figure 2.1.

Patent searches

To be valid, patents have to cover inventions that are sufficiently novel and not obvious (in Europe, they must have a sufficient "inventive step"). A company planning a substantial investment in a new product line should ask:

- If the product is brought to market, can a third party claim patent infringement?
- Can the company obtain patents that would protect the product in the marketplace because the invention embodied in the product is new and not obvious?

Answers to these questions can be obtained through two kinds of searches: a "freedom to operate" search; and a "prior art" or "patentability" search. These searches used to be carried out by skilled patent searchers, who would look through the libraries of patents and publications associated with patent offices and use various searching methodologies to track down relevant documents, including the ways in which patent offices classify technologies into certain categories. Many thorough searches are still carried out in this way. However, as more and more patents and publications are available online, to save costs searches of varying degrees of thoroughness may be carried out remotely anywhere in the world over the internet. The internet has also provided new methods of finding prior art, such as crowdsourced prior art search services (that is, a search for pre-existing relevant patents and other publications in the field).

The US Patent and Trademark Office has an extensive website (www.uspto.gov) with many tools to search for pending and issued patents. Similar resources are available on the European Patent Office website (www.epo.org). Patent searching is a sophisticated field and much information has to be sifted through. For instance, taking the example of the power controller in Chapter 1, a simple word search on uspto.gov reveals that there are many issued US patents with the term "power controller" in the title. One belongs to Sony and is entitled "Power Controller and Power Control for a Portable Contents Player". That patent could possibly be relevant. However, a search would go far, far beyond the title of patents; indeed, their titles are often not a useful guide to what they cover.

A prior art or patentability search is in many ways easier to conduct than a freedom to operate search. For example, in the case of the power controller, the idea of the invention is a plug-in device that regulates power fluctuations. A search may be carried out in a patent office and over the internet to see whether that idea or refinements of it have been patented before, and how close the design and technology are to those of the new device. A freedom to operate search to guard against infringement of third-party patents is much harder. This is because infringement may not come from the basic idea of the device itself, but from a single feature of the product, such as a patent covering use of the USB connection as a power supply. Furthermore, the scope of patents is always open to interpretation so their boundaries may often be unclear.

However, rather than boiling the ocean, freedom to operate searches can be focused by, for example, looking at patents owned by specific competitors that may be likely to sue for infringement. And searches for prior art can focus on prior work by businesses known to be active in the field.

Searches have significant cost implications and, particularly in the US, potential legal implications. Some patent filers take the view that the patent office will carry out a prior art search when a patent application is filed, so why go to the expense of an independent search before filing for a patent? Patent filers worry that any relevant prior art that is known to an applicant for a patent is, broadly, required to be disclosed to the US patent office when seeking a patent.

What matters, however, is not just obtaining a patent, but obtaining a patent that is strong, which is why investors should look at the patents of start-ups with a critical eye. A strong patent is one which is granted after all the relevant prior art has been put before the patent office and overcome, so there is less likelihood of it being challenged later on the grounds of invalidity (see below). Furthermore, a search may reveal commercially useful information about third-party patents and products.

But even before a search is started, there are a number of legal issues to be considered (see Chapter 16).

Who drafts the patent document?

Patent applications are technical documents and are usually drafted by a patent agent or patent attorney, although in the US and some other countries a provisional filing may be made where more informal documents may be submitted to the patent office. This can be done to avoid a loss of patent rights when timing is crucial; for example, before disclosure of a new machine at a trade show, when a first draft may be put together by the scientist or engineer involved.

Description of technology
Patents contain a "specification" or "description" that describes the technical aspects of the invention and often the current technological background. A specification may be detailed and lengthy and is required by law to contain certain information.

Patent claims
The specification of a patent is followed by a series of "claims". This part of a patent sets out the scope of rights granted to the patent owner. It comprises a number of usually short paragraphs identifying the features of a product or process that must generally be present to infringe the rights of the patent owner, that is, the scope of the invention that will be granted protection from copying. For example, one of the claims in the patent at issue in the *Ariosa v Sequenom* litigation mentioned above reads as follows:

> A method for performing a prenatal diagnosis on a maternal blood sample, which method comprises:
> - obtaining a non-cellular fraction of the blood sample
> - amplifying a paternally inherited nucleic acid from the non-cellular fraction
> - and performing nucleic acid analysis on the amplified nucleic acid to detect paternally inherited fetal nucleic acid.

The interpretation of such a claim is discussed below.

Where to file for a patent
Typically, inventors will file in their home country patent office, or in Europe through the European Patent Office, but that is not an absolute requirement. For example, certain types of invention may be better protected in the US and a filing could be made solely in that country (which may also be the most material commercial

market), or recent Supreme Court cases could mean that broader patents could be obtained outside the US. Special filing requirements apply to applications under the Patent Cooperation Treaty (PCT – see below). Note that the ability to obtain patents and their worth vary by country, so do not have too parochial a view when considering patenting. However, for a type of invention that would not be protected in major markets, also note that a decision could be made to rely on trade secret protection (see Chapter 6).

Seeking international protection

The decision on where to file for patents internationally is usually driven by market size, free-trade areas, realistic enforcement in that country and costs. It should be noted that strict deadlines apply to the decisions to file internationally. A number of international treaties govern matters such as allowing the earliest date of filing in one country to be used as the "priority date" in another country so long as certain deadlines are met. Obtaining the benefit of the earlier filing date (the priority date) is extremely important because the filing date may cut off third-party rights and limit prior art.

Patent applications may be filed in several countries based on an original priority (or first) filing, but they can be filed simultaneously in most countries under the PCT. The home office of the applicant usually acts as the receiving office for the application and carries out a preliminary search of prior art. The application may then be filed in all countries designated by the applicant. Brazil, Russia, India and China are all PCT member states. (A map of the PCT countries is available on the World Intellectual Property Organisation's website, www.wipo.int.)

Utility models and petty patents

"Utility models" and "petty patents" are names for forms of patents that are available in some countries. They give protection to certain types of invention (generally not processes but including mechanical devices), but are often not subject to full patent office examination and are obtained quickly and cheaply for a limited term. A European example would be a German *Gebrauchsmuster*. Utility models are important in China because these have been successfully enforced in the past and are a cost-effective method of protection much used by the Chinese themselves.

The examination process – scope of claims

Securing a patent is essentially a bargaining process where the scope of the rights to be granted to the patent owner as set out in the claims may be narrowed in order to get a patent. In most countries, patents are examined to determine whether the invention is sufficiently inventive over the current state of the art (or prior art) so that it is both novel (that is, no one has made the invention before) and not obvious. A patent is generally not granted for a routine improvement that a person of average skills working in the field would have found it obvious to make. A 2014 study showed that around 30% of patent applications filed in the US patent office are turned down.[1]

The examiner in the patent office will carry out a search of publications, and the applicant then has to distinguish their invention from the prior inventions that the examiner has located. As a result of this back-and-forth negotiation between the patent examiner and the applicant, the final set of claims is written. Depending on the prior art, these claims may be narrow or broad (that is, limited to a specific product or covering all products of a particular type). A broad claim is usually shorter and more descriptive with fewer subparagraphs or subparts, which are known as "limitations".

Whether or not a claim has many limitations (and so is lengthy) is important to the rights given to the patent owner. This is because to infringe a patent (that is, act in a way that is forbidden under the patent statute) a third party must, broadly, have a product or process that contains all the features specified in each limitation.

Maintenance fees

Once a patent is granted a fee is payable, followed by annual or other periodic fees to keep the patent in force (see Chapter 9).

The rights granted by a patent
Geographical/national rights
Patents generally exist country-by-country depending on where applications have been filed and the patent granted. The new European unitary patent will create a patent right of unparalleled scope across the 25 EU countries that have chosen to participate in the arrangement (importantly, excluding Italy and Spain), and some are now regarding it with trepidation.

Where patents are obtained is the choice of the applicant. Generally, a patent in a country will give rights only in that country. Patent applications filed in the European Patent Office will, if granted, create national patent rights in each country designated by the applicant. However, in December 2012, agreement was reached on a unitary patent package, which after decades of discussion will create a pan-European patent as an option in most of the EU. When it is implemented (which depends on ratification by at least 13 member states including France, Germany and the UK), this international patent right – although initially an optional form of protection that will be created and exist on top of the current national and European systems – is likely to revolutionise patent protection in Europe by creating the possibility of a decision on a patent in one country having an effect across most of the EU. This has caused concern that Europe could become a venue for litigation by PAEs looking for favourable jurisdictions within Europe in which to obtain judgments covering most of the EU. As a result, there has been discussion about the standards under which the new court will issue injunctions, including those where only a feature of a larger product infringes a patent.

Duration
Generally, the right to enforce a patent and prevent others from using the patented invention does not come into being until the patent is issued by the relevant patent office – that is, there is an official grant of the patent. After that, a patent exists for a specified period, usually 20 years measured from the date of the patent application, so long as maintenance fees are paid (see above).

In many countries there are provisional rights where once a

patent has been granted, some compensation may be obtained for infringement during the period after a patent is published and before it is officially issued. These rights are limited and "infringement" during the long process of obtaining a patent can be a significant commercial problem; this should be considered when deciding the value of patent protection.

Adjustments may be made to the effective term of a pharmaceutical patent in the US to compensate for delays in obtaining regulatory approval. In Europe rights to patents covering certain regulated products may also be extended through "supplementary protection certificates".

Scope of legal rights

The basic rights granted to the owner of a patent are to exclude others from making, selling or using the invention. The specific rights to exclude others granted to the owner of a patent are set out in the patent laws in the relevant country. In the US, the law states (35 USC 271(a)):

Whoever without authority makes, uses, offers to sell, or sells any patented invention within the United States or imports into the United States any patented invention during the term of the patent therefor, infringes the patent.

As well as its provisions on geography and the duration of patent rights, the US law covers other forms of infringement such as inducing infringement, supplying non-staple components of patented inventions, and import of a product made by a process patented in the US.

The equivalent language that governs patent infringement in the UK is as follows (Patents Act, 1977, c. 37, §60 (Eng.)):

[A] person infringes a patent for an invention if, but only if, while the patent is in force, he does any of the following things in the United Kingdom in relation to the invention without the consent of the proprietor of the patent, that is to say ... where the invention is a product, he makes, disposes of, offers to dispose of, uses or imports the product or keeps it whether for disposal or otherwise.

How is a patent infringed?

As discussed above, each feature of a patent generally has to be found in an accused product or process for the patent to be infringed. The scope (interpretation) of the claims of a patent may be strongly contested because of its business importance – the wider the scope, the more valuable the patent.

Direct infringement

The types of activities that infringe the rights of the patent owner depend on the scope of the patent. To infringe a patent a third-party product or process generally has to infringe each feature of a patent claim as properly interpreted. For example, in the *Ariosa v Sequenom* litigation discussed above, one claim reads:

> A *method for performing a prenatal diagnosis on a maternal blood sample, which method comprises:*
>
> ■ *obtaining a non-cellular fraction of the blood sample*
> ■ *amplifying a paternally inherited nucleic acid from the noncellular fraction*
> ■ *and performing nucleic acid analysis on the amplified nucleic acid to detect paternally inherited fetal nucleic acid.*

According to the general principle, the patent would not be infringed by a prenatal diagnosis unless all the described steps of the method were carried out. This raises two issues.

First, how are the terms in a claim interpreted? What is needed for each step? This was litigated in the case between Ariosa and Sequenom. The district court construed "amplifying" to mean "increasing the concentration of a paternally inherited nucleic acid relative to the other DNA in the sample". However, the Court of Appeals disagreed:

> *To the contrary, the claim language requires "amplifying" paternally inherited nucleic acid, without any mention of an effect on the quantity of other nucleic acid …The claim does not state that paternally inherited nucleic acid is "selectively" or "only" amplified".*

The appeals court bolstered this plain reading by looking at the specification of the patent (the description of the invention), which it noted also undermined the district court's interpretation because it did not require amplification to change the proportions of paternal or maternal nucleic acids. It also looked at the history of prosecution of the patent to reach the same conclusion. This is a good illustration of an approach whereby claims are initially interpreted by looking at their language, with questions or ambiguities then being addressed by looking at the description of the invention in the patent – and, at least in the US, looking at dealings with the patent office during the application process.

Second, what happens if the accused device or method does not exactly match the claims of the patent as properly interpreted? For example, what if there were no "amplification" of nucleic acid or if the accused infringer used a different method? Interpretation of patents is fodder for much litigation, as is the question of how close a product must come to the claimed invention to infringe the owner's rights. Infringement where there is an exact fit is known as literal infringement. Infringement where the fit is not exact is known in the US as infringement under the doctrine of equivalents. This type of infringement occurs where, broadly, an accused product performs substantially the same function, in substantially the same way, to achieve substantially the same result. The law in Europe is somewhat different. It is not so much that protection may extend beyond the literal meaning of the claims, but rather a matter of how the scope of the claims is interpreted.

Infringement by equivalents is a contentious issue. It pits the public need for clarity and notice as to third-party patent rights against the legitimate desire of the patent owner that a potential infringer does not make inconsequential changes to the patented invention and thus avoid infringement through such minor changes. As stated in a 2014 UK case:

> The law recognises that drafting patent claims is a difficult and imprecise art and that third parties should not be allowed to exploit infelicities of drafting where it is reasonably clear that those infelicities should not affect the scope of the claim. This is in order

to provide *"fair protection for the patent proprietor"*. *The law also recognises, however, the countervailing consideration that third parties are entitled to rely on the drafting of the claim when deciding on a commercial course of action. There is no tort of avoiding a patent claim. Thus it is also necessary to provide "a reasonable degree of legal certainty for third parties". The problem, of course, is that what is fair protection to one person is legal uncertainty to another.*

As well as these philosophical debates, there is a real business issue underlying the determination of the scope of the patent. The more broadly a patent owner can claim infringement, the more valuable is the patent.

Indirect infringement
Companies that enable infringement by a customer or other person may also be liable for indirect infringement. Where a patent is infringed, it is not just the direct infringer that may be liable, but also third parties that contribute to or induce that infringement. Indirect infringement is codified by statute in the US and Europe with differing legal standards.

Remedies for patent infringement
A review of news stories on patents over the past few years brings up many articles on "patent trolls" and "phone wars" and discussions about whether, at least in the world of technology, patenting and patent litigation have got out of control. Litigation and the involvement of antitrust and competition authorities mean that today, in some countries, the nature of the owner of a patent and the commitments to license made by that owner or its predecessors affect the remedies that the patent owner may obtain in litigation. Before addressing remedies in general, two types of patent owner need to be differentiated: those, often referred to as patent trolls, that have no operating business and buy and assert patents purely for financial gain; and those that develop technologies that become industry standards, enabling entirely new classes of products to be marketed, and that obtain patents covering those industry standards.

Patent trolls and US patent reform

As noted in Chapter 1, in a phenomenon still largely limited to the US but growing in Germany and other countries, patents may be acquired by investors purely with a view to generating revenue through making infringement allegations that are usually settled for a negotiated amount (as are most patent cases), or are sometimes taken to a trial seeking damages for infringement. This phenomenon of patent acquisition for enforcement appears to be both a cause and an effect of the market in patents that has grown up in recent years.

A number of patents, especially in the area of e-commerce, became available through business failures after the 2001 dotcom collapse, and nowadays in any insolvency the patents of the company may be auctioned off. Moreover, since the early 2000s companies have sought to obtain cash by divesting unwanted patents, and there has been significant use of auctions and patent brokers to trade patents. (The market for patents is discussed in Chapter 15.) But contrary to common perception, this is not an entirely new development, as research by economic historians suggests that an active patent market and such activities were prevalent in the 19th century.

This not-so-new phenomenon is alluded to in President Obama's June 2013 report, *Patent Assertion and US Innovation*, which quotes from Senator Isaac Christiancy in 1878 (45 CONG.REC.3079 (1878)), who was in turn quoted in an article by Gerard Magliocca, a professor at Indiana University's Robert H. McKinney School of Law:[2]

> *Among a host of dormant patents, some will be found which contain some new principle ... which the inventor, however, had failed to render of any use in his own invention. And some other inventor, ignorant that such a principle had been discovered ... had the genius to render it of great practical value ... when, lo! the patent-sharks among the legal profession, always on the watch for such cases, go to the first patentee and, for a song, procure an assignment of his useless patent, and at once proceed to levy blackmail upon the inventor of the valuable patent.*

These days, however, companies that acquire patents for enforcement are not known as "sharks" but rather "trolls", non-practising entities (NPEs) and most recently, by the US Federal Trade Commission (FTC), patent assertion entities (PAEs). That PAEs are a political issue in the US is apparent in a 2011 report prepared by the FTC, *The Evolving IP Marketplace: Aligning Patent Notice and Remedies with Competition*, the 2013 White House report mentioned above, a 2013 report on intellectual property by the US Government Accountability Office and, even more so, in President Obama's comment quoted in Chapter 1 and his subsequent actions aimed at helping companies sued by PAEs.

PAEs are a major cost to technology companies. Some PAEs sue under old, ambiguous and low-quality patents that were purchased "for a song". Some have hidden their true identities behind shell entities, pursuing litigation or campaigns of threats of infringement without a reasonable basis against numerous defendants that had no knowledge of the asserted patent, are locked into technology alleged to infringe the patent, and may be small, unsophisticated companies. Some are regarded not as pursuing meritorious claims of clear infringement but profiting from the inefficiencies, uncertainties and expense of US litigation to force settlements. Lastly, a claim by a PAE is one-sided because, unlike a claim by a competitor, there is no counterclaim for infringement that can be made, and given that most PAEs are shells they suffer few operational or reputational costs in bringing litigation.

The activities of PAEs have undoubtedly put an increasingly heavy cost burden on technology and software companies over the past decade and these companies have been vocal in their views. Although the America Invents Act 2011 provided new means of challenging the validity of patents and limited certain PAE tactics, such as suing a host of unrelated defendants in one litigation, there have been continuing calls for further action.

A number of legislative initiatives have focused on issues such as the level of detail required to make an accusation of patent infringement, requiring litigants to reveal those parties having a financial interest in the claim (to avoid effective use of shell companies in litigation). Other initiatives make it harder to sue retail-level customers of devices such as internet routers rather than the manufacturer, which is the real party in interest; making patent litigation less expensive for defendants; and providing for the prevailing party to receive its fees. There is a concern that steps taken with PAEs in mind that weaken patent rights may reduce the incentive to innovate. In addition, some consider that a thriving market for patents should help innovators obtain a reward for their innovation.

However, even without legislation, there has already been a shift in the attitude of the courts, arguably resulting in a weakening of patent remedies. Decisions in recent years in the US courts have reduced the availability to PAEs that did not invent the patent of injunctions that stop a defendant from marketing an infringing product; made large awards of damages more difficult to obtain; and made it easier for a defendant to obtain fees from the plaintiff as a result of litigation misconduct. Arguably, the need for legislation has diminished, as these decisions have made US patent litigation less onerous for defendants.

Standard essential patents

Participation in technical bodies that set industry standards brings with it obligations to license patents on fair, reasonable and non-discriminatory (FRAND) terms to competitors as well as antitrust and competition law scrutiny.

Many industries such as telecoms are dependent on industry participants agreeing technical standards so that devices such as mobile phones can operate with each other. Some industries have standard-setting bodies and industry members can choose to participate in developing technical standards. These bodies generally have rules that require participants in the standard-setting process to declare patents they own that are required for compliance with a standard (essential or standard essential patents – SEPs) and to offer those patents for licensing on FRAND terms (or in some cases reasonable and non-discriminatory – RAND – terms).

There is thus a quid pro quo between the strategic advantages of being able to sell products under a standard that a patent owner has influenced, and the royalty revenue to be obtained through having patents needed for use of that standard, and an obligation to license on reasonable terms. An owner participating in a standards organisation is thus making a decision that within certain parameters a proprietary model will not work, and that revenues will be maximised by participation in a larger standardised market. Of course, a particular company may have patents needed for use of the standard and other patents on consumer features that are not part of the standard. These feature patents may be licensed or not as determined by the patent owner.

Remarkably, until recently there was little or no legal precedent on how royalties were to be calculated under FRAND-encumbered portfolios of standard essential patents, whether injunctions could be obtained against an unlicensed infringer under such patents as opposed to seeking damages and a royalty, and the extent to which contract and antitrust and competition law governed the negotiation process, the royalty amount and the basis on which that royalty could be calculated. The flood of litigation over FRAND-encumbered patents in the phone wars, which began in around 2011 (see Chapter 11), was in some ways unsurprising against a background where new entrants disrupted the modus vivendi that had grown up among existing market participants. A few years on, case law and actions by antitrust and competition authorities have begun to provide some clarity.

Even beyond the lack of legal precedent, the system of standards and FRAND licensing is complex. A new market entrant will have to negotiate with many patent owners. There is also no requirement that the owner of patents relevant to a standard should agree to license those patents unless that owner participates in the standard-setting organisation. Thus certain patent owners may wait out the standard-setting process and then assert their patents later. However, it is now clear that injunctions to prevent infringement of SEPs may be obtained only in limited circumstances. The differences between standard and non-standard essential patents are discussed below.

US damages

The remedies for patent infringement are set out in the applicable patent statute. In the US, the statute provides for a civil action with the remedies of damages and an injunction against further infringement. Damages should be "adequate to compensate for the infringement, but in no event less than a reasonable royalty for the use made of the invention by the infringer". But it is important to note that in the US the plaintiff has the option that the damages be decided by a jury, which means they can be extremely high – for example, over $1.5 billion was awarded in 2014 in favour of Carnegie Mellon University against Marvell, a chip manufacturer.

The way patent damages are calculated has been highly controversial in the US because there is a strong sentiment among technology companies that damages have become too large and that this has led to the rise of PAEs. In US patent litigation, broadly speaking, unless stringent requirements are met where a plaintiff can demonstrate that it would have made the sales actually made by the infringing defendant, damages are calculated by reference to a "reasonable royalty", which the parties would have agreed just before the date of infringement in a hypothetical negotiation. This royalty is used to calculate a lump-sum damages figure based on the amount of infringing sales. The royalty is assessed taking into account what are known as the Georgia-Pacific factors, which are as follows:

■ *The royalties received by the patentee [the patent owner] for the licensing of the patent in suit, proving or tending to prove an established royalty.*

■ *The rates paid by the licensee for the use of other patents comparable to the patent in suit.*

■ *The nature and scope of the license, as exclusive or non-exclusive; or as restricted or non-restricted in terms of territory or with respect to whom the manufactured product may be sold.*

■ *The licensor's established policy and marketing program to maintain its patent monopoly by not licensing others to use the invention or by granting licenses under special conditions designed to preserve that monopoly.*

■ *The commercial relationship between the licensor and licensee, such as, whether they are competitors in the same territory in the same line of business; or whether they are inventor and promoter.*

■ *The effect of selling the patented specialty in promoting sales of other products of the licensee; the existing value of the invention to* the licensor as a generator of sales of its non-patented items; and the extent of such derivative or convoyed sales.

■ The duration of the patent and the term of the license.

■ The established profitability of the product made under the patent; its commercial success; and its current popularity.

■ The utility and advantages of the patent property over the old modes or devices, if any, that had been used for working out similar results.

■ The nature of the patented invention; the character of the commercial embodiment of it as owned and produced by the licensor; and the benefits to those who have used the invention.

■ The extent to which the infringer has made use of the invention; and any evidence of the value of that use.

■ The portion of the profit or of the selling price that may be customary in the particular company or in comparable companies to allow for the use of the invention or analogous inventions.

■ The portion of the realizable profit that should be credited to the invention as distinguished from non-patented elements, the manufacturing process, business risks, or significant features or improvements added by the infringer.

■ The opinion testimony of qualified experts.

■ The amount that a licensor (such as the patentee) and a licensee (such as the infringer) would have agreed upon (at the time the infringement began) if both had been reasonably and voluntarily trying to reach an agreement; that is, the amount which a prudent licensee – who desired, as a business proposition, to obtain a license to manufacture and sell a particular article embodying the patented invention – would have been willing to pay as a royalty and yet be able to make a reasonable profit and which amount would have been acceptable by a prudent patentee who was willing to grant a license.

These factors sound reasonable and businesslike. The difficulty in the technology industry (but not in the biotechnology and pharmaceutical industries, which are reliant on the strength of one or a small number of patents) is that these factors give little guidance on real economics and awards are made that exceed the economic value of a patent, not least because little account is taken of the many hundreds of patents covering a modern electronic device.

The detailed US patent legislation passed in 2011 did not address the issue of damages, but the courts responded by requiring higher evidentiary standards to support damages awards, meaning that there must be evidential proof of the royalty base and royalty amount claimed, and that the royalty should be based on apportionment of the actual incremental profit attributable to the patented feature, particularly where the patent covers only a small component or a minor improvement. Where the patent owner has repeatedly licensed a patent, this can be good evidence of the applicable royalty – a so-called "established royalty". Evidence of royalties under truly comparable licences is also helpful. In the absence of this type of evidence, royalties are based on economic and accounting analyses by experts hired by each party, with the judge or jury being left to decide between them.

In certain circumstances, damages in the US may be increased up to three times in case of wilful infringement. (This is addressed in Chapter 16 because the law affects strategies on investigating third-party patents.) To establish wilful infringement, a patentee must show that the infringer acted despite an objectively high likelihood that its actions constituted infringement of a patent and knew, or should have known, of that risk.

Where no injunction is granted, courts may also award a continuing royalty to the patent owner.

Calculation of FRAND damages

FRAND damages should aim to compensate patent owners fairly for their contribution to an industry standard (thus encouraging innovation). However, manufacturers are technologically locked into a standard in order to sell a particular type of product and may therefore in theory be required to pay an unfairly high royalty (this is called holdup). There is also a risk that because standards may incorporate thousands of patents manufacturers may have to pay royalties to many patent owners, which when all added up would prevent them from operating profitably (this is called royalty stacking).

How to calculate FRAND royalties was finally addressed by the applicable Court of Appeals in the US in late 2014.

The Court of Appeals took a middle course between lower court approaches that had allowed a jury great latitude to establish FRAND royalties and those that had established prescriptive lists of factors to be taken into account in all FRAND cases, including patent holdup and stacking royalties. The court held that an initial determinant of damages was the actual wording of the FRAND obligation that the patent owner had entered into (the wording of these obligations varies between standards). Beyond that, the royalty award for patented technology must be based on the incremental value of the invention, not the value of the standard as a whole. ("Just as we apportion damages for a patent that covers a small part of a device, we must also apportion damages for SEPs that cover only a small part of a standard."). That value must also be separated from any increased value the patented feature gains from its inclusion in the standard. ("We merely hold that the royalty for SEPs should reflect the approximate value of that technological contribution, not the value of its widespread adoption due to standardisation.")

The court also held that patent holdup and royalty stacking could be introduced to further reduce royalties only if there were actual evidence of these issues in the case being decided. However, it seems that the analysis required should take into account the existence of multiple patented features making up a standard and require that the patented feature be valued without taking into account the impact of standardisation.

Given the huge amounts of money involved in the phone industry, litigation continues over the exact contours of FRAND royalty calculation. An example is litigation filed in 2015 between Apple and Ericsson after the existing licence from Ericsson to Apple expired.

European damages

In Europe, measures of damages can include an accounting of the profits of the defendant, which is different from the US approach except in the case of design patents. The general rules for remedies are set out in EU Directive 2004/48/EC on the enforcement of intellectual property rights and provide other ways of calculating damages.

One is similar in general approach to the US and provides for calculation of lump-sum damages based on a royalty for use of the patent. Alternatively, lost profits and other damages may be claimed, including – unusually from a US perspective – damages for "moral prejudice", which is a form of non-economic damage. Legal costs and seizures of infringing products may also be awarded. For example, the UK Patents Act, Section 61 (which is supplemented by regulations to ensure the approach is in line with EU law), states:

> A claim may be made ...
>
> (a) for an injunction or interdict restraining the defendant or defender from any apprehended act of infringement;
>
> (b) for an order for him to deliver up or destroy any patented product in relation to which the patent is infringed or any article in which that product is inextricably comprised;
>
> (c) for damages in respect of the infringement;
>
> (d) for an account of the profits derived by him from the infringement;
>
> (e) for a declaration that the patent is valid and has been infringed by him.

Efficient or just risky infringement

One strategic question is whether the royalty awarded by a court would essentially be the same as that arrived at in a commercial negotiation, thus in essence making patent infringement a low-risk activity, and indeed a rational alternative to seeking a licence because the infringer may never be sued (this is referred to as efficient infringement). In most jurisdictions, this is not the usual result. Rather, patent infringement is risky because the damages awarded by a court may be higher than the royalty arrived at on an arm's-length basis – one reason being that at the time of a judgment there is no debate about infringement or validity. Indeed, in the US a deliberate course of infringement may lead to a higher award of damages for wilful infringement. Most important, there is also the risk of an injunction being granted to prevent the continuance of the infringing activity (see below). An injunction can literally shut down a one-product business.

Patent marking

Innocence is generally not a defence against patent infringement, but certain legal systems have limitations on damages for infringement depending on knowledge of the patent or whether the patent owner's product has been marked. Thus in the US, 35 USC 287 provides that if patented products have not been marked with the applicable patent number, damages may not be recovered if the defendant was not otherwise aware of the patent:

> In the event of failure so to mark, no damages shall be recovered by the patentee in any action for infringement, except on proof that the infringer was notified of the infringement and continued to infringe thereafter, in which event damages may be recovered only for infringement occurring after such notice. Filing of an action for infringement shall constitute such notice.

Similarly in the UK, Section 62(1) of the Patents Act 1977 states:

> In proceedings for infringement of a patent damages shall not be awarded, and no order shall be made for an account of profits, against a defendant or defender who proves that at the date of the infringement he was not aware, and had no reasonable grounds for supposing, that the patent existed; and a person shall not be taken to have been so aware or to have had reasonable grounds for so supposing by reason only of the application to a product of the word "patent" or "patented", or any word or words expressing or implying that a patent has been obtained for the product, unless the number of the patent accompanied the word or words in question.

However, great care needs to be taken on patent marking because false claims of patents or pending patent applications may also be penalised – a case of potentially being damned if you do and damned if you don't. For example, Section 110(1) of the UK Patents Act 1977 states:

> If a person falsely represents that anything disposed of by him for value is a patented product he shall, subject to the following provisions of this section, be liable on summary conviction to a fine not exceeding level 3 on the standard scale.

Injunctions

A big risk to an infringer is an injunction because of the effect it has on a company's ability to carry out its business. Recent cases have made it harder to obtain a patent injunction in the US but the risk remains, especially when action is being taken against a competitor of the patent owner. Injunctions are more readily granted in some European countries.

An injunction may be either preliminary (that is, granted before a full trial) or permanent (that is, granted after a full trial). Because of the effects an injunction has, the circumstances in which one will be granted are much contested in the courts and have varied over the years.

Until 2006 in the US, a permanent injunction was the general remedy for patent infringement, thus making patents a powerful competitive weapon and, in the right circumstances, valuable property. However, in *eBay v MercExchange*, the Supreme Court decided that:

> [The test for an injunction] requires a plaintiff to demonstrate: (1) that it has suffered an irreparable injury; (2) that remedies available at law [ie, damages] are inadequate to compensate for that injury; (3) that considering the balance of hardships between the plaintiff and defendant, a remedy in equity is warranted; and (4) that the public interest would not be disserved by a permanent injunction.

In the US, a preliminary injunction is "an extraordinary remedy that may only be awarded upon a clear showing that the plaintiff is entitled to such relief". A plaintiff seeking a preliminary injunction must establish: the likelihood of success on the merits; that it is likely to suffer irreparable harm in the absence of preliminary relief; that the balance of equities tips in the plaintiff's favour; and that an injunction is in the public interest. To demonstrate a likelihood of success on the merits in a patent infringement case, a plaintiff must establish that it is likely both to prove that the defendant infringes the patents and to withstand the defendant's challenges to the validity and enforceability of these patents. Under English law, although the wording of the legal test is different, the approach is broadly similar.

By contrast, in continental Europe, an injunction has often been the primary remedy sought in patent litigation. The perceived readiness of European courts to grant preliminary and permanent injunctions has led to multinational litigation where actions are filed, for example, in Germany with a view to obtaining early injunctive relief.

In the US, injunctions are more readily granted when competitors are at odds with each other. For example, in March 2014 BlackBerry obtained a preliminary injunction before trial in California under both a design and a utility patent against Typo Products, a maker of a keyboard that works with an iPhone. However, since the Supreme Court decision in *eBay v MercExchange*, it has become harder for companies that purchased a patent for investment purposes to obtain injunctions in the US. This is because it is felt that such financial players can be adequately compensated by damages.

In cases involving competitors in the technology field, where a patent does not cover the whole product, the US courts have looked at the impact of infringement on consumer demand for the plaintiff's products when assessing whether a competing product carrying an infringing feature may cause the necessary irreparable injury to the plaintiff to support the granting of an injunction. This has become a crucial issue in the phone wars, where an infringing feature is only one of many on a personal device such as a phone. In *Apple Inc. v Samsung Electronics Co Ltd*, the US Court of Appeals stated:

> *Apple must show some connection between the patented feature and demand for Samsung's products. There might be a variety of ways to make this required showing, for example, with evidence that a patented feature is one of several features that cause consumers to make their purchasing decisions. It might also be shown with evidence that the inclusion of a patented feature makes a product significantly more desirable. Conversely, it might be shown with evidence that the absence of a patented feature would make a product significantly less desirable.*

The analysis in the UK is different and focuses on the effect of the injunction. Indeed, Mr Justice Arnold, a UK judge, in *HTC Corporation v Nokia Corporation* stated at the end of 2013:

So far as the future effect of an injunction is concerned, I cannot see that the mere fact that the injunction only relates to a small component of a larger whole is significant.

Looking at the principles of the EU Enforcement Directive, he granted an injunction to Nokia on the ground that just one feature of a phone, which had many patents applicable to it, was infringed by HTC. For Arnold, the effect of an injunction would not be "disproportionate" based on the availability of non-infringing alternatives. By contrast, were the impact to be disproportionate, an injunction should not be granted.

The grant of a final injunction would not be disproportionate. It would not deliver HTC to Nokia "bound hand and foot, in order to be made subject to any extortionate demand" Nokia may make, because HTC already had some non-infringing alternatives available to it, could have had more if it had acted promptly when first sued by Nokia, and will in any event have more non-infringing alternatives available to it in a period which is significantly shorter than the remaining term of the patent.

The US approach to standard essential patents
Owners of standard essential patents (SEPs) are subject to antitrust and competition law constraints. These constraints make it hard to obtain an injunction under FRAND patents unless a defendant refuses to participate in negotiations with the patent owner.

In US litigation between Apple and Motorola Mobility, Judge Posner, a highly respected US Court of Appeals judge and University of Chicago economist, took the position that patents licensed under a standard and required, for example, for a mobile phone to function should not be subject to an injunction because the patent owner had committed to license the patents to anyone willing to pay a FRAND royalty.

The Court of Appeals for the Federal Circuit took a more nuanced and potentially flexible approach using the factors laid out in *eBay v MercExchange* (see above) for granting an injunction, stating that an injunction may be justified where, for example, an infringer unilaterally refused a FRAND royalty or unreasonably delayed in negotiations with the patent owner.

The German approach

In Germany, the view of the court in the Orange Book Standard case (May 9th 2009) was in effect that the owner of a patent essential to a standard is entitled to an injunction unless the user of the technology made a royalty offer that the patent owner would be prevented from rejecting under competition law principles, and that the user has been complying with the terms of the applicable licence.

Antitrust and competition law limitations

Antitrust and competition law actions on both sides of the Atlantic have made clear that whatever the approach of patent law, in the case of competition and antitrust law FRAND obligations mean that injunctions under FRAND-encumbered patents are generally obtainable only after a potential licensee refuses to negotiate. Thus Motorola Mobility has entered into a consent judgment in the US limiting its ability to seek an injunction to circumstances where a licensing process and arbitration have failed to result in a licensee paying a royalty. Similarly, in the EU, investigations by the European Commission into Samsung's and Motorola's patent assertion practices with respect to SEPs resulted in Samsung offering an undertaking to comply with a similar mechanism, and a decision that Motorola had breached EU competition rules. In a press release dated October 17th 2013 seeking industry comments on Samsung's proposal, the concern of the Commission was well expressed:

> The Commission considers that the seeking of an injunction based on SEPs may constitute an abuse of a dominant position if a SEP holder has given a commitment to license its SEPs on Fair Reasonable And Non-Discriminatory (FRAND) terms and where the company against which an injunction is sought is willing to enter into a licence agreement on FRAND terms.

In a press release dated April 29th 2014 relating to both Samsung and Motorola, the Commission stated:

> [T]he Commission's aim is to prevent SEP holders from using SEP-based injunctions in an anticompetitive way, in order to extract licensing conditions that may restrict competition and ultimately

harm consumers. At the same time, SEP holders should be entitled to appropriate remuneration for their SEPs. ...

The Motorola decision provides a "safe harbour" for standard implementers who are willing to take a licence on FRAND terms. If they want to be safe from injunctions based on SEPs by the patent holder, they can demonstrate that they are a willing licensee by agreeing that a court or a mutually agreed arbitrator adjudicates the FRAND terms.

US International Trade Commission

As injunctions have proved harder to obtain in the US courts, firms have sought to get the International Trade Commission (ITC) in Washington, DC, to issue orders to exclude imported infringing products from the US.

Although it is specifically a US tribunal, the ITC is an important forum for international patent disputes whatever the nationality of the plaintiff. It may be used to seek exclusion orders – called Section 337 proceedings (Tariff Act of 1930) – against infringing goods. An action in the ITC is against the products themselves, so jurisdiction over defendants from outside the US is not required. An exclusion order means that the goods cannot be imported into the US. The requirements for a Section 337 proceeding include a US "domestic industry" that relates to the infringing goods, but these requirements have still permitted many companies based outside the US to take advantage of the ITC. In particular, Section 337 allows a domestic industry to be based on "substantial investment in ... licensing", meaning that a non-manufacturing organisation can take advantage of the tribunal. This has caused controversy with regard to claims by PAEs (see below).

ITC proceedings have become much more prominent because of the increasing difficulty in obtaining injunctions against patent infringement in the US courts since the 2006 eBay case (see above). So far, the ITC does not have to follow the eBay decision, and the effect of an exclusion order against imported goods (such as mobile phones) may be devastating to a defendant and thus be a powerful tool to force a settlement.

ITC cases have therefore featured prominently in the phone wars litigation (see Chapter 10); according to an article in the *Financial Times* in October 2012, "The battleground of choice in patent wars", every smartphone-maker was involved in an ITC dispute as either a plaintiff or a respondent in 2011.[3] As these cases progressed, the results varied depending on whether the patents asserted were patents covering specific features, or patents covering features that were essential to the use of a technical standard needed for mobile telephony and subject to an obligation by the patent owner to license the patent under RAND or FRAND (see above). In the latter case, in a much-publicised move in August 2013, President Obama vetoed an exclusion order obtained by Samsung against Apple on the basis that it was against public policy to issue an exclusion order under a FRAND-encumbered SEP. By contrast, in October 2013 Obama refused to intervene in an exclusion order obtained by Apple against Samsung under feature patents.

The ability to use the ITC has been limited by actions under US antitrust (competition) laws. The US Federal Trade Commission (FTC), one of the agencies charged with enforcement of the antitrust laws, takes the position that the threat of an exclusion order is so great that it may enable the owner of a patent essential for use of a technical standard to negotiate for a royalty higher than is justified under a FRAND commitment. In a consent order finalised in 2013, the FTC obtained an agreement from Motorola Mobility that required the company not to seek a court injunction or ITC exclusion order under FRAND-encumbered SEPs until a required licence negotiation and arbitration procedure had been followed.

The increased use of the ITC, including by patent assertion entities, has also prompted concern and associated lobbying among manufacturing companies that its procedures and the threat of an exclusion order prohibiting imports may be used to extort larger settlements.

International patent enforcement

Where international litigation ensues, differences in patent law and procedure among countries mean that effective co-ordination requires a high degree of legal sophistication and practical management. The basic landscape of patent litigation may be similar, but there are significant differences in the criteria used for deciding whether a patent has been infringed and in the remedies that will be applied if it has. Thus when faced with international infringement, consideration must be given to where and when it will be most effective to take action. Litigation may be pursued in several jurisdictions with the hope of forcing settlement by being the first party to obtain a damaging injunction against an opponent.

In the US and UK, a trial normally covers both infringement and patent invalidity. In Germany this is not the case, and invalidity of a patent is decided in a separate court. Because of this and the speed with which an injunction may be obtained compared with countries such as the US, plaintiffs often prefer to use German courts. However, it is hard and expensive to co-ordinate several litigations. The danger is that a tactical litigation in a small market may mess things up in a big, commercially important market and result in an adverse decision. For example, sworn testimony that may prove useful in winning a case in country A may be used against its proponent in country B with devastating effect. As a result, pleadings and filings in each jurisdiction need to be reviewed and co-ordinated by one central legal team.

Limits on patent enforcement

Being issued by a patent office does not necessarily make a patent valid. In the US a patent has a statutory "presumption of validity", which means that invalidity must be proved by clear and convincing evidence in litigation, but validity is still open to challenge. Research by John Allison, professor of business, government and society at McCombs School of Business, University of Texas at Austin, Mark Lemley, professor of law at Stanford Law School, and David Schwartz, a professor at Chicago-Kent College of Law, shows that there is on average only a somewhat better than even chance of a US patent being adjudicated valid in litigation (57%).[4] There are also procedures under the laws of many countries to challenge the validity of patents in the patent office. In Europe, these are known as opposition and revocation procedures. In the US, as well as the possibility of invalidating a patent in litigation, there are, following the enactment of the America Invents Act 2011, three such procedures: a "post-grant review" available during the nine months after patent issue; an "inter-partes review" available thereafter; and a special procedure for challenging business method patents available to those charged with infringement under such patents (one of the aspects of the 2011 legislation drafted with PAEs in mind).

The grounds for invalidation of a patent in a post-grant review are much broader than those available under prior law outside patent litigation in court and thus this is a new departure in US patent practice. The inter-partes review is an invalidity proceeding brought by a patent challenger on the basis of prior patents and printed publications. The challenger must establish a reasonable likelihood that at least one claim of the patent will be found invalid. If this is established, what is essentially a small litigation takes place in the patent office to determine whether the patent is invalid or not.

In Europe, patents are subject to an established post-grant opposition procedure. Any third party may challenge the validity of a patent within nine months of notice of grant of the patent. This may be on the basis of prior art, prior use or for technical reasons.

A patent may be revoked or invalidated in a legal or patent office proceeding if a prior publication (or publications) describing the invention ("prior art") is discovered, or more rarely if the patent office did not properly understand the impact of a piece of prior art. The grounds on which patents can be invalidated are hotly contested because of the risk of loss of patent rights.

Inventiveness

In many cases a patent is a development in an already crowded field of technology. For example, it may cover a rapid-release form of an already known painkiller. A challenger may argue that the new formulation is simply obvious in light of prior work.

In the words of the US patent statute (35 USC 103 (a)):

A patent may not be obtained ... if the differences between the subject matter sought to be patented and the prior art are such that the subject matter as a whole would have been obvious at the time the invention was made to a person having ordinary skill in the art to which said subject matter pertains.

In the case of *KSR v Teleflex*, the US Supreme Court was confronted with a patent covering an adjustable vehicle pedal coupled to an electronic sensor. Each element of the invention – mechanical vehicle pedals and electronic sensors – was known, but not in combination. The court found that there was "a strong incentive to convert mechanical pedals to electronic pedals" and that "the prior art taught a number of methods for achieving this advance":

> *When there is a design need or market pressure to solve a problem and there are a finite number of identified, predictable solutions, a person of ordinary skill has good reason to pursue the known options within his or her technical grasp.*

The patent was thus invalid as obvious because of the small number of options and the motivation to combine them. In other words, the available options were obvious to try out and there was the incentive to do so. Thus, where there are a small number of known obvious choices to solve a problem, a patent relying on one of those choices may be invalid.

The concern over this obvious-to-try approach is that things may look obvious in hindsight that were far from obvious at the time of the invention. The Supreme Court stated that hindsight should be avoided, but these issues remain hotly litigated and are of huge significance, particularly in the pharmaceutical industry where individual patents may protect blockbuster drugs.

In addition to lack of inventiveness, often a patented invention may be challenged as not being novel at all. In US parlance, the patent is "anticipated" because the claims encompass technology that was developed before the priority date of the patent. If proven, this is in essence a direct hit on the patent.

Other challenges to patent validity

The large number of possible legal challenges to a patent is the reason that much patent litigation is protracted and expensive. It is also a reason why companies assemble portfolios of patents, which give them a greater number of potential "shots on goal".

Absolute novelty

As noted above, in many countries an invention cannot be revealed to the public before a patent application has been filed, which is called absolute novelty. Filing a patent after prior disclosure is an area rife with own goals, even by large and sophisticated companies, where patent protection is lost through early publication or sales of prototypes. Depending on the period of delay, however, a patent filed after a publication was made could be invalid in Europe but valid in the US and some other countries, as patent rights and grace periods may vary by geography.

Technical requirements

Patents must effectively describe an invention. Under Section 112 of the US patent statute, a patent must have an adequate description of the invention and of the best method known to the inventor of carrying out the invention. The claim must also be sufficiently definite:

> *The specification shall contain a written description of the invention, and of the manner and process of making and using it, in such full, clear, concise, and exact terms as to enable any person skilled in the art to which it pertains, or with which it is most nearly connected, to make and use the same, and shall set forth the best mode contemplated by the inventor or joint inventor of carrying out the invention ... The specification shall conclude with one or more claims particularly pointing out and distinctly claiming the subject matter which the inventor or a joint inventor regards as the invention.*

In Europe, the European Patent Convention requires a "description" of the invention. A patent may be challenged on the basis that the European patent does not disclose the invention "in a manner sufficiently clear and complete for it to be carried out by a person skilled in the art" or that "the subject matter of the European patent extends beyond the content of the application as filed".

The research exemption

In a number of countries, research activities may be exempt from infringement liability. In the US, except in the area of research necessary to submit a drug for regulatory approval, the exemption is "very narrow and limited to actions performed for amusement, to satisfy idle curiosity, or for strictly philosophical inquiry". In other words, research use is not a free pass to infringe a patent.

In the UK, the exemption is arguably slightly broader. It covers "experimental purposes relating to the subject matter of the invention" and, similar to the US, exempts certain activities related to drug approvals.

Patent exhaustion

If a company buys a product that is covered by a patent and uses that product, can it be sued for patent infringement? Generally, the answer is no. This is because rights under a patent are stated to be exhausted by the first sale of the patented item by the patent owner or a licensee acting within the scope of their licence, which is called an authorised first sale. This means that a subsequent purchaser may not be sued for patent infringement.

The scope of patent rights and what rights are exhausted by a sale are important in razor-blade companies: those that sell a device but make their real money from the sale of items used with it. An example is the supply of capsules for use with patented coffee-makers, where third parties step in to sell competing capsules. The sale of a patented coffee-maker has been found to exhaust the applicable utility patents on use of the coffee-maker.

Patent exhaustion is also a potential defence when an owner of patents relating to microchips makes a claim against a customer of a chip fabricator who may be licensed by the patent owner. Complex issues may arise in industries such as microchips with international supply chains and licensing structures regarding whether a first sale was actually authorised and whether an authorised sale in one country will exhaust patent rights in another.

Inequitable conduct

In the US, the process of applying for a patent may give rise to issues of patent enforceability. Essentially, a patent applicant must disclose relevant prior art to the patent office during the patent application process. Intentional failure to disclose material prior art may amount to so-called inequitable conduct, rendering the patent, once granted, unenforceable. Recent changes in US patent law have made this less of an issue than it was, including the possibility of trying to fix the problem after the event by a further patent office proceeding, but it makes no sense not to disclose relevant prior art to the patent office.

Patent misuse

Certain anti-competitive licence practices may render a US patent unenforceable in litigation under the doctrine of patent misuse until the practice has been terminated (see Chapter 12).

Patent ownership and enforcement

The ownership and licensing of a patent may affect who has the right to bring an infringement suit and what remedies in terms of damages and an injunction may be obtained. In many countries an exclusive licensee may be able to bring suit, but only if the patent owner is also a party. Where complex ownership and licensing structures are set up for tax or other reasons, care should be taken to understand what impact those structures may have on litigation remedies, such as the ability of the owner to sue for lost profits.

Delay

Even a small delay in enforcing a patent may result in loss of the right to a preliminary injunction. Longer delays may prevent any action under an applicable statute of limitations that prohibits claims of infringement too long after that infringement has occurred. The applicable period is six years in the US and the UK and the policy is that pursuing stale claims is unfair to a defendant. Delay may also prejudice the right of the patentee to a remedy where the delay is unreasonable, or a defendant has suffered prejudice or been lulled by the patentee into a false sense of security. These rules (known as laches and estoppel in countries with legal systems that are descended from English case-based common law) are complex and differ by country, and a patent owner facing an infringement that it does not wish to pursue should find out what the consequences of failing to take action may be.

Risk and settlement in patent litigation

The use of patents in litigation is discussed in Chapter 11. But given the risks for the patent owner of successful defences such as patent invalidity or non-infringement, and the risks for the defendant of damages or an injunction, most patent litigations are settled through an agreement between the parties and few make their way to trial and judgment.

Validity and value

Although investors generally consider them to be valuable assets, patents are not well understood. There may be a significant difference between the commercial value of a product and the legal strength of the intellectual property protecting that product. Classic examples of this occur in the pharmaceutical industry. A patent covering a blockbuster drug could be legally weak. The invention that led to the drug may have been the result of routine and obvious development work building on an existing product that did not rise to the level of invention protected by a patent. Mistakes could have been made during the patent application process, or the invention inadvertently disclosed before a patent application was filed.

The difference between the commercial value of a patented pharmaceutical and the potential weakness of the patent protecting it is one reason there is so much litigation in the pharmaceutical industry.

The converse proposition is also true. That is, a legally strong patent may not be worth anything because it covers an invention of little use in the marketplace. As research by Mark Schankerman, a professor at the London School of Economics, and others in the field shows, most patents are of little or no monetary value. In many countries, once a patent is obtained, fees have to be paid to the patent office to maintain the patent rights and prevent them from being abandoned and put into the public domain. Studies of patents where owners consider it worthwhile to maintain them for a number of years indicate that the value of patents granted is skewed; in other words, only a few patents are valuable and most are worth little. Over time, around 50% of patents are allowed to lapse. Surveys of patent owners on the patents they own also indicate the same skewed distribution of value.[5]

The commercial value of a patent is a function of the scope of the claims of that patent and whether a commercial product, or features of such a product, will fall within that scope. For example, many potential antiviral drugs have a broadly similar overall structure but differ in terms of the detailed structure of the molecule. In the search for a drug, hundreds of different variants may be synthesised and tested. If the particular drug chosen has the right clinical effect and the right safety profile, and is covered by a patent, that patent is valuable. However, if a patent covers a similar product that turns out not to work in humans, that patent is worthless.

Methods of estimating the financial value of intellectual property are discussed in Chapter 14.

What makes a patent legally strong?

If a patented product appears to have commercial value, the next question is whether the patent obtained on that product is legally strong. The legal strength of a patent covering an invention can be affected by:

- whether the invention arises from actual experimental or engineering work;
- whether the patent was filed before public disclosure of the invention;
- whether there is a significant inventive step over the current state of the technology in the field (this can be judged indirectly by, for example, looking at the number of times the patent has been cited as prior art in later patents);
- whether the patent has been properly drafted and processed by the lawyers or patent agents involved in the various national and international patent offices, with all the relevant prior art having been reviewed by the patent office;
- whether the patent has claims that do not require a large number of features to be infringed (that is, where the claims are broad and not easy to circumvent by making minor changes in a product, as opposed to narrow claims with many required

features) as well as a cascade of narrower claims that are more likely to withstand validity challenges;

- how detailed the patent is and how many claims it has;
- whether there have been major changes in the law regarding patent subject matter and validity since the patent was obtained;
- whether the patent has already withstood a litigation challenge;
- whether the patented product has been successful in the marketplace or has been widely adopted through licensing.

Patent portfolios and thickets

The numerous potential attacks upon patents mean that a patent is subject to a statistical risk of invalidity. Furthermore, the scope of a patent is subject to interpretation. The research by Allison, Lemley and Schwartz cited above shows that in the US patent owners have on average only a 26% win rate against infringers when a case is fought by a defendant to the bitter end. As a result, companies try to assemble portfolios of patents that cover the desired field in different and complementary ways. The pejorative term for such a portfolio, although now more often used to describe an industry-wide series of portfolios, is a patent thicket.

A final thought

To draw an analogy, patents are the tanks of the IP army. Their firepower is formidable. However, the correct analogy would be to tanks made by a sometimes unreliable manufacturer. They are complex, are expensive to acquire and run, require a team of mechanics, may have weak spots and are therefore best used in groups as opposed to individually. And like the tanks used in the heavy mud of Flanders in the first world war, they can easily get bogged down when used on the wrong ground. So a clear and carefully thought through strategy is required before they are employed in offensive activity on behalf of a business.

3 Trademarks

THIS CHAPTER ADDRESSES the trademark rights that protect many of the ways businesses and products are identified. It covers how they are obtained and the rights they give to the owner to prevent third parties from activities that are likely to be confused with those of the trademark owner. The brand of a business is often that business's most valuable IP asset, and at the heart of most brands is a trademark that identifies – in possibly a variety of ways – products or services as originating from a particular company or source.

Trademark law is a broad concept. It may provide protectable rights in respect of traditional product trademarks such as Cadbury or Hershey for chocolate. But it goes far beyond that, giving protectable rights in respect of the names of companies, names or marks under which services are provided (service marks) and other distinctive features of products, sometimes including shape, smell, sound and colour, as well as their overall distinctive appearance. Under the broad scope of trademark law, protection may be given to everything from single words such as Microsoft or Ford to the shape of the traditional glass Coca-Cola bottle or Heinz tomato sauce bottle, the distinctive look of a luxury handbag or the layout of an Apple store.

Historically, a trademark represented and identified a particular manufacturer. The distinctive red triangle for beer from the Bass brewery was the first registered trademark in the UK and is still in active use. In recent years, the word "brand" has been used in the

For a quick summary of points to note and strategic considerations, go to page 285

context of trademarks, sometimes interchangeably but often more broadly. A brand originally referred to the mark branded on livestock to identify the owner. Now, however, a brand may represent to consumers a certain lifestyle or image, or aspirations.

A trademark may be the symbol of a brand, but the brand is a much broader form of intangible asset representing in part the consumer experience with a company. If it is successful and satisfying, this gives the company a competitive edge over rivals with less strong brands. A brand may have value in many different areas: for example, a variety of products and services are sold under the Virgin brand. Some luxury-goods brands have expanded into perfumes and even hotels. In this context, a trademark may be seen as a symbol not of the quality of a specific product such as beer, but of a much broader consumer or customer experience.

Unlike a patent, which may be challenged and declared invalid, the strength and value of a trademark from a legal perspective is closely related to its commercial strength and value. The legal strength of a trademark generally depends on the amount and type of use, how distinctive the mark is and how famous it has become, coupled with good legal housekeeping. It is possible that a brand becomes so well known that it becomes a generic term, such as escalator, and therefore loses its value, but that is rare.

In general, a major brand is a much more valuable asset than any but the rarest and most valuable patent. A brand may apply to many products across many geographies for decades or longer, but to remain valid (and valuable) it must be registered, used, policed and maintained.

How is a trademark obtained?

In countries with common law jurisdictions (England and countries that adopted the English legal system), legal rights to trademarks are obtained through first use of the trademark by an organisation and the trademark's association by the public with a known and trusted source of goods or services. In countries with civil law jurisdictions, rights to a trademark are generally obtained through first registration. This is one of the major differences in intellectual property protection between common law countries and those such as France and

Mexico that follow a civil code. Thus companies intending to adopt a worldwide brand must make sure that their registration and marketing strategy provides appropriate international protection.

Before applying for registration of a trademark, the following should be addressed:

■ Does the applicant have the right to use and file for registration of the trademark? That is a question of both ownership of a mark and whether others have previously established ownership rights through prior use or registration. It is closely linked to whether is it possible to register the mark given pre-existing marks for which registration has been sought by third parties.

■ Is the mark of a type that may be registered?

■ Is the registration filing timely? This is not normally a problem with trademarks unless a third party steps in and registers the mark first.

■ Where is the application filed?

■ How is international protection obtained?

■ How much will the process cost?

Does the applicant have rights to the trademark?

The trademark owner will normally be the party that has commenced first use of a new, original mark in a common law country or first registered that new, original mark in a civil law country. Ownership issues with respect to trademarks are addressed in Chapter 8. But determining whether the trademark has been previously used or registered by a third party may be resolved through trademark searches.

Trademark searches

Professional trademark searches include not only registrations but also other uses. Separate searches may be needed to reserve domain names and company (corporate) names. Adoption of a new trademark is an international process: checking the proposed mark is available for registration in major markets, and adopting a trademark and domain name filing strategy that provides international protection.

Trademark searches are generally simpler than patent searches.

Search services costing several hundred dollars will look for all prior trademark registrations and applications for registration of a proposed mark in a particular country or region, as well as uses of that mark in sources such as trade directories and on the internet. These unregistered uses are important in common law countries where use of a trademark may give legal rights without a registration.

It is hard to find a unique new trademark that is appropriate for worldwide use. If a consumer-oriented brand is being considered, brand specialists can be retained to propose trademarks and help in their selection. If numerous ideas are being considered, search costs can mount quickly. To reduce costs, initial searches may be carried out online using trademark office search facilities to determine whether direct-hit prior registrations exist. If similar but not identical marks or marks in a different product or service area are being considered, legal advice is recommended because the pre-existing trademark rights of third parties are often a matter of legal interpretation.

A simple first step in discovering whether a trademark has already been registered or used is to check trademark websites such as the United States Patent and Trademark Office (USPTO – www.uspto.gov), the UK Intellectual Property Office (www.gov.uk/government/organisations/intellectual-property-office), or the Office for Harmonization in the Internal Market (OHIM – https://oami.europa.eu/ohimportal/en/home), which issues Community Trade Marks. To check out available domain names go to a service such as www.whois.com.

Company names
When starting a new company, as well as trademark and domain name, the availability of the desired company name has to be checked. In the UK this can be checked at www.companieshouse.gov.uk. In Delaware, the US state most often used for incorporation, the place to look is http://corp.delaware.gov/directweb.shtml.

Can a trademark be protected and registered?
Trademark registration may be refused for marks that are descriptive and not sufficiently distinctive, or that would deny others the right to functional elements necessary to compete. Other grounds for refusal include deceptiveness or offensiveness.

Fanciful, arbitrary, suggestive, descriptive, generic marks

The most common trademark criterion that companies come up against is that of descriptiveness. This is because a descriptive phrase may be a significant marketing advantage. It is normally not possible to trademark purely descriptive marks (for example, milk chocolate) because that would remove needed words or phrases from the public domain. Nor may it be possible to trademark something that is not sufficiently distinctive, such as a common product feature.

Traditionally, the trademark significance of words has ranged from highly protectable to unprotectable. At one end of the spectrum are fanciful marks, such as Exxon, which are made-up words. Next are arbitrary marks, which are known words but have no connection to the underlying product. For example, Virgin has no connection in meaning to any of the services offered under it and is a strong mark.

Then come suggestive marks, which suggest some characteristic of the particular product or service. As the US *Trademark Manual of Examining Procedure* puts it:

> Suggestive marks are those that, when applied to the goods or
> services at issue, require imagination, thought, or perception to reach
> a conclusion as to the nature of those goods or services.

Thus a suggestive term differs from a descriptive term, which immediately says something about the goods or services. Often a suggestive mark is attractive from a marketing perspective, notably, for example, Microsoft – a brand that suggests software for microcomputers.

As noted above, trademarks that are purely descriptive of the goods or services they cover are hard to protect. Fast Laptop, for example, is unlikely to be protectable in any country. In some countries, a descriptive mark may be registered if it can be shown that it has achieved "acquired distinctiveness" or "secondary meaning", that is, association by the public with the owner. Descriptive marks may be valuable from a marketing perspective so many attempts are made to protect them.

However, an important point to note is that choosing a trademark that has no connection to the underlying product can save time and lawyers' fees later because there are likely to be fewer competitors trying to use the same or similar marks or words.

A generic mark is one that the public regards as being the name of the type of product, such as escalator. Such marks are completely unprotectable.

Deceptive and rude marks

Trademarks may be refused registration because they are deceptive in some way, allegedly scandalous or, for example, use the names of national institutions. Under US law a trademark may not be disparaging to persons, which is why the trademark "Redskins" owned by the Washington, DC, Redskins professional football team was cancelled during 2014.

Functional marks

Trademark law generally cannot protect something that is functional and where providing trademark rights would significantly undermine competition in the marketplace. An example is the limited rights of Louboutin, famous for its red-soled shoes, where protection was granted in the US but only where the red sole contrasted with a different coloured top of the shoe, not to red shoes generally – thus not restricting the public from buying red shoes as they historically have done.

Non-traditional marks

There may be difficulties when trying to register a non-traditional mark such as a colour or shape. For example, Nestlé and Cadbury have fought over the registrability of the purple colour used for Cadbury's Dairy Milk chocolate and the three-dimensional shape of the Kit Kat bar. However, the potentially indefinite duration of trademark rights and their legal strengths mean that the efforts required may be worth it, as evidenced by major consumer companies' battles over these types of trademark rights.

Geographic indications

Lastly, there are special rules dealing with particular categories of trademarks such as geographic indications, particularly in the wine and food industries. Geographic indications are covered in the Agreement on Trade-Related Aspects of Intellectual Property Rights (TRIPS). The business consideration is that the law protects producers in particular regions associated with a product from products wrongly claiming or implying that they are also from that region.

When and where to file a trademark registration

In most countries, there is no time limit for filing a trademark application, although it is wise to file early as most countries have a first-to-file priority system. In the US, a trademark filed by a domestic applicant cannot be registered until it has actually been used. However, it is possible to file what is known as an "intent to use" application where there is a bona fide intent to use a trademark in the future. This matures into a normal trademark application when evidence of use is filed with the trademark office.

A trademark registration application may be filed in the local trademark office of the applicant, or it may be made online. The application document is fairly simple, requiring the trademark to be set out in letters or in a drawing, together with the classes or types of goods or services for which the mark is used, as well as other information required under national law – in the US, the date of first use of the trademark in commerce.

As noted above, applications are made for trademarks by reference to classes of goods or services. In other words, a trademark for shoes is in a different category from one for boats. However, the classes do not easily take into account current business models, such as ones with both real and online aspects; and for many products multiple classes may be needed, thus increasing expenses.

In the EU an application may be made not only to a national office but also to the OHIM in Alicante, Spain. Through a Community Trade Mark (CTM) filing, a single trademark can be obtained that is effective in all EU countries. Use is not required for registration, but genuine use must be made of the mark in the EU within five years after registration.

International trademark protection

In many countries, international treaties can be used to file trademark registration applications. As well as the CTM process described above, the Paris Convention and Madrid Protocol allow central international trademark filing if specified procedures are followed;

after registration, the trademark is effective in all the countries that have been designated by the applicant. An application is generally filed in the trademark office of the country of the applicant. Once a trademark application has been filed there is a six-month time limit for filing international applications based on the priority of that first filing under the Paris Convention and the Madrid Protocol.

The registration process

Trademarks may be rejected by a trademark office on formal grounds, because the application is considered not to be registrable, or in some systems because of prior third-party rights. Other systems require the owner to keep a watch on conflicting marks that may be filed by competitors or others.

As with a patent, an application for a trademark is generally subject to examination at the trademark office of the relevant country. Trademark applications are filed for different classes of goods, based on the idea that protectable rights for a trademark generally extend only to the particular sector of goods or services in which it is used.

The trademark examiner will review the trademark and determine whether it is registrable. In some systems such as the US, the examiner will also search for identical or similar marks for each class of goods or services for which an applicant has filed a registration application. So, for example, an applicant for the trademark Cadbury for chocolate would in such a system be refused registration because of the pre-existing registrations for that mark. However, an applicant for a similar mark, such as Cadberry, should also be refused registration on the basis that the applicant's mark is confusingly similar to the already registered Cadbury mark.

Some trademark offices search for third-party prior rights but rely on the applicant to withdraw its application or for third parties to file oppositions. The OHIM, which issues CTMs, follows this system.

Opposition procedure

Brand owners need to be vigilant and watch out for registration of conflicting marks. In many systems, once a mark has been accepted for registration it may also be subject to an opposition period, where members of the public who believe that they will be harmed by the registration of the mark may oppose its registration. This may lead to a litigation-type procedure before the issue of who has rights is decided by the trademark office.

Geography

Trademark registrations are obtained for particular jurisdictions: a country, groups of countries, or, in the case of CTMs, the EU. Trademarks are enforced territorially. Rights in a particular country have generally depended on whether the trademark owner does business in that country under the mark or has a registration there, and whether the defendant uses the mark on goods or services related to those of the plaintiff. Broader geographic rights may be granted to famous or well-known trademarks in some countries on the basis that their reputation transcends national boundaries.

Duration of rights

Unlike patents, which have a set duration, trademarks – although issued for a specific number of years – may be renewed indefinitely. For example, in the US the initial period of registration is ten years, with successive ten-year renewal periods. By the end of the sixth year after registration, and before every renewal, an affidavit of use must be filed setting out the goods or services in respect of which the mark is used and providing samples of use. In the EU under the CTM, registrations last for ten years after application with ten-year renewals, subject to cancellation for failure to use.

The rights of a trademark owner

Trademark registrations are issued for particular classes of goods or services, and a trademark owner has the right to prevent others from infringing use of its trademark within those classes, although famous trademarks enjoy wider rights (see below). Under the laws of most countries, infringement is measured through a standard of "confusing similarity" or "likelihood of confusion". A trademark owner may sue to prevent a third party from using a trademark that would be likely to confuse the public into believing that the goods or services are actually those of the rightful trademark owner. Trademark infringement has its complexities, especially when applying EU law, but that is the basic concept.

One example of such litigation is a court decision in the UK in 2013 that Microsoft's cloud storage service, under the name SkyDrive, infringed BSkyB's Sky trademarks. Microsoft subsequently changed the name of SkyDrive to OneDrive. Another is litigation in the UK, the US and Canada between Thomas Pink, a London-based men's shirtmaker owned by Louis Vuitton, and Victoria's Secret, a well-known lingerie company which as one of its lines sells predominantly teenage products under the Pink brand. In the UK, Thomas Pink succeeded in its claim of infringement of its rights. In the US and Canada, Victoria's Secret is seeking a declaration that its use of Pink does not infringe Thomas Pink's rights on the basis that there is no likelihood of confusion.

Famous trademarks

Traditionally, trademark rights did not extend beyond the particular types of goods sold by the owner of the trademark. However, famous marks are subject to broader protection, which in the US is referred to as "dilution". In this situation, protection is granted beyond the scope of goods or services offered by the trademark owner. An example would be the broad protection granted to McDonald's in the US for "Mc" marks on unrelated products.

Remedies for trademark infringement

Injunctions, seizures and damages

The typical remedy in a trademark action is an injunction preventing further sale of the infringing goods and damages. In many jurisdictions, the right to seize infringing goods may also be granted. The UK Trade Marks Act states:

> *In an action for infringement all such relief by way of damages, injunctions, accounts or otherwise is available as is available in respect of the infringement of any other property right.*

In trademark litigation, the ability to obtain a speedy injunction (a preliminary injunction) is important because of both the impact on the marketplace of sales of infringing goods and the difficulty of calculating the damages suffered by a trademark owner as a result of infringing sales; a preliminary injunction may also give the plaintiff the only remedy it really needs. Many cases end after the award of a preliminary injunction.

Stopping infringing goods at the border

In a number of countries including the US, infringing materials may be stopped at the border through customs enforcement. This is cheap and effective. A mark that is registered at the USPTO or a registered copyright may be recorded with US Customs and Border Protection (CBP), an agency of the Department of Homeland Security. Images of protected rights may be uploaded through the department's electronic recording system so that customs officers can identify the goods. The CBP will also accept guides to the goods, and rights owners may provide training sessions for officers. This is often a highly effective form of enforcement.

Similarly, in the EU infringing products may be stopped at the border under Customs Regulation (608/2013), which sets out procedures applicable in each member state. Measures are being strengthened to include seizure of goods in transit through the EU. The US International Trade Commission (see Chapter 2) may also be used to obtain orders excluding infringing trademarked goods from the US.

However, counterfeiters are protean in form and in November 2014 the *Wall Street Journal* reported that the success of customs enforcement at ports meant that counterfeiters were shifting to sales over the internet directly to consumers.[1] Such websites may nevertheless be seized by law-enforcement agencies.

Counterfeiting

Counterfeiting is trademark infringement whereby the infringing products are sold as the products of the trademark owner and are similar or identical, that is, fakes or knock-offs. Counterfeiting of trademarked goods is a crime in many countries, including the US where statutory damages of up to $2 million may be obtained.

Governments and police are increasingly interested in these practices. For example, the US government has established a website (www.stopfakes.gov) and the City of London police have an intellectual property crime unit.

Online sales of knock-offs

As discussed in Chapter 7, in many countries take-down procedures are part of the laws applicable to internet service providers (ISPs) that protect them from claims of copyright infringement involving customer content. Many online marketplaces have similar procedures for trademarked goods. Under a take-down procedure, an owner of an IP right may contact the ISP's agent and provide a notice of infringing material and that material will be taken down. An example is the eBay VeRO (Verified Rights Owner) programme (http://pages. ebay.com/help/tp/vero-rights-owner.html).

Where products are sold through independent websites as opposed to online markets, as well as seizures by law-enforcement agencies noted above, website-blocking injunctions may be obtained in the UK and some other countries. Internet issues are discussed in Chapter 7.

International trademark enforcement

Trademarks are generally enforced nationally, so although a brand may be international in scope, its protection in each country will be under local law and procedure. The first step of an international enforcement programme is to make sure that registrations have been obtained in the main markets. Then, based on those registrations, the various local remedies available need to be assessed to determine which are most useful: civil litigation; seizing goods at the border (customs); preliminary measures such as injunctions and seizures; co-operation with law-enforcement agencies and government where trademark infringement may be a criminal offence.

Limits on trademark enforcement

Certain uses of a trademark may be found neither to infringe nor to dilute that mark if they are uses that simply correctly describe an item or the trademarked item itself, or, under the laws of some countries, if they are parodies of a trademark (US law may currently be more generous to parodists than EU law). "Grey-market" sales of genuine products from another country are discussed in Chapter 12.

Delay

Delay will cause the loss of urgent (pre-trial) remedies. Further delay may cause the loss of rights against a particular infringer. A trademark owner should be especially careful of any actions that may make an infringer think it will not be accused in the future.

As noted in the previous chapter, most legal systems have a concept of a statute of limitations, which prevents a suit for infringement occurring too long after the infringement occurred. However, there are also concepts of unreasonable delay, or delay coupled with prejudice to the defendant, or actions by the trademark owner which lull a defendant into an understanding that it will not be sued (in common law known as laches or estoppel), that may limit or prevent the trademark owner's remedies against an infringing party.

The crucial point for trademark owners is that if a serious infringement occurs and an immediate remedy is required, the ability to obtain an injunction before full trial (a preliminary injunction) may be lost through any delay.

Value and strength

A trademark is valuable when it has high and positive consumer or customer recognition, in both the business and legal sense, and when it has significant goodwill.

As discussed in Chapter 2, the value of a patent is a highly complex issue; the value of a trademark or brand is far more intuitive. Thus, for example, the value of the Coca-Cola, Mercedes or Sony brand is apparent from widespread knowledge of them and their association with high-quality products. Damage to a brand's value can occur through adverse publicity, particularly that reflecting the quality of the products sold, but also that affecting the brand owner as a whole.

In general, the legal strength of trademarks is a function of their business strength. A legally strong trademark is one that is distinctive, protects a well-known brand, has been used with high-quality products, is registered throughout the major world markets, and is properly and consistently used and policed. The more famous the mark, the greater is the breadth of protection against infringing uses.

Trademarks are associated with quality. Failure to sell quality goods or provide quality services will damage a brand as both a legal and business matter. In common law countries, trademarks are associated with product quality and the goodwill associated with a brand. Thus the trademark's value will diminish, and the trademark rights may even be lost, if the owner does not maintain and police the quality of any licensed trademark use. This is because the trademark will no longer be associated with a single source of quality products and services.

Trademark guidelines

Trademark guidelines aim to make sure that the trademark is used only in the approved form and that over time it does not become generic or descriptive of the goods or services. In this context, trademarks are often indicated as being trademarks by use of the ® symbol (if registered) or ™ (if not registered).

Changing trademarks over time

Sometimes trademark owners decide to "refresh" their trademarks by changing their appearance or wording. This has to be approached with caution because in common law countries rights may be lost if a mark is changed sufficiently, and throughout the world new registrations may be required. In addition, any new variation has to be reviewed to ensure that it does not infringe third-party rights.

Third-party use

Trademark owners need to police the way third parties use their marks to make sure that such marks retain their function as identifiers of the owner's goods. This has at least three aspects.

First, a trademark owner needs to watch for third parties using the same or similar marks and seeking registrations for those marks. As noted above, opposition to registrations may need to be filed. When dealing with legitimate businesses selling non-competing products, so-called "co-existence agreements" may be reached where each trademark owner agrees not to seek registrations for or use a trademark for the products of the other party. However, third-party use of similar or identical trademarks is a difficult area because of the many issues that need to be addressed over time, especially if a trademark contains a word that others may legitimately want to use. Resources are always limited, even for large companies, but trademarks may be used for decades and current compromises may risk limiting trademark rights in the future as a business expands. In some circumstances, there may be no alternative to filing an opposition or taking action in court for infringement.

Second, a trademark owner may need to monitor how trademarks for its products and services are used in the media and elsewhere. At its most extreme, a trademark may suffer "genericide" through rampant unauthorised and improper use and become open for use by all as a generic term for a product. Famous brands that have become generic names include zipper, aspirin and escalator.

The Securities and Exchange Commission filings for Twitter have included the following as a risk factor:[2]

For example, there is a risk that the word "Tweet" could become so commonly used that it becomes synonymous with any short comment posted publicly on the internet, and if this happens, we could lose protection of this trademark.

This is an unusual disclosure, perhaps driven by the seeming impossibility of controlling language use on the internet. However, claims of genericide, though rare, are not theoretical. For this reason, companies with famous marks are well advised to put in place a process for monitoring media use of these marks. A formal notice of complaint should be sent to any organisation that uses the marks in a purely descriptive way or without acknowledging that it is a registered mark. Such complaints will be valuable evidence should the validity of the marks ever be challenged.[3]

Third, as well as making sure that uses that are controllable are correct, trademark owners have to deal with infringers. There are "watch services" that can be used to search for infringing uses. In the past, trademark policing usually involved a fairly rigorous process of pursuing infringers through cease-and-desist letters and occasional litigation. However, the advent of the internet has led to massive amounts of infringement of consumer brands. Take-down procedures can be used with online marketplaces, but for many brand owners these are round-the-clock activities, and for reasons of cost and speed are now automated.

The sheer volume of infringement and piracy means that many consumer companies have difficult decisions to make. The distinctiveness of a trademark needs to be maintained for a mark to retain both its legal and business strength, but pursuing every infringement would be prohibitively costly. As discussed in Chapters 7 and 16, prioritisation may be possible, based on the proximity of the infringement to the business of the trademark owner, but ignoring infringement carries risks. Enforcement may be coupled with a variety of legal and non-legal strategies, such as ensuring pirated products do not come from the brand owner's own suppliers; enforcement in the country of manufacture; working with reputable online markets and internet service providers; working with customs and law-enforcement agencies; advertising and other forms of publicity and education to ensure that the trademark continues to be associated with the business of the trademark owner and that consumers understand about counterfeits and their risks. Often these activities may be co-ordinated with other affected members of the industry.

Licensing: lack of quality control

Widespread licensing of a brand for low-quality goods may tarnish the brand's image. Licensing a trademark without the licensor trademark owner controlling the quality of the goods or services sold under it may render the trademark subject to challenge and potential invalidity. The theory is that the trademark no longer represents a single source of quality products or services. This means that where permission is granted to a third party to use a trademark, the licence contract should in most circumstances contain the right to review, approve and control how the mark is used and the quality of the goods and services of the licensee, and such rights should be exercised by the licensor.

Assignments: lack of goodwill

Under older concepts in common law countries, a trademark could not be assigned separately from the business to which it related because that would separate the trademark from the source of products to which it related and thus mislead consumers. This developed into a concept still in existence in the US that a trademark cannot be assigned without the goodwill of the business to which the trademark relates, the idea being that there should be some continuity of product type and quality. However, in the UK, the Trade Marks Act 1994 provides in Section 24 that a registered trademark may be assigned with or without goodwill, and Article 21 of the TRIPS treaty makes similar provisions. Some countries have a requirement for advertising a transfer without goodwill (the position under previous UK law), and others do not have a requirement to transfer goodwill. However, when entering into a transaction where a trademark is treated separately or is transferred separately from other company assets, and especially if the products covered by the trademark are going to change, specialist legal advice should be obtained.

Trademark holding companies

Trademark or IP holding companies need to be properly structured from an IP perspective. For example, it may be advantageous from a tax perspective for IP to be owned by an entity in a particular jurisdiction and for royalties to flow to that jurisdiction. Alternatively, a company may decide to transfer IP to an entity to avoid a risk of bankruptcy or creditor claims. In common law countries in particular, companies should make sure that the appropriate assets are transferred and that the entity is able to, and does, exercise quality control over the use of trademarks by its affiliates and third parties.

Loss of rights through non-use

Trademarks may be lost after a long period of non-use. Brands of a particular company may be discontinued, or a company may be liquidated or taken over and the name of the company discontinued. The original brand owner may have allowed or been required to let its registrations lapse for lack of use.

In such circumstances, even though the name or brand may still be recognised, it may be possible for a third party to revive the brand or name by filing for registration. In recent years companies have been created to revive abandoned brands that have some resonance with the public. There may be little that the original brand or name owner can do about this beyond, perhaps, claiming some form of unfair competition based on confusion. Companies that are aware of this risk try to maintain some continued use of largely discontinued names and brands.

The limited use of marks may also be for competitive purposes. For example, as a result of a tangled history, the Marlboro brand is owned in Canada by BAT and elsewhere by Philip Morris.

Trade dress and passing off

In a number of countries there are areas of law closely allied to trademark law that may protect unregistered rights that signify a source of goods to the public such as the distinctive appearance or packaging of a product. This is known as "trade dress" in the US or "get up" in the UK. An example is a designer handbag that the public associates with a particular fashion house. Under US law, a claim may be made for infringement of trade dress where elements of the design are not functional, where those rights have acquired secondary meaning (that is, they are associated by the public with a particular source of goods) and where there is a likelihood that the public will be confused about the source of the infringing goods. Such rights may also be subject to dilution (see above).

As well as common law claims, in the US there are federal statutory claims including dilution of trade dress. Notable among the claims brought by Apple against Samsung in 2012 as part of the phone wars were claims for infringement and dilution of Apple's trade dress rights in the iPhone and iPad.

In the UK, the similar concept of passing off may be used (no person may pass off his goods as those of another). As stated in *Reckitt & Colman v Borden, Inc.* (the Jif Lemon case):

> First, [the plaintiff] must establish a goodwill or reputation attached to the goods or services which he supplies in the mind of the

purchasing public by association with the identifying "get-up"
(whether it consists simply of a brand name or a trade description,
or the individual features of labelling or packaging) under which
his particular goods or services are offered to the public, such that
the get-up is recognised by the public as distinctive specifically of
the plaintiff's goods or services. Second, he must demonstrate a
misrepresentation by the defendant to the public (whether or not
intentional) leading or likely to lead the public to believe that goods
or services offered by him are the goods or services of the plaintiff
... Third, he must demonstrate that he suffers or ... that he is likely
to suffer damage by reason of the erroneous belief engendered by
the defendant's misrepresentation that the source of the defendant's
goods or services is the same as the source of those offered by the
plaintiff.

Similar concepts also exist in many civil code countries under
unfair competition statutes. Unfair competition law protection is
required under Article 10 of the Paris Convention for the Protection
of Industrial Property.

Using other people's trademarks

It is fairly obvious that use of a competitor's trademark on identical
goods is asking for a legal claim, and most trademark owners will
object to use of their trademarks by third parties without consent.
The more valuable a trademark the more important that it is used
correctly and in ways that have been authorised and do not wrongly
imply endorsement by the trademark owner.

Start-ups that plaster their websites and press releases with logos
of larger businesses with which they have some relationship may
simply cause the trademark owners to feel that their name is being
traded on. As noted above, some uses of trademarks are permissible
– for example accurately describing a product, or, in some countries,
in a work of art or a parody – but sensitivity should be expected from
trademark owners with respect to any use of their trademarks that
may be regarded as derogatory or taking business advantage.

4 Copyright

THIS CHAPTER DISCUSSES COPYRIGHT, which protects creative works from being copied or otherwise used without permission. It shows that copyright is an easy and almost costless form of protection and therefore should be part of any business's IP strategy.

Copyright is a statutory or, in some countries, constitutional right granted to the author of an original work. Copyright covers the creative expression of literary works, musical works, dramatic works and accompanying music, pictorial, graphic and sculptural works, motion pictures and other audio-visual works, sound recordings and architectural works that have been written down or otherwise fixed in a medium. Copyright protection arises as a matter of law when a work is created and fixed. As the name suggests, the essence of copyright is the legal right to prevent copying of the particular work. Thus copyright prevents the duplication of a CD or a work of art, and allows fees to be charged for the performance of a piece of music, or the copying of a musical score. A literary work need not, however, be particularly literary to be protected by copyright; most countries protect software as a literary work. The creative elements of business documents such as brochures and customer manuals may also be protected by copyright.

Copyright is a robust form of intellectual property. Copyrights may be bought, sold and licensed independently of an underlying business. Indeed, probably the earliest form of monetisation of

---

For a quick summary of points to note and
strategic considerations, go to page 287

IP occurred in the musical copyright field where music publishers amassed and licensed catalogues of musical compositions.

Limitations

Copyright has its limits and these are important to understand in a business context. Copyright does not protect pure ideas or factual information where their expression has no creativity. The World Intellectual Property Organisation (WIPO) Copyright Treaty states: "Copyright protection extends to expressions and not to ideas, procedures, methods of operation or mathematical concepts as such." Nor does copyright generally protect the design of a purely utilitarian object. Protection of such designs is the subject matter of design rights, or design patents in the US. However, rules vary among countries, and where a utilitarian object has sufficient artistic originality, or has separable artistic features, it is possible in some countries that both copyright and design right protection could exist in the same object.

Complexities

Beyond the question of the scope of copyright and whether copyright will protect a company's investment, the crucial policy and political issue today is the fight for control of pirated content on the internet between owners of copyright content and online companies, which benefit from light regulation and easily meet standards for avoiding legal liability for transmitting and housing pirated content (see Chapter 7). There are also emerging issues involving new technologies that threaten traditional copyright-based business models; in the US the concept of fair use of copyrights is used to defend such models.

There are complex schemes for licensing rights in different types of broadcast transmission and performance that are beyond the scope of this book. Copyright and licensing structures struggle to adapt to new forms of distribution. And for those outside the field, it can be hard to determine either what IP rights are needed for a particular project, or where a company is being purchased, what rights that company has. For example, separate rights exist for the author of a musical work, the lyricist and the performer of that work. This has created tension in the area of streaming music over the internet where the appropriate division of royalties between these separate owners of copyright is being disputed. Equally, acquiring a library of celluloid film may transfer no rights in the underlying copyrights. As stated in the US Copyright Act:

> *Transfer of ownership of any material object ... in which the work is first fixed, does not of itself convey any right in the copyrighted work embodied in the object.*

Rights may need to be obtained from a number of different individuals and companies involved in the film's production. Where rights have been obtained, those may also be insufficient for a new medium or form of distribution such as the internet.

Copyright protection exists for long periods of time; legal protection may change over time. For example, before 1972 copyright for sound recordings in the US came under state not federal law, which has led to issues today concerning liability for infringement of those recordings on the internet. In a number of countries, ownership of copyright may revert to an author or their heirs during the period of protection. Although the principle of copyright is simple, there may be huge complexities in obtaining necessary rights to acquire or use pre-existing works such as films and recordings of music, as well as in determining who owns copyright in a particular work (there are "orphan" works where the owners of copyright cannot be found). Thus dealing in copyrightable works is often a matter either of detailed fact finding or of disappointed hopes and litigation.

Reform

As this chapter explains, new technology and the internet have made copyright even more complex and contentious. Litigation is slow in defining the boundaries and the rules that apply in a digital world. In March 2013, Maria Pallante, the US Register of Copyrights, urged Congress in prepared remarks to "think about the next great copyright act" and "think big."[1]

Bear knuckle tussle – tiddely pom

Many of the complexities of copyright are revealed in the 21-year-long legal saga surrounding the character Winnie the Pooh, and the huge revenues resulting from commercialisation of the character by Disney. These included the sheer duration of copyright, old agreements that were claimed not to address valuable new business models and new products that arose over the decades, and therefore arguments over royalties, differing rights splits between three parties, disagreements over whether a crucial agreement was an assignment or a licence, and the possibility of reversion of copyright to the author's heirs – all fuelled by the huge value of the rights involved.

The story involves the following:

- A.A. Milne writing the Pooh stories in Sussex, UK, in the 1920s;
- Stephen Slesinger sailing from New York to meet Milne and in 1930 obtaining exclusive merchandising and other rights in the US and Canada "for and during the respective periods of copyright and renewal thereof";
- a 1961 agreement transferring rights to Walt Disney Productions;
- the possibility under the 1976 Copyright Act that the author or his heirs could terminate a grant of rights to copyright made prior to 1978 (see below);
- a new agreement by Disney with the owners of copyright in 1983 to resolve that issue;
- litigation brought in 1991 by Slesinger's successors claiming breach by Disney of the 1983 agreement by failing to pay royalties due;
- enactment of the Sonny Bono Copyright Extension Term Act in 1998;
- an unsuccessful attempt in 2002 by the author's heir, Clare Milne, joined by Disney, to terminate the rights of Slesinger's successors to the Pooh works based on that new law;
- further litigation in the 2000s by Slesinger's successors for royalties and for infringement of rights allegedly retained by them and cancellation of trademarks owned by Disney (which was defeated by Disney in 2012), with an appeal by Slesinger's successors to the US Supreme Court being denied in 2013.

How is copyright obtained?

Unlike patents or trademarks, copyright generally does not have to be registered for the right to exist. If a work is eligible for copyright protection, that protection arises upon creation and fixation. The US Copyright Act grants copyright to "original works of authorship ... fixed in any tangible means of expression". A tangible means of expression means anything "now known or later developed, from which [the work] can be perceived, reproduced, or otherwise communicated, either directly or with the aid of a machine or device". The act thus intends to cover all forms of electronic media. Under the Berne Convention, the primary international copyright treaty, the requirement that a work be fixed in a material form may vary from country to country. UK copyright legislation states: "Copyright does not subsist in a literary, dramatic or musical work unless and until it is recorded, in writing or otherwise."

In many countries there are no filing or registration requirements, and none are necessary under the Berne Convention. However, the US is an outlier and registration in the US is required if US copyright holders want to assert their rights in the courts. Registration has advantages for non-US copyright owners as well. Similarly, recording or registering copyrights may help when asserting ownership or other rights in other countries. Registration of copyrights in the US is comparatively simple, and the Copyright Office has an online registration service.

Use of a copyright notice (as set out at the beginning of this book) indicates a claim of ownership of copyright but under the Berne Convention does not have a legal implication. However, under the laws of some countries, including the US, a notice may defeat a claim of innocent copyright infringement. The form of the notice should be: Copyright or © [the year of first publication] and [the name of the copyright owner].

As a business matter, whatever the limitations of copyright protection, copyright's near costless creation suggests that all businesses should take the trouble to own the copyright in the work they create or commission and should claim copyright through notice where such a right may exist. Ownership of copyright is addressed in Chapter 8.

Copyright subject matter

Ideas

Copyright does not protect ideas or inventions. As stated in the US Copyright Act:

> *In no case does copyright protection extend to any idea, procedure, process, system, method of operation, concept, principle or discovery.*

Thus a description of an invention may be protected by copyright but that does not protect use of the invention. It may prevent copying of the drawings or text relating to an invention but not the ideas disclosed in them. Protection of those ideas is the domain of either patents or confidentiality agreements.

Software

The particular form (expression) in which a computer program may be written is generally the subject of copyright, but at some level of abstraction the idea or methodology or functionality of the program is not protected.

The extent of copyright protection for computer software continues to be explored in litigation. Google and Oracle have been in litigation over the Android phone operating system and the extent to which Java program headers and application programming interfaces that allow one program to operate with another are subject to copyright protection. The US trial court decided that copyright protection for utilitarian programs was limited, but the Court of Appeals held that copyright protection requires only a limited degree of originality and, looking at the expressive choices available at the time of writing the programs, held that the compilation of program headers and the structure, sequence and organisation of the programs were subject to copyright. At issue is whether Google's use of the copyright material constitutes fair use (see later).

At the same time, the European Court of Justice has held in Case C-406/10, *SAS Institute Inc. v World Programming Ltd*, Court of Justice (May 2nd 2012) that there are significant limits to the scope of copyright protection of computer code, at least where the alleged copier did not have access to the source code of the relevant program but rather studied its functionality. In that situation, unless there is line-by-line copying of the code, copyright infringement may be hard to establish.

However, like other products, software may be protected by multiple forms of IP: copyright at a more detailed level; patent at a functional level; and trade secret for aspects kept confidential.

Facts and data

Copyright does not protect facts, although courts sometimes try to find a way to prevent blatant free riding. For example, in the US, under the "hot news" principle, a tort of misappropriation may in certain limited circumstances prevent competitive copying and dissemination of time-sensitive factual information such as news feeds.

However, although copyright may not protect facts, it may protect creative arrangements of facts. As stated in the WIPO Copyright Treaty:

> Compilations of data or other material, in any form, which by reason of the selection or arrangement of their contents constitute intellectual creations, are protected as such. This protection does not extend to the data or the material itself and is without prejudice to any copyright subsisting in the data or material contained in the compilation.

The European Database Directive provides unique protection to databases. It defines a database as:

> A collection of independent works, data or other material arranged in a systematic or methodical way and individually accessible by electronic or other means.

The selection or arrangement of the contents of the database is protected by copyright. The Directive also provides sui generis protection for a database-maker based in Europe who shows that there has been:

> Qualitatively and/or quantitatively substantial investment in either the obtaining, verification or presentation of the contents ... [to] prevent extraction and/or re-utilization of the whole or of a

substantial part, evaluated qualitatively and/or quantitatively, of the contents of that database.

In the US there is no such protection for the "sweat of the brow"; instead, copyright protection for databases depends on the general copyright law and the database must have the necessary minimum degree of originality for protection. Japan and China have also been reluctant so far to enact a law giving protection similar to the EU Database Directive, so for the time being this remains a purely European form of IP protection.

Nevertheless, databases not qualifying for copyright or *sui generis* protection may generally still be protected through contractual terms and conditions of use, such as a non-disclosure agreement or contractually binding terms and conditions of a website allowing access to that database.

Semiconductor topographies
In 1984, the US Semiconductor Chip Protection Act was passed. It protects the topographies or layouts of semiconductor chips (mask works), which arguably were not protected under copyright law as utilitarian in nature, and is a registration-based system. Similar legislation exists in other countries, and Part II, Section 6 of the Agreement on Trade-Related Aspects of Intellectual Property Rights (TRIPS) now requires protection of semiconductor topographies.

Useful objects
Historically, garments, for example, have not been subject to copyright protection in the US, but fabric designs have been. The US fashion industry is lobbying for specific legislation that will protect fashion designs. As noted above, a specific form of protection for the look or shape of a useful object is a design right or, in the US, a design patent (see Chapter 5).

International protection
Copyright is protected internationally by treaty, including the Universal Copyright Convention, the Berne Convention and the WIPO Copyright Treaty. Most major countries are signatories to one or more of these conventions. A copyright owner who is a citizen of a

country that is a party to a treaty can generally enforce their copyright in a work published in a treaty country in the courts of another treaty country where infringement occurs. However, the litigation in the country of infringement would generally be under the legal standards and procedures existing locally in that country.

Duration of copyright

The duration of copyright in a work depends on a number of factors: the type of literary, musical or artistic work in question; whether or not the author was employed to create the work; whether, when and where the work has been published; and the country in which the question is being asked. Not all copyrights have the same duration even in the same work, for example a recording of music. The copyright in a sound recording may have a duration based on a fixed number of years, whereas the copyright in the musical score may depend on the life of the author.

International copyright treaties lay out default rules, but the trend in recent years at a national level has been for legislation to increase the duration of copyright. The practical conclusion is that it should not be assumed that a work is in the public domain.

Questions often arise about copyright in old works of art in museums. Complications can arise when the image to be copied is not the original one but a newer digital image in which copyright may be claimed (although that claim may be weak), or where photography is forbidden under the terms governing access to where the work is located.

Links to government and other resources on copyright duration are listed in Useful resources at the end of the book.

The rights of the copyright owner

In general, under US law, the copyright owner has the exclusive right to control copying, distribution, public display and performance of the copyright work as well as the preparation of works derived from the copyright (known in the US as derivative works). Under English law, the owner of a copyright has the exclusive right to copy the work; issue copies of the work to the public; rent or lend the work to the public; perform, show or play the work in public; communicate the work to the public; and make an adaptation of the work or do any of the above in relation to an adaptation. Complex rules govern rights and licences in music and broadcasting.

Infringement

Copyright is infringed through copying the elements of a work that are original and protectable expression. Copyright may also be infringed by unauthorised exercise of any of the other rights of a copyright owner such as distribution. Determining which elements are original and protectable and whether they have been copied or otherwise infringed may be complex.

A person may also be liable for secondary copyright infringement through, for example, encouraging or inducing another to infringe. In the context of peer-to-peer distribution of music over the internet, it was decided in 2005 by the US Supreme Court in the Grokster case that:

> One who distributes a device with the object of promoting its use to infringe copyright, as shown by clear expression or other affirmative steps taken to foster infringement, is liable for the resulting acts of infringement by third parties.

Similarly, those who circumvent technological measures such as encryption taken to protect copyright are liable for infringement. As set out in Article 11 of the WIPO Copyright Treaty of 1996:

> Contracting Parties shall provide adequate legal protection and effective legal remedies against the circumvention of effective technological measures that are used by authors in connection with the exercise of their rights under this Treaty or the Berne Convention and that restrict acts, in respect of their works, which are not authorised by the authors concerned or permitted by law.

For example, copyright legislation in the US prohibits "circumvention" of "technological measures" that "effectively control access" to copyright works.

Remedies for copyright infringement

UK copyright law provides broad remedies:

> In an action for infringement of copyright all such relief by way
> of damages, injunctions, accounts or otherwise is available to the
> plaintiff as is available in respect of the infringement of any other
> property right.

In the US, damages may include the infringer's profits as well as profits lost by the copyright owner. There is also a scheme of statutory damages based on a dollar amount per infringed work ($750–30,000) as determined by the court, provided that the infringed work has been registered in a timely manner. Statutory damages for wilful infringement may be increased to $150,000 per infringement and reduced for innocent infringement (see below). Attorneys' fees may also be awarded in certain circumstances. Certain types of copyright infringement may also be a criminal offence in the US.

In many countries, infringing printing press plates and copies may be impounded during the course of litigation and destruction ordered as a part of a final judgment.

Customs services may be used within the EU to stop import of infringing goods. In the US, another advantage of registering copyright is that it may be recorded with US Customs and Border Protection.

Limitations

The defences granted to internet service providers (ISPs) and the limited usefulness of the remedies provided to owners of copyrights with respect to infringing material hosted by ISPs are covered in Chapter 7. From the perspective of the owners of copyright, these are a major hindrance to enforcement of copyright against infringement enabled through the internet.

Fair use and new technologies

The concept of fair use is part of the US Copyright Act, which states that fair use of a copyright work for purposes such as criticism, comment, news reporting, teaching, scholarship or research is not an infringement if it is fair, taking into account factors such as whether the use is commercial or not, the nature of the copyright work, the amount of the copyright work used (a fact-specific test where, for example, copying of small but highly important parts of the work may be problematic) and the effect of the alleged fair use on the market for the original copyright work.

The battle over new technology, fair use and copyright infringement dates back to the 1984 Supreme Court case *Sony Corp. of America v Universal City Studios*. The court upheld the legality of consumers recording television programmes using Betamax VCR technology for later viewing at their chosen time. This was based on a finding that any such copying was a fair use.

A more recent example of the fair use analysis involves long-running litigation over Google Books. In November 2013 a judge in New York found (in a case still in litigation) the Google Books scanning project to be a fair use. The judge acknowledged that Google had scanned and copied millions of books, but the only issue was whether the copying was fair use. The judge held that the factors enumerated in the statute are "non-exclusive and provide only 'general guidance'; they are to be explored and weighed together, 'in light of the purposes of copyright'". The judge then said:

> *In my view, Google Books provides significant public benefits. It advances the progress of the arts and sciences, while maintaining respectful consideration for the rights of authors and other creative individuals, and without adversely impacting the rights of copyright holders. It has become an invaluable research tool that permits students, teachers, librarians, and others to more efficiently identify and locate books. It has given scholars the ability, for the first time, to conduct full-text searches of tens of millions of books. It preserves books, in particular out-of-print and old books that have been forgotten in the bowels of libraries, and it gives them new life. It facilitates access to books for print-disabled and remote or underserved populations. It generates new audiences and creates new sources of income for authors and publishers. Indeed, all society benefits.*

Hence the acknowledged copying was found legal.

The outcome of any fair use case depends on the specific facts, but one thing the US courts consider in cases where there is commercial use of copyright material is whether that use of the copyright work as a result of the new technology is "transformative" by adding something new or different in terms of use, function or expression.

The Berne Convention has a fair use concept:

It shall be permissible to make quotations from a work which has already been lawfully made available to the public, provided that their making is compatible with fair practice, and their extent does not exceed that justified by the purpose, including quotations from newspaper articles and periodicals in the form of press summaries.

However, compared with the flexible approach of the US to fair use, the UK and other countries generally have a more rigid system of specific "fair use" or "fair dealing" exceptions to the rights of a copyright holder – although the UK in 2014 widened what will be permissible fair dealing.

New distribution models

In 2012 a US service introduced by Aereo, a start-up company, streamed television content over the internet. Aereo provided on behalf of each user what amounted to a tiny antenna at a remote location that picked up local TV broadcast signals and allowed the user to view, store and download that content. This was hugely important to the broadcasting industry because given the widespread availability of legal TV and movie programming for download or streaming over the internet, for many viewers the only reason they stayed with expensive and generally unpopular cable TV providers was to obtain access to broadcast TV. Multiple litigations against Aereo ensued and were taken all the way to the US Supreme Court.

The issue was whether the Aereo service infringed the public performance right of the copyright owners. Aereo lost and in 2014 filed for bankruptcy. The Supreme Court issued a majority opinion on behalf of the broadcasters finding that the high similarity of the Aereo service to cable TV meant that Aereo infringed the networks' rights:

Insofar as there are differences, those differences concern not the nature of the service that Aereo provides so much as the technological manner in which it provides the service.

The dissenting judges derided this as a "looks-like-cable-TV" analysis.

Aereo was in some ways a departure from previous cases on copyright and new technology because the Supreme Court took it upon itself to plug what the dissenters described as a legal loophole with its broad approach. The decision leaves uncertainties for providers of new internet-enabled technologies, but the lesson of the saga may be that courts do not look kindly on new technologies that directly take income from a copyright owner without providing something very different for consumers.

The first sale doctrine

The first sale doctrine allows, for example, the owner of a book to give or sell it to someone else without infringing the copyright holder's rights. But things get complicated with digital files.

In the US ReDigi litigation, the issue was whether the first sale doctrine should apply to resale of second-hand digital files such as legally downloaded music. The reseller, ReDigi, had been sued by Capitol Records, which claimed infringement. At the same time there were reports that Amazon was planning to set up a company selling second-hand digital media. The District Court in New York determined that the ReDigi system on a technical level involved impermissible copying of the copyright material of Capitol Records.

In the EU, as well as general principles of copyright law, software protection is governed by the European Software Directive, which provides for protection of computer programs but also puts certain limits on the rights of the owner of the software. In particular, the Directive provides that the first sale of a computer program exhausts the right of the owner to limit distribution. This limitation was the subject of a 2012 case in the European Court of Justice involving Oracle, a large US software company. Prior case law had determined that a lump-sum licence to use a piece of software for an indefinite period was considered to be a sale of goods, and under the Directive the owner's restrictions on the transfer of the physical copy of the software were not enforceable. The question in the Oracle case was whether this would apply to situations where the owner distributed, and the user downloaded, the software on the internet.

The court held that once a copyright holder makes a copy of the software available to a user (in either tangible form as a CD-ROM or intangible form as a downloadable program) in exchange for a fee, under a licence agreement that allows use of the copy for an unlimited period, the copyright owner is essentially selling the copy to the user, and exhausts its exclusive distribution right. Even if the licence agreement prohibits further transfer of the program, the copyright owner cannot prevent the resale of the copy. This does not appear to be the position in the US, where it has been held that the first sale doctrine does not apply to software licensed with restrictions on use.

The issue of whether there is exhaustion of rights in the EU when distributing digital files generally (as in ReDigi) has led to differing decisions. This issue and its scope will ultimately be determined by the European Court of Justice, although the indications from a 2015 Court of Justice case suggest that outside the software field, exhaustion applies only to physical not digital distribution.

Limits on enforcement

As noted in the previous chapters on patents and trademarks, most legal systems have a concept of a statute of limitations, which prevents suing for past infringement after a particular period of delay. For copyright in the US, no more than three years must elapse before filing a lawsuit; but new acts of copying start another three-year period. In the UK the limitation period is six years. However, as noted above, in addition to limitation periods, there are concepts such as unreasonable delay, or delay coupled with prejudice to the defendant, or actions by the copyright owner which lull a defendant into an understanding that it will not be sued, which may limit or prevent the copyright owner's remedies against a party that is infringing.

In *Petrella v Metro-Goldwyn-Mayer*, the US Supreme Court narrowed the applicability of these doctrines and stated:

> It is hardly incumbent on copyright owners ... to challenge each and
> every actionable infringement. And there is nothing untoward about
> waiting to see whether an infringer's exploitation undercuts the
> value of the copyrighted work ... Even if an infringement is harmful,
> the harm may be too small to justify the cost of litigation.

This seems the right approach in a world of multiplying infringement, but rules differ by country and even in the US following *Petrella*, depending on the facts, rights may be modified or lost as a result of delay or misleading conduct.

Value and strength

Copyright value depends on how many people want to have, or listen to, or view, the copyright work. Copyrights may lose value when widespread infringement occurs that cannot be stopped, or when new technologies create ways of exploiting copyright in a manner not covered by the applicable copyright legislation. As discussed in Chapter 7, the battle between the owners of content protected by copyright and ISPs and other distributors of content over the internet is a major issue in IP law today, simply because of the huge economic cost involved.

Copyrights are subject to fewer legal challenges than patents. Copyright enforcement may be complex where line-for-line copying is not involved and there are questions about whether the copied elements are protectable, but where there is direct and substantial copying of the work it is fairly straightforward. The legal maxim that "what is worth copying is worth protecting" has been used with great effect in many copyright cases where the copyright owner can prove that the original work was actively used in the production of the secondary work. In contrast, with a patent there may be legal issues of patent scope, validity and enforceability.

A copyright is legally strong when it protects a piece of software or a creative work that many people would like to copy or otherwise exploit in ways that are clear infringements of the owner's legal rights. Thus, for example, the copyrights to the Microsoft Word program in which this book is written are hugely valuable. Equally, the rights to the works of famous photographers such as Annie Leibovitz and David Bailey will be valuable.

The copyrights to a sophisticated word-processing software program or a specific image do not lose value because of the limits of copyright protection. Creating a new software program would require an immense amount of work, and an inexact recreation of a scene in a photograph would not have the same visual effect. In both instances, copyright is an effective form of protection. However, the copyright in this book as a factual piece of writing is less valuable not only because it may be of less widespread interest or use, but also because the facts and ideas in it may be copied so long as my particular way of expressing those facts and ideas is not copied. In other words, copyright protects how facts and ideas are expressed, not the facts and ideas themselves.

Open-source and copyleft software

Open-source software is software where the source code is made available free of cost for third parties to use, modify or distribute, but on specified licence terms. Such software is not in the public domain in the sense that the authors have not abandoned their rights. Nor is open-source software necessarily the same as freeware or shareware, which may be available free of cost but subject to proprietary licence terms. Rather, open-source software is software that the author has made available on specific terms, such as requiring that any modified source code created and distributed (even in machine readable form) by the licensee be made publicly available.

Open-source software has the philosophical underpinning that copyright prevents creative modification of programs and that a community of users may improve a program through their individual efforts if the source code is made freely available to that community. A dichotomy exists, however, in that those in the open-source community tend to view intellectual property with at best suspicion, whereas those in business software worry that even inadvertent use of "viral", "copyleft" open-source software may throw their software into the public domain.

Copyleft is a concept that has arisen with respect to open-source software. The most prominent form of copyleft licence is the GNU General Public License or GPL developed by Richard Stallman, founder of the Free Software Foundation. The GNU website (www.gnu.org/licenses/licenses.html) sets out the philosophy behind open-source (or free) software and explains why modifications and extended versions of an open-source program should be made public.

However, the requirement to make such derivative works available to the public has been categorised as "viral", and it is this aspect of open-source software that has created concern among companies that sell or license proprietary software. Their worry is that by using open-source software with proprietary code and thereby modifying the open-source code, the owner of the proprietary code will be forced to put its proprietary code into the public domain in source-code form, thus effectively losing both copyright and trade secret protection.

This concern covers not only deliberate use of open-source software but also the risk that employees or contractors have used copyleft open-source software without informing management. Open-source software is freely available to software engineers on the internet and they may "borrow" useful code as shortcuts in program development.

The difficulties are compounded by the fact that the nuances of how open-source software interacts with proprietary software and the legal consequences of that interaction are highly technical, in terms of both software engineering and the applicable and sometimes vague legal language of licences. Thus cautious lawyers may become fearful of any open-source use. For example, in the financing of a proprietary software company or a major software licence granted by a software developer, third parties such as a bank or licensee may seek contractual assurances about the use of open-source software.

Use of open-source code in proprietary code may be detected by scanning that code using commercial tools. In many circumstances it is possible to "remediate" the use of open-source software in a proprietary context, meaning that open-source code can be removed from all copies distributed by the software publisher and replaced with proprietary code.

Where a software development company is bought by a larger company, or a technology company is planning to use third-party code in a critical application, it is becoming more common to carry out these sorts of scans. However, it is always best to address the issues concerning the use of open-source software in a proprietary company before using it.

Authors' moral and other rights

In the US, the copyright statute provides that the transfer or licensing of a copyright executed by the author after January 1st 1978 is subject to termination in certain circumstances 35 years after the date of execution of the grant (that is, the provision of the statute started to take effect in 2013). In certain countries and for certain older works the rather splendidly titled "British Reversionary Right" also provides a right of reversion.

Closely allied to copyrights are moral rights. Even when an author has assigned rights in a copyright, he or she may continue to have a right to attribution as the author or to prevent further modification of the work. Moral rights are considered stronger in civil law countries than in common law countries. The distinction arises because the civil law is more concerned with the human element in the creation of copyright works rather than the commercial aspects of their exploitation. However, the law on moral rights has not been harmonised within the EU and varies considerably even between civil law countries. The practical consequence is that a business should ensure that it has a written waiver of moral rights from the creator as well as any assignment of the copyright in the work concerned.

Furthermore, in some countries (and California under a law subject to challenge) artists may be entitled to a royalty on subsequent sales of their works of art under the doctrine known as *droit de suite* (right to follow).

Clearing rights

Many questions arise on the use of third-party material in a business context. Technology has enabled multimedia documents to be created with images, film clips and music all available for download on the internet.

Images and music are in some ways easier than text. Someone will probably own copyright in an image, a musical composition and the recording itself. If a piece is simply being copied, it is likely that permission is needed. Because a copyright work is available to download does not mean that it is available to copy. Furthermore, the subject matter of an image may bring requirements for other permissions depending on how it is used, including rights of publicity or personality of a person photographed and potentially trademark rights or further copyright rights in the object photographed (such as a work of art).

There are exceptions for fair use, but the principles are open to interpretation. For example, there has been litigation over the use of "thumbnail" pictures in internet search results.

Where text is concerned, short quotations and similar use may often be fair. The questions that have to be considered include the amount taken and any competition with the copyright owner, as well as acknowledgement of the source.

Lastly, nearly all websites and many institutions such as galleries and museums have terms and conditions governing access. Even where something may seem to be in the public domain under copyright law, contract restrictions may still apply.

5   Design rights

THIS CHAPTER ADDRESSES forms of IP that protect the shape and look of objects. They cover designs as diverse as those for hoodies and ice cream vans, and are an increasingly important and low-cost form of IP.

That design rights have become increasingly important has been highlighted by the "phone wars". Design patents and design rights have been at the heart of Apple's litigation against Samsung relating to the iPhone and iPad. Design rights are also becoming more used in the fashion industry, and changes in the UK law in 2014 have made design rights stronger there.

It is also the case that although the extent to which 3D printing will spread remains unclear, IP rights that protect the shape of "things" are likely to grow in importance. This is because 3D printing could, if predictions come true, lead to consumers being able to replicate and print objects on their own. Thus there is the possibility of design files specifying a particular object being shared peer-to-peer, as music was shared over the internet to the great detriment of music publishers, with the objects that are the subject of the design files being printed all over the world.

As noted in the previous chapter, copyright protection is generally not available for utilitarian objects (as opposed to the drawings from which they are made) and the protection of such objects under trademark law can require evidence that the product features are

For a quick summary of points to note and
strategic considerations, go to page 289

distinctive. Design rights (or industrial design rights) are intended to fill this gap and are a useful form of protection for objects from cars to toys to components of complex industrial machines, as well as for items such as distinctive computer interfaces.

How are design rights obtained?

Europe

To be protected in Europe, a design must be novel. Registration may be obtained through the Office for Harmonization in the Internal Market (OHIM) in Spain, which is also the filing office for Community Trade Marks. Registrations are obtained for five years with the possibility of up to four renewals. Unregistered rights also exist for three years after the design is first made public, but unlike registered designs, for infringement of an unregistered right, copying is required to be shown. Design rights are also protected on a national level under the World Trade Organisation's Agreement on Trade-Related Aspects of Intellectual Property Rights (TRIPS).

European registered design rights have been at issue in the litigation by Apple against Samsung relating to the iPhone and iPad in Europe. In 2012 the High Court of Justice of England and Wales issued a judgment that Samsung's Galaxy tablet computers did not infringe Apple's applicable registered design, including the now famous phrase that the Samsung product was "not as cool" as the Apple design. In Germany, a court had issued a conflicting preliminary injunction, which was overturned by a decision in the Court of Appeal of England and Wales in favour of Samsung that was held to be applicable throughout Europe. This decision, by Lord Justice Jacob, is instructive about the scope of registered IP rights where a popular product such as the iPad is involved and shows how they are different from trademark rights or copyright:

> Because this case (and parallel cases in other countries) has generated much publicity, it will avoid confusion to say what this case is about and not about. It is not about whether Samsung copied Apple's iPad. Infringement of a registered design does not involve any question of whether there was copying: the issue is

*simply whether the accused design is too close to the registered
design according to the tests laid down in the law. Whether or not
Apple could have sued in England and Wales for copying is utterly
irrelevant to this case. If they could, they did not. Likewise there is no
issue about infringement of any patent for an invention.*

*So this case is all about, and only about, Apple's registered design
and the Samsung products. The registered design is not the same as
the design of the iPad. It is quite a lot different. For instance the iPad
is a lot thinner, and has noticeably different curves on its sides. There
may be other differences – even though I own one, I have not made
a detailed comparison. Whether the iPad would fall within the scope
of protection of the registered design is completely irrelevant. We are
not deciding that one way or the other. This case must be decided as
if the iPad never existed.*

United States

Design patents were somewhat forgotten in the US until around
2008 when they became recognised as offering potentially valuable
protection at reasonable cost. Case law in that year meant that the test
for infringement is less complex than it was. Furthermore, although
there is a trend towards lower awards of damages in the US courts
in utility (invention) patent litigation, design patents have a different
measure of damages under Section 289 of the Patent Act providing for
payment of the profits of the infringer:

> *[Whoever] ... sells or exposes for sale any article of manufacture
> to which such design or colorable imitation has been applied shall
> be liable to the owner to the extent of his total profit, but not less
> than $250, recoverable in any United States district court having
> jurisdiction of the parties.*

These aspects of design patents were the basis of large damages
awards to Apple in its US litigations with Samsung, which have been
the subject of appeal.

Design patent applications are really no more than a set of
professionally made drawings with little text and thus are much

less expensive to draft than utility (invention) patents. The costs of filing and obtaining a design patent are also lower than for utility (invention) patents (see Chapter 9), and they may be obtained more quickly. The same bars apply to late filing of design patents as apply to utility patents (see Chapter 2).

Design patents filed after May 13th 2015 have a duration of 15 years from the date of grant.

International protection

The Hague Agreement concerning the International Registration of Industrial Designs provides for international protection. The Patent Law Treaties Implementation Act 2012 brought this treaty into effect in the US, which has been a late adopter of the Hague Agreement. The US patent office is working on rules that will enable it to be part of this international system. These changes will integrate the US into an international filing system and should allow international design rights to be filed much more simply and cheaply than is currently the case.

Other forms of protection

Protection of a designer handbag or an elegantly designed mobile phone may be obtained at a number of levels – not just design rights, but also the branch of trademark law known as trade dress or get-up, and in some countries under unfair competition rules. It may also be possible to obtain a three-dimensional trademark registration (see Chapter 3), and some countries are more generous than others in allowing copyright protection for utilitarian objects.

Value and strength

Design right (or patent) litigation is surprisingly technical because it often addresses both the extent to which a design merits protection in terms of originality or novelty and whether the protectable elements of that design have been infringed. The more novel a design, and the stronger the appeal of the design in the marketplace, the more valuable is the design right. Conversely, incremental design improvements may not be as valuable (or indeed valid). Yet given that in many countries there are unregistered design rights, just as with copyright, the virtually costless nature of such protection means that any limitations should not preclude obtaining ownership of those rights. And although design patents or registered designs are not cost free, they are much less expensive than utility (invention) patents.

6 Trade secrets

THIS CHAPTER ADDRESSES the protection of secret information. Confidentiality of information and security of IT systems are basic precautions and protections for most businesses.

The competitive edge of many companies is based on keeping information confidential. Confidential information includes not only the famously secret formula for Coca-Cola but also particular fermentation methods in biotechnology and databases of information that have been laboriously created (note that in Europe, databases are subject to their own form of *sui generis* copyright-like protection). Where an industry has only a small number of large manufacturers, such as the aircraft industry, trade secrets will be the first choice for protection of many aspects of production, because the market participants are unlikely to license patents to each other and the filing of a patent would alert competitors to the new innovation.

To be protectable, information must be kept confidential. This requires physical and IT precautions such as secure buildings, rooms or computer systems, and contract protections such as agreements by employees and collaborators to keep information confidential. There is concern about the practical aspects of keeping information truly confidential given allegations of state-sponsored spying on internet traffic, industrial espionage and employees' use of their own insecure IT devices as well as the cloud for data back-up and services.

Concerns about cyber-security have led to proposals in a number

*For a quick summary of points to note and
strategic considerations, go to page 290*

of countries to increase protections for trade secrets. In November 2013 the EU introduced a proposal for an EU-wide Directive "on the protection of undisclosed know-how and business information (trade secrets) against their unlawful acquisition, use and disclosure". Various legislative efforts are also under way in the US, including the aptly named Defend Trade Secrets Act.

What is a trade secret?

The concept of a trade secret may encompass many types of information that are important to a company, from technical to strategic to financial. Article 39 of the Agreement on Trade-Related Aspects of Intellectual Property Rights (TRIPS) states:

> 2. Natural and legal persons shall have the possibility of preventing information lawfully within their control from being disclosed to, acquired by, or used by others without their consent in a manner contrary to honest commercial practices so long as such information:
>
> a) is secret in the sense that it is not, as a body or in the precise configuration and assembly of its components, generally known among or readily accessible to persons within the circles that normally deal with the kind of information in question;
>
> b) has commercial value because it is secret; and
>
> c) has been subject to reasonable steps under the circumstances, by the person lawfully in control of the information, to keep it secret.

In most US states, New York being a notable exception, trade secrets are covered by the Uniform Trade Secrets Act (UTSA). Unlike patents and copyrights, which are created under US federal law, trade secrets are generally a matter of US state law, although expanded federal legislation is under consideration.

A trade secret is defined in the UTSA as:

> Information, including a formula, pattern compilation, program, device, method, technique, or process, that: derives independent economic value, actual or potential, from not being generally known to, and not being readily ascertainable by proper means by,

*other persons who can obtain economic value from its disclosure
or use, and is the subject of efforts that are reasonable under the
circumstances to maintain its secrecy.*

Personal information

Some successful internet companies monetise personal information
about their users through advertising or other means. However,
misuse or loss of personal information including security breaches
risks heavy legal, financial and reputational damage.

Personal information is information about individuals that may
include their date of birth, address, contact details, national insurance
or social security numbers, financial information such as credit-card
and bank account numbers, medical information, or information
obtained through following their internet or mobile device activities.

Personal information may not technically be secret (for example,
your neighbours know where you live and your employer knows
how much you earn), and the rights relating to personal information
are not generally intellectual property rights. However, its use may
be commercially valuable and its misuse harmful to an individual.
Laws governing the use of personal information by third parties
are generally separate from trade secret laws and have grown up
as information technology and the internet have enabled data
to be collected, transmitted and shared including across national
boundaries – and used for good or ill (see Chapter 7).

How are trade secrets created?

Trade secrets are created by developing something novel and
valuable in a confidential environment where those with access to
the information are under obligations of confidentiality. Thus, for
example, a group of employees may develop a new formula for a
chemical product and keep that formula confidential. Until disclosure,
the formula would be a trade secret.

The same or a similar trade secret may be developed
independently by independent groups. Moreover, independent
creation may not prevent a claim of patent infringement by someone
who has filed for a patent not knowing of the trade secret. Although

many countries have some sort of prior user defence, which protects the use of an invention predating the patent filing, this is often factually and legally difficult to prove. The burden may be on the defendant to prove its prior use and such a defence is not always available. (One solution to this issue that loses all IP protection is a defensive publication, a method of clearly putting an invention into the public domain to avoid problems with a third party patenting the same invention.)

Development of trade secrets through unauthorised access to the trade secrets of others is generally problematic. This may arise through often inadvertent misappropriation of trade secrets belonging to others, where employees or consultants are hired who may have worked for a competitor and may bring with them that competitor's trade secrets. Thus steps should be taken to ensure that employees or consultants working on a project do not do this, for example by investigating their prior work and obtaining statements from them that they can work on the project without using other people's confidential information.

How are trade secrets protected?

There is no form of registration applicable to trade secrets. They maintain their value through being kept confidential.

Each individual who may develop or receive the trade secret must agree to keep it confidential. Precautions should be taken to safeguard the secret information against misuse, loss or theft. As well as contractual agreements with employees and others who may have access to the information, precautions include keeping material under lock and key, physically secure facilities and appropriate IT security guarding against unauthorised network or internet access to computers where the information may be stored.

Given that much of a company's value lies in its internal information, a potential buyer will look closely at the precautions taken to ensure that its confidential know-how cannot simply "walk out of the door" at any time. This will involve a review not only of physical and IT security, but also of agreements with employees and third parties.

Trade secrets are usually lost through inadvertence, such as allowing public access to the information, or through careless or wrongful acts by employees or third parties. Readers of reports on loss of data will marvel at how often unencrypted laptops are lost.

The cloud

Many companies now store data and operate programs remotely through third-party services, a business model loosely known as the cloud. Some services provide security from intrusion that would be hard for a small company to replicate itself, but such services should be investigated before use on at least three levels:

■ What do the terms and conditions of use say about confidentiality and access by the service provider and its employees?

■ What are the actual security systems and measures that prevent third-party intrusion?

■ If this is a concern, under what circumstances could the service provider be required to give access to data in response to a legal or government order?

Protecting trade secrets

Elements of a thorough trade secret and personal information protection programme include the following:

■ Understanding what information is secret and valuable and what other types of information the company holds, such as personal, health or financial information about customers, it is crucial to protect.

■ Understanding and complying with particular laws that govern security and access to different types of information, such as personal, health or financial information about customers as well as complying with contracts with third parties governing information provided to the business.

■ Employee policies and training covering good practices on storing of confidential information, laptop security, use of e-mail (including training on how to handle e-mail that may contain malware), use of the internet and social media, and access to and use of confidential information outside the office, including control over use of memory sticks and other easily lost or stolen computer media, as well as use of personal devices such as laptops, smartphones and tablets.

- Policies on use of open-source software.
- Policies on review of publications for patentable inventions prior to publication.
- Policies on marking of information as confidential (ie, appropriate documents are stamped or headed "Confidential").
- Education of employees on use of non-disclosure agreements (see later).
- Entrance and exit interviews with employees emphasising confidentiality obligations.
- Secure facilities, including access procedures and sign-in logs, key cards and other measures, and secure areas with no visitor access for critical material.
- Use of encryption.
- Disposing of unneeded or duplicate documents or data through shredding or destruction of computer media. Note that computer media containing data may be found in copiers, scanners, employee devices and even cars that download the content of personal devices.
- Secure internal and external networks, with access limited on a need-to-know basis to sensitive information, with both perimeter security and, ideally, methods of detecting unauthorised activities within networks. (If senior management cannot understand the terminology of and information from their IT department, a consultant or other "translator" should be hired.)
- Crucially, audit of the security procedures of contractors, which are often a weak link.
- Plans for dealing with a breach of security that comply with applicable laws governing the type of information held by the

company, including required notices to third parties and attempts to mitigate the likely consequences.

Chapter 7 addresses privacy, data protection laws and cyber-security risks. However, data security is by no means just an internet issue. Major data breaches have resulted from the theft of network access credentials held by a contractor and the misuse of employee access credentials. Some of these risks may be mitigated through cyber-liability insurance.

Trade secret versus patent

There may be a choice between keeping certain information as a trade secret and protecting it under a patent. A failed patent application that is rejected after publication will result in any trade secret protection being lost. Thus the two forms of protection cannot coexist in the long term, except to the extent that a company has trade secret information different from that disclosed in a patent.

There are certain requirements, as well as advantages and disadvantages, for each form of IP protection (see Figure 6.1):

■ Patent protection is advantageous for inventions that can be reverse engineered or where the invention is plain to see. If a third party can take a device and eventually deduce the process by which it works, that process cannot be maintained as a trade secret. Trade secret protection may, however, be used for manufacturing processes not accessible to third parties.

■ Patent protection requires that any invention be novel and non-obvious and satisfy other statutory requirements not required for trade secrets. A patent search revealing that the chances of obtaining a valuable patent are low may lead to consideration of trade secret protection.

■ If a patent is obtained, it will have a specific term. By contrast, a trade secret can in theory have an indefinite duration, so long as it is not inadvertently disclosed and is kept secret.

■ Patents are simply not available for certain types of secret information that does not fall within the subject matter of patent protection.

■ There is a time lag between publication of a patent and the patent coming into force.

■ Patents are expensive, but so is a complete programme of trade secret protection given the complexity and cost of employee policies and contractual, physical and IT protections that are required to maintain confidentiality.

■ The increasing number of network security breaches has led some to question how effectively a valuable trade secret can be protected from government, criminal or competitor espionage. Others, however, argue that changes in the US patent system are weakening patents and so argue in favour of more reliance on trade secrets.

■ Keeping a valuable invention secret and not filing for a patent has certain legal risks, as a third party could independently discover the same invention. That third party could also file for a patent itself.

Some people draw the conclusion from the foregoing that trade secret protection may be considered for less important developments or for products with a short market life and early obsolescence, because of the cost of patenting in major markets and the time taken for a patent to issue.

Unauthorised use or disclosure

Unauthorised use or disclosure of trade secrets lays the offender open to a variety of civil legal actions – and in some countries and in some circumstances criminal liability.

A breach of contract claim with regard to a trade secret is a claim for breach of an agreement (for example, by an employee) to keep information confidential, or by a third party to use information only for a particular purpose. There may be criminal liability as well as a civil claim; for example, in the US certain forms of taking of trade secrets are also a crime under the Economic Espionage Act 1996.

Article 39 of the TRIPS agreement prohibits taking trade secrets in "a manner contrary to honest commercial practices", which means "at least practices such as breach of contract, breach of confidence and

FIG 6.1 **Patent versus trade secret and other IP**

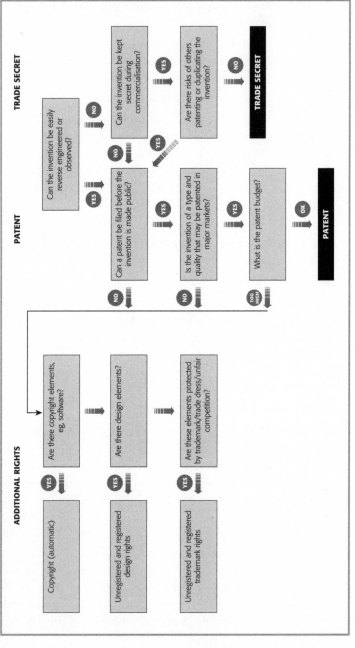

inducement to breach, and includes the acquisition of undisclosed information by third parties who knew, or were grossly negligent in failing to know, that such practices were involved in the acquisition".

The proposed EU trade secret legislation includes the following litany of bad acts:

The acquisition of a trade secret without the consent of the trade secret holder shall be considered unlawful whenever carried out intentionally or with gross negligence by:

(a) *unauthorised access to or copy of any documents, objects, materials, substances or electronic files, lawfully under the control of the trade secret holder, containing the trade secret or from which the trade secret can be deduced;*

(b) *theft;*

(c) *bribery;*

(d) *deception;*

(e) *breach or inducement to breach a confidentiality agreement or any other duty to maintain secrecy;*

(f) *any other conduct which, under the circumstances, is considered contrary to honest commercial practices.*

The wrongful taking of a trade secret is in the US a form of misappropriation. In the UTSA misappropriation is defined as follows:

"Misappropriation" means: (i) acquisition of a trade secret of another by a person who knows or has reason to know that the trade secret was acquired by improper means; or (ii) disclosure or use of a trade secret of another without express or implied consent by a person who (A) used improper means to acquire knowledge of the trade secret; or (B) at the time of disclosure or use, knew or had reason to know that his knowledge of the trade secret was (I) derived from or through a person who had utilized improper means to acquire it, (II) acquired under circumstances giving rise to a duty to maintain its secrecy or limit its use, or (III) derived from or through a person who owed a duty to the person seeking relief to maintain its secrecy or limit its use; or (C) before a material change of his [or her]

position, knew or had reason to know that it was a trade secret and that knowledge of it had been acquired by accident or mistake.

The typical legal remedy sought for these types of activity is an injunction to prevent further misuse or dissemination of the trade secret. As set out in the UTSA:

Actual or threatened misappropriation may be enjoined. Upon application to the court, an injunction shall be terminated when the trade secret has ceased to exist, but the injunction may be continued for an additional reasonable period of time in order to eliminate commercial advantage that otherwise would be derived from the misappropriation.

However, if there has been a disclosure to the public by the time of the litigation, the "horse has left the barn" and the owner of the trade secret is left with a claim for damages with the often hard task of proving the amount of loss he has suffered.

Value and strength

A commercially valuable trade secret protects something secret of great value to a company's competitors but not available to them. Examples include the formula of Coca-Cola, the method of manufacturing a pharmaceutical and software used by an investment bank to measure risk.

The legal strength of a trade secret depends on its secretness and the ability to argue in court that it is not generally known. Under the TRIPS agreement, legal action for taking a trade secret requires proof of the information not being generally available to the public, its value and the steps taken to keep the information confidential.

Non-disclosure and employment agreements

Non-disclosure agreements (NDAs) with third parties and employee confidentiality agreements are crucial parts of a programme to protect trade secrets.

In many countries, employees may be under duties implied by law to maintain an employer's information as confidential, but these duties are generally much strengthened by being put in writing. Without a written NDA, third parties to whom confidential information is provided may be under limited constraints, if any. Those who sign NDAs agree not to disclose confidential information to others and preferably to use such information only for specifically limited purposes.

Employee confidentiality agreements and NDAs may cover a number of IP issues where the underlying law may lead to ambiguity. For example:

- What types of information are regarded as being confidential?
- When is confidential information regarded as coming into the public domain?
- Precautions (agreements, physical protections and IT protections) to be taken to ensure confidentiality is maintained.
- The obligation of confidentiality and the limits on persons to whom confidential information may be disclosed, in what circumstances, and with what requirements (for example, that recipients have to accept confidentiality restrictions themselves).
- Permitted and prohibited uses of confidential information.
- Ownership and assignment of intellectual property developed through use of confidential information and under the agreement (or the employment relationship).
- Return of confidential information and destruction and deletion of files.
- Legal requirements on use, processing, security, disclosure or export of personal information as a result of laws governing personal information identifying individuals, information relating to the health of individuals or information relating to financial transactions.
- Obligations to report any breach of confidentiality or security.

Confidentiality and collaboration

Modern informal collaborations, particularly in respect of the internet and e-commerce start-ups, and open research collaborations often do not mix well with a traditional focus on intellectual property. Where a patentable invention is made, it may be disclosed publicly, thus possibly fatally damaging patentability. And ownership disputes may arise over business models, as was the case in the litigation regarding the founding of Facebook by students at Harvard. Although not the case with Facebook, the involvement of employees of a university may lead to claims of ownership by the university itself as a result of its employment policies or use of its facilities. Entrepreneurs should educate themselves as to the risks of informal collaborations where matters such as ownership rights are not defined in writing even if they accept them.

Submission of ideas

Many people come up with ideas that they wish to submit to a company, be they new technologies for cars or the concept for a new television programme or film. The unsolicited submission of ideas is problematic for all involved. The established company may already have a similar idea under development. Individuals may be aggrieved that their idea is not accepted; and if they later see a similar product, they may believe that they have been cheated.

The basic problem is that ideas are not usually protected by copyright and many ideas are not patentable. That leaves confidentiality, but confidentiality normally requires some express or implied agreement.

In the US, attempts have been made in a number of cases in New York and California (centres of the entertainment industry) to resolve these issues and arrive at fair results through various legal theories. These are too complex to discuss here, but a few common-sense guidelines apply:

- If submitting an idea, be wary of companies' idea submission forms. These are usually designed to remove legal rights.
- Disclose as little as possible.
- It is generally a good idea to include a copyright notice and a confidentiality notice.
- Always try to negotiate a non-disclosure and limited-use agreement.

■ If receiving an unwanted idea, limit disclosure within your organisation and send the communication straight back, disclaiming any duties. Possibly keep a copy in a legal archive unavailable to business people and let the discloser know that.

Agreements not to compete

Non-competition provisions in employment agreements are useful, but to ensure enforceability legal advice should be taken.

An employee non-compete agreement may restrict that employee from gaining employment in a competing company for a defined period of time. Such agreements are useful in that they may prevent former employees, who have knowledge of a company's trade secrets or other confidential information, from going to a competitor or using the information for their own benefit. Not permitting an employee to work for a competitor for a period of time may be more secure than relying on the agreement of an employee not to disclose a previous employer's confidential information while in future employment.

However, most countries do not allow enforcement of an employee covenant not to compete that is unreasonable in scope, due to the excessive territory covered or an overly long duration, because it will essentially put an employee out of work. California, a centre of the technology and entertainment industries, goes further and states in Section 16600 of the Business and Professions Code that a contract "by which anyone is restrained from engaging in a lawful profession … of any kind" is "to that extent void". There is, however, significant case law surrounding the provision and particularly its intersection with trade secret law.

7   IP and the internet

ENTIRE BOOKS ARE DEVOTED to the law of the internet. The aim of this chapter is to identify some of the business (and political) issues posed by the internet in the context of intellectual property protection and risk, and, in conjunction with Chapter 16, proposes strategies for dealing with IP issues.

Trademark and domain name strategies

Domain names are a comparatively recent form of intellectual property. At its most basic, a domain name is an address for a website on the internet, obtained through a contract with a domain name registrar. Domain names are the combination of a second-level domain name, such as profilebooks, and a top-level domain (TLD), such as .com or .co.uk, to create a domain name: profilebooks.com. The Internet Corporation for Assigned Names and Numbers (ICANN) manages much of the domain name system and has contracted with companies that have rights to act as registrars. Domain names can be obtained through a company providing registration services for the desired TLDs. Registering is a simple online process. Rights to a domain name are largely a matter of the contract between the applicant and the registrar.

In 2012, ICANN set up a process for issuing generic top-level domain names (gTLDs) to anyone able to act as a registrar at a cost of $185,000 per application. As well as opening up new domain names

For a quick summary of points to note and
strategic considerations, go to page 292

for the public, this allows companies to use a brand name as a TLD, or to have control over a generic term that has business significance, such as .search. ICANN has also set up a trademark clearing house, which will contain a verified database of trademark information supporting the new gTLDs. Registered trademark owners are able to record their marks in the registry and thereby obtain certain protection against or notice of cybersquatters (see below). The gTLD and clearing-house procedures open up new fields of domain-name-related law and practice.

Domain name and trademark strategies should be interlinked but often are not. This is usually because lawyers or trademark agents handle trademark filings and business people or advertising agencies handle the acquisition of domain names. Ideally, selection of a new trademark would involve both a search of prior trademark rights and an assessment of available domain names. A trademark filing programme would also be linked to a domain name registration programme, as the two rights are legally intertwined.

Some common mistakes occur in obtaining domain names. First, they are so simple to obtain that they may be purchased by employees or agencies acting in good faith who forget to transfer ownership to the employer or client, or to keep track of renewal notices, which go to the employee or client. Second, although trademark lawyers are punctilious in recording deadlines for the renewal of trademarks, domain name renewals are sometimes forgotten, with the result that a third party may come in and purchase the domain name.

Companies typically try to protect a name or brand by registering a number of major TLDs (such as .com and .net) and local markets where the name or mark will be important (such as .co.uk or .de or .jp). Some companies also register variants that may be caused by typographical errors or to protect against an adverse use of the name (for example, in US slang, xxxxsucks.com, or the new TLD .sucks). Third-party companies provide domain name management services enabling domain names to be managed as a portfolio.

Cybersquatting

Obtaining a domain name is simply a matter of availability, but there are laws and procedures to protect individuals and companies whose names are wrongfully taken. Domain names have been the subject of IP disputes as a result of cybersquatting, which involves the acquisition of a domain name for a brand, company name or celebrity before the legitimate owner acquires that domain name. Other forms of abuse involve typo-squatting, where a variant of a famous name is registered, or the acquisition of inadvertently lapsed domain names.

Generally, a cybersquatter that adopts a domain name identical or confusingly similar to a trademark in which someone has rights may be prevented from using it. Thus protection of domain names is essentially derived from trademark rights. The Uniform Domain Name Dispute Resolution Policy (UDRP) is an arbitration procedure administered by the World Intellectual Property Organisation (WIPO) and some other organisations. Under this procedure the owner of a registered trademark may obtain transfer of a cybersquatter's domain name that is identical or confusingly similar to the registered trademark.

Although other laws, such as the US Anticybersquatting Consumer Protection Act 1999, enable objections to wrongful domain name registrations, the UDRP usually provides a quicker, less expensive resolution. The remedies available to a trademark holder are cancellation of the wrongful domain name or the transfer of the registration. Filing a case with the UDRP does not prevent either party from filing suit in a national court. ICANN is also establishing a new and simpler procedure, the Uniform Rapid Suspension System, which it says offers "a lower-cost, faster path to relief for rights holders experiencing the most clear-cut cases of infringement".[1]

Geographic and field-of-use rights

In general, except in the case of famous or well-known trademarks, the same trademark can be registered by different companies for, say, crackers and hotels (Ritz). However, a domain name does not on its face indicate what goods and services it covers. A problem arises when different companies, each with a legitimate trademark, wish to use the same domain name. There is only one web address available for that trademark with a particular TLD. Which company obtains this domain name has been based on first come, first served, with the later registrant having to use another TLD or a variant of its trademark.

For example, Merck & Co, a US pharmaceutical company, has since the first world war been separate from its original German parent, Merck KGaA. The domain name merck.com is used by the US company and merck.de by the German one. The latter forwards US users to an English-language website, which contains a disclaimer: "In the United States and Canada the subsidiaries of Merck KGaA, Darmstadt, Germany, operate under the umbrella brand EMD."[2] This is not cybersquatting, which involves an attempt in bad faith to acquire rights to a domain name before the rightful trademark owner has a chance to register it. In this instance, there are two or more rightful trademark owners. And as noted, steps may need to be taken to avoid customer confusion.

Websites, e-commerce and privacy

The laws relating to websites and the laws relating to personal data are not IP laws as such. However, although the laws relating to personal data establish obligations on the holders of that data, there is no doubt that a large database of personal information may be a hugely valuable intangible asset.

Risk mitigation

Establishing an internet-based business involves potential risks, obligations and liabilities, often of an international nature. A simple website set up in the UK to sell a product may collect personal information about its customers, including credit-card information, and may be subject to comprehensive regulation under EU rules on contracting, data protection and privacy. For example, uses of devices such as cookies (messages given to a web browser by a web server) are subject to EU regulation.

However, if that website sells to US customers as well, it may be subject to federal and state laws governing privacy and security. There has also been much patent litigation in the United States brought by patent assertion entities (PAEs) and others over various aspects of e-commerce. Companies offering goods, services or software for licence over the internet to US-based customers may risk a claim of patent infringement.

This is an example of where the borderless nature of the internet may result in the risk of potential claims being made. One solution is to build an internet business in a series of steps, starting with the home country and then, through the use of differing domain names and TLDs (for example, .co.uk rather than .com), directing customers to websites created for and tailored to the risks and regulations in a particular country or region. An example is a UK website that does not take orders from customers in a particular country (such as the US), but directs them to an affiliated site established to cater for specifically US issues.

Terms and conditions and architecture

New websites are often created in a haphazard manner. For example, there is a general understanding from review of other websites that there may need to be terms and conditions of use and a privacy policy. But these are often borrowed from some other context and are sometimes spectacularly inapplicable to the business model and technology. There is also typically little co-ordination between the technical architecture of the website and the legal and contractual aspects, so that customers purchasing a product may never have had to agree to terms and conditions of sale, and even if they did, there may be no record of that agreement.

Furthermore, the terms and conditions and privacy policy of the website may bear no resemblance to its business and data practices. Each website generally needs terms and conditions of use, and a privacy policy developed in conjunction with a legal review of how third-party, customer or employee personal information is handled. In the US, the Federal Trade Commission may investigate complaints about companies that are alleged not to live up to their privacy policies using its powers under Section 5 of the Federal Trade Commission Act – and it has done so in cases involving major internet businesses.

Correctly establishing the terms and conditions and the internal and external technical architecture of a website should enable an internet company to mitigate a number of risks, comply with the most immediately applicable regulatory schemes and attempt to control its international exposure. The website architecture should be as secure as possible from third-party hacking and intrusion, and should comply with applicable laws governing security of customer data, including credit-card information.

As well as establishing a secure legal and technical framework, a well-executed website should also address IP issues through correct use of trademarks, copyright notices, and terms and conditions that make clear what is and is not permissible use. The copyright in the content of the website, in terms of text and illustrations, should as far as possible be owned by the website owner so that remedies are available in the event of third-party copying. This may protect a website when competitors or others copy its designs and features; although truly novel web-based operations may also be protectable through patents.

Privacy and data protection laws

Companies and individuals that have access to individuals' personal information may be under legal obligations concerning use of that information, even if it is not strictly confidential. Examples would be a person's name, address, e-mail address, identification number, employment, medical and financial information, religious affiliation and ethnicity, credit-card numbers and so on. Collection and use of such information on website users, customers and employees may be regulated or prohibited. Companies new to international operations (particularly over the internet), or new to gathering and using personal information, should focus particularly on regulatory and technical (IT security) compliance in the major jurisdictions where they do business.

Over 100 countries now have data protection laws in force and these, as well as companies' own undertakings given through privacy policies on their websites, may limit or restrict the use, disclosure, export or processing of such information, and require minimum standards for confidentiality and security. They may also require notices to customers of security breaches and unauthorised access by third parties.

Applicable legal regimes are complex. In the US, for example, regulation depends on the industry involved and regulation may occur at both the federal and state level, depending on the industry. In the EU, there is a comprehensive regime that covers the "processing" (itself covering most acts you can think of) of "personal information" (which is also broadly defined). Similar regimes have been adopted in Canada, Japan and many of the free-market countries of Asia, Africa and South America. Thus data protection is something that all internet businesses are forced to recognise and grapple with.

Compliance is a significant cost and administrative burden for companies. In general, outside the area of health care, regulation is lighter in the US than in the EU, but a remarkable decision of the European Court of Justice in May 2014 illustrates the reach and power of data protection law. The court held in *Gonzalez v Google* that Google was responsible for compliance with data protection law in Spain and had to ensure that links to a newspaper article mentioning Gonzalez were disabled in Google's search engine. The implications of the case are still to be worked through, but it shows how control over personal information remains ultimately with the individual not the data collector.

A classic problem for companies based outside the EU is moving personal data about customers or employees in the EU through networks to locations outside it in contravention of EU laws. A proposal to create a new Data Protection Regulation – a uniform but stringent set of privacy standards across the EU – has raised significant concerns among US companies that rely on data collection and use, such as Facebook and Google. The proposed regulation contains a provision that would subject businesses to fines for infringement based on a percentage of their worldwide turnover, in the way that antitrust sanctions have been enforced for a number of years. Whether the eventual percentage enacted proves to be 10%, 5% or 1%, the consequences for breaching this new regulation will be severe. Hence there has been a record level of lobbying against it. Furthermore, the issue of transatlantic data access has been accentuated by the Snowden revelations of US government surveillance.

Even within the US there is unease over data collection and aggregation practices. The commercial incentive to track behaviour on the internet and combine online and offline databases to create "big data" is huge given the holy grail of efficiently targeting online advertising to consumers. As a saying attributed to more than one notable businessman puts it: "Half the money I spend on advertising is wasted; the trouble is I don't know which half." Tracking consumer habits and likes on the internet helps answer that question: hence its great commercial value.

In general, loss or misuse of customers' personal data is a major reputational, legal and financial issue for a corporation, and maybe even disastrous. In the US, there is the possibility of class actions for damages, where individual plaintiffs sue on behalf of all the affected customers, as well as actions by state and federal regulators. Breaches of the existing data protection laws in Europe may involve fines or imprisonment. For any company, customer data use and protection should be on every list of major compliance and risk management issues.

Blogging, social media and IP risks

Employees' use of their own tablets or smartphones for business purposes, the use of cloud-based services to store or back up data, social media, websites, blogging and other internet activities bring with them a variety of IP risks. Proprietary information may be removed from corporate networks and made public or placed in insecure locations. Personal accounts may be set up rather than corporate accounts that can be monitored and terminated. Weak links are created.

When managers or other employees are permitted to blog, or post content, there is a risk that confidential information may be disclosed to the detriment of the company, or statements made that may be legally troublesome in the future. Product launches may be disclosed before patent filings have been made; trademarks may be used in an incorrect manner; statements may be made about patents or other intellectual property that are not correct; and so on. Policies should be developed to address these issues. And security policies should address the use of personal devices and cloud-based services.

Linking and framing

Linking is where one website connects to another through a link, taking the user to another website. Framing occurs when the second website may be viewed through the original website, so that the user is presented with the original website and the second website on one page. Linking and framing may raise issues under trademark or unfair competition rules if, for example, users are likely to become confused as to the association between the two websites, or if logos of the linked site are used. The terms and conditions of a linked website may also prohibit certain activities.

These practices may also be challenged under copyright law. As a business matter, however, challenges to linking have occurred in contexts where the effect of the link is arguably to divert revenue from the owner of the website. In Germany, this resulted in legislation being passed on ancillary copyright, which was aimed at enabling newspapers to share the revenue of news aggregators, such as Google and Yahoo, which publish small amounts of text in news listings with links to the original site.

Use of trademarks in metatags and search terms

Various online practices aimed at driving traffic to websites or providing targeted advertising using competitors' trademarks are subject to litigation over their legality. The outcome depends on the facts of each case, such as how trademarks are used, what types of advertisements are called up by use of those trademarks and what trademarks those advertisements contain.

For example, in a 2013 case in the UK, Marks & Spencer was found to have infringed Interflora's registered trademark by purchasing "Interflora" as a search term in Google Adwords, thus triggering the display of a link to Marks & Spencer's flower delivery service in a way that on the facts was held to be confusing as to the source of the service. The decision was overruled on appeal in 2014 on the basis that the burden of proof was on the trademark owner:

> [T]o establish that the advertisement complained of does not enable normally informed and reasonably attentive internet users, or enables them only with difficulty, to ascertain whether the goods

*or services referred to by the advertisement originate from the trade
mark proprietor ... or, on the contrary, originate from a third party.*

The use of a trademark in meta elements (or metatags – which
provide information about webpages that is readable by a search
engine) to drive searches to a website not owned by the trademark
owner has been found to be a basis for possible trademark
infringement in the US. In the case in point, a company marked its
website with a competing company's brand so that search engines
would pick up the brand and drive traffic to the company's website.
However, this type of "initial interest confusion" was found not to be
part of EU law by the UK Court of Appeal in the Interflora case.

Cybercrime, trade secrets and hacking

The internet is often the vehicle for cyber-attacks, for example through
"spear phishing", where an e-mail to an employee if opened enables
malicious code to invade a network. From an IP perspective, use of
the internet and public networks presents a risk of loss of trade secret
information that needs to be addressed as a part of business planning.
Risk identification and mitigation are now regarded as board-level
obligations within companies. At a political level, cyber-security and
national security cause discord between governments and internet
companies and users, who have very different interests in privacy
and regulation.

At the administrative level, following a 2013 order from the
president, the US National Institute of Standards and Technology
issued in February 2014 its *Framework for Improving Critical
Infrastructure Cybersecurity*, which provides broadly applicable
guidelines on best practices. A 2015 presidential order encourages
sharing of information on cyber-security threats. However, there
has been significant opposition to proposed legislation to combat
hacking and cyber-security threats. The US Cyber Intelligence Sharing
and Protection Act is aimed at sharing information about hackers
and attacks, but there are concerns about the transfer of personal
information to the government in the course of cyber-security
investigations. Nevertheless, there is support for creating a federal
cause of action for trade secret misappropriation (federal procedures

are generally more effective than their state law counterparts) and closing loopholes in existing applicable criminal legislation such as the US Economic Espionage Act and the US Computer Fraud and Abuse Act.

In the EU, there is also legislation pending that seeks to address similar issues. Under the proposed legislation, providers of "critical infrastructure", such as energy, transport, health care and financial services, would be subject to various obligations relating to security, including that breaches of security would have to be reported to the authorities.

Copyright and piracy

The internet has enabled enormous piracy of copyright material and the easy sale of knock-offs of branded goods. The economics of the music industry have been fundamentally changed by the combination of the digitisation of music, the internet as a means of copying and transmission, and the availability of massive amounts of low-cost digital memory. Pirated copies of TV programmes and films are freely available. Legitimate companies are also pushing the boundaries of copyright law. For example, websites aggregate news stories from news services. And the Google Books project fundamentally alters the publishing industry by copying into digital form millions of books and making those copies searchable. From a US perspective, a number of these issues touch on the doctrine of fair use (see Chapter 4), and the boundaries of the law are constantly being challenged.

The sheer quantity and ubiquity of infringing material on the internet means that owners of content or branded products are involved in a never-ending effort to stop such piracy. This has led to owners of IP trying to attach liability to internet service providers such as search engines and marketplaces.

The internet has therefore become the main battleground where the rights of copyright owners are tested. It is in some ways a battle between advocates of freedom of speech and a free internet (or business advocates seeking loose internet regulation sheltering behind free speech concerns) and content industries such as music, publishing, software, TV and film. Even within the US the interests of different regions diverge; northern California, notably Silicon Valley, is home to companies focused on the internet and benefiting from loose regulation and loose liability standards, whereas southern California, around Los Angeles, and New York are home to content industries. These conflicting interests continue to clash over proposed legislation and treaties aimed at reducing piracy.

Liability of ISPs and online markets

Many legitimate companies enable the advertising and sale of pirated products, yet liability is hard to prove and regulation remains lax, being based on a legislative balance between the remedies of IP owners and freedom of the internet that is hotly debated. Under the Digital Millennium Copyright Act (DMCA), which amended US copyright law to address internet and digital issues, a network service provider may avoid liability for copyright infringement as a result of content posted by users, provided that the service provider:

(A) (i) *does not have actual knowledge that the material or an activity using the material on the system or network is infringing;*

   (ii) *in the absence of such actual knowledge, is not aware of facts or circumstances from which infringing activity is apparent; or*

   (iii) *upon obtaining such knowledge or awareness, acts expeditiously to remove, or disable access to, the material;*

(B) *does not receive a financial benefit directly attributable to the infringing activity, in a case in which the service provider has the right and ability to control such activity; and*

(C) *upon notification of claimed infringement ... responds expeditiously to remove, or disable access to, the material that is claimed to be infringing or to be the subject of infringing activity.*

The protections are conditional upon the service provider designating an agent to receive notices of claimed infringement. So long as the service provider complies with the statutory requirements and takes down the infringing material upon being notified by the copyright owner, it may avoid liability and be inside what is often called a "safe harbour".

Similar legislation applies in the EU under the E-commerce Directive (2000/31/EC), where Article 14(1) states that liability may not attach if:

(a) *the provider does not have actual knowledge of illegal activity or information and, as regards claims for damages, is not aware of facts and circumstances from which the illegal activity or information is apparent; or*

(b) *the provider, upon obtaining such knowledge or awareness, acts expeditiously to remove or disable access to the information.*

Although this may seem fair, infringing copyright material is rife on the internet and the burden of enforcement is on the IP owner. In practice, IP owners may employ people or services to police the internet continually for infringing material. Many legal challenges have been mounted by suppliers of copyright content throughout the world claiming that ISPs are failing in their duties, ignoring red flags indicating infringing material or being wilfully blind, and that they should be liable for enabling the sale of counterfeit products. These challenges have had mixed results, with the decisions tending to support the ISPs.

The increasing amount of internet piracy has led to intense lobbying and political pressure from providers of copyright content, such as the music and entertainment industries, to enact new legislation and enter into IP-focused treaties. Such efforts have been vigorously opposed by telecommunications and internet companies, which often argue that such legislation would curtail free speech.

In the UK in 2011 and 2012 there were legal challenges to provisions of the Digital Economy Act 2010 which required ISPs to send notices to suspected infringers and potentially to cut off service to them. In Ireland, a 2012 government order providing for the possibility of injunctions against ISPs raised significant concerns. In the US, the Stop Online Piracy Act (SOPA), introduced in 2011, aimed to strengthen the ability of US law enforcers to fight online infringement and infringing sales. The legislation came up against well-organised lobbying and protest from technology companies, which claimed that it could stifle the freedom of the internet, particularly with regard to provisions that might require ISPs to block access to sites that provide infringing material, or stop search engines linking to such sites. The Anti-Counterfeiting Trade Agreement (ACTA) encountered similar opposition in the US and the EU, where it was rejected by the European Parliament. The ACTA was claimed to embody the agenda of the motion-picture industry in particular. It addressed various remedies against copyright infringement and counterfeiting and would require all signatory countries to have similar levels of intellectual property protection.

Similarly, efforts to attach liability to online marketplaces that allow the sale of "knock-offs" have generally not been successful in the US so long as the site is willing to take down infringing products, and have had mixed results in Europe.

However, in the UK under Section 97A of the Copyright, Design and Patents Act, which predates the Digital Economy Act 2010, the court has the power to grant an injunction against a service provider to block a website "where that service provider has actual knowledge of another person using their service to infringe copyright". This provision has been successfully used to block access to websites infringing copyright, and in 2014 a similar remedy was granted to block websites selling goods that infringed trademark rights.

Working with ISPs

In the absence of court or legislative victories, the film, music and fashion industries have turned to negotiating with major industry players such as Yahoo! and Google to voluntarily take steps to reduce piracy. In September 2013, Google issued a report, *How Google Fights Piracy*. At more or less the same time the Motion Picture Association of America issued its report, *Understanding the Role of Search in Online Piracy*, pointing out the pivotal role of search engines in providing access to pirated material. Google's report is a thoughtful presentation of the issues involved and is worth studying. One example of the focus of ISPs is "following the money". A number have adopted notice and take-down procedures to remove infringing sites from their advertising programmes, which provide revenue for those sites.

Reducing demand for counterfeit products

Current thinking on piracy focuses initially on whether it is being driven by aspects of a company's marketing strategy that may be modified to limit the incentives for counterfeiters, such as simultaneous worldwide publication of a copyright work as opposed to creating unsatisfied demand in certain regions. The music industry is using services that make legitimate digital copies of a copyright work available online at a reasonable price and allowing music to be available through legal streaming services. Over time, the ready availability of legitimate and convenient channels may reduce demand for piracy.

Where tangible products are sold over the internet, supply chain and supplier relationships are audited and examined to determine whether the goods come from genuine suppliers who do not have exclusive supply obligations. Attempts can be made to bring these suppliers into the anti-counterfeiting strategy.

Technological measures can also be used. For example, where copyright files such as software are distributed, licence keys and passwords may assist in limiting copying.

An internet infringement strategy

Infringement of rights over the internet remains a huge and frustrating problem. Solutions differ across industries, but here are some questions to ask:

- Are aspects of the company's worldwide marketing or pricing strategies encouraging piracy through unmet demand? Can these strategies be changed so that online content is available conveniently and legally?

- Are there sources of counterfeit products from within the company's supply chain that can be stopped?

- Are the problems industry-wide? Are there trade association resources that can be marshalled? Can a trade association negotiate with legitimate ISPs or lobby government? What can be done co-operatively with competitors suffering the same problems? Are there steps that a legitimate ISP can be persuaded to take (for example, reducing the prominence of certain websites or removing infringing sites from advertising programmes)?

- Are ISPs or other intermediaries that do not seem to be legitimate or to be following the normal rules being used? Could they be the target of litigation under current case law?
- Are there technological solutions to piracy that can be used, such as licence keys?
- How can infringement issues be prioritised? For example, which internet activities lose revenue or may threaten ownership of IP rights or their value?
- How can targets be prioritised? For example, which activities are carried out by legitimate companies (which may be the easiest to pursue), which by customers and which by illegitimate companies?
- Can the company make transactions or settlements with legitimate companies using its IP?
- Where are identifiable infringers located?
- Are the company's IP rights registered in these places?
- What is the strength of the applicable legal rights in the company's home country and in other countries? Do any countries have laws that favour particular industries?
- Are any of the activities potentially criminal in any affected jurisdiction? Can law enforcement assist by, for example, seizing infringing websites?

8   Who owns IP?

THIS CHAPTER ADDRESSES the rules relating to the ownership of IP. They are important because the default rules usually fail to meet business expectations, and not least because disputes over IP ownership are frequent. Typically, they arise between:

- employers and employees where the employer is surprised not to own IP rights;
- companies and independent contractors, including software writers and website developers, where the party paying for a project discovers that it does not own the IP;
- collaborating parties where the default joint ownership rules do not implement common ideas of what is meant by "joint" action;
- companies and universities and university employees where the university claims an ownership interest;
- manufacturers and international distributors where the distributor claims ownership of the manufacturer's trademark in the distributor's country;
- individuals and companies where the name of an individual is used as the name of the company and there is a later parting of the ways.

Each type of IP has somewhat different default rules governing

---

For a quick summary of points to note and
strategic considerations, go to page 294

ownership in the absence of a written agreement, and these rules vary among countries, so there should always be a written contract setting out the deal on ownership.

Patents

In the US and Europe, the inventors of a patent are the original owners of the patent although they can assign that right. In the US, an application for a patent is filed by the inventors with an oath of inventorship. Deciding who is an inventor of a patent can be complex, because it depends on who made a necessary inventive contribution to the actual inventions claimed in the patent.

Article 60 of the European Patent Convention states that:

(1) *The right to a European patent shall belong to the inventor or his successor in title. If the inventor is an employee the right to the European patent shall be determined in accordance with the law of the State in which the employee is mainly employed ...*

(3) *For the purposes of proceedings before the European Patent Office, the applicant shall be deemed to be entitled to exercise the right to the European patent.*

However, the applicant need not be the inventor and can be a successor. No oath of inventorship or similar document from an inventor is required.

Rights of employers and employees

Under US law, in the absence of an agreement, an invention will belong to an employer only if the employee is hired to invent. Otherwise, in the absence of agreement, an employer may have only what is called a "shop right", a non-exclusive right to an invention made during the course of employment that may not be non-transferable, with the employee even having the right to license a competitor. Even where hired to invent, a written assignment from the employee to the employer is required.

In the UK, an employer would generally own inventions made during the normal course of employment where an invention may be expected. In Germany, under the German Act on Employee Inventions, an employee has to disclose an invention to their employer and the employer has to claim rights to "service inventions" (or rather, not waive those rights), subject to compensation (see below). China also has a service invention rule, but apparently with a twist that an employee may have a pre-emptive right to purchase the patent if it is sold by the employer.

Obviously, the rules differ among countries, and within countries rules and classifications are not precise. Therefore the only sensible course is to have written contracts with employees covering ownership of IP, notwithstanding that some aspects of laws protecting employees may not be waived by contract. (Other benefits of employee agreements are discussed in Chapter 6.)

Employee compensation

In certain countries, such as Germany, France, Japan, China and the UK, inventors may be entitled to economic compensation for use of their inventions by their employers. Again the rules differ: in the UK, an invention of outstanding benefit to the employer is necessary for a right to compensation; in Germany, the rule is one of reasonable compensation.

Rights of joint owners

The ownership of IP created in a collaboration between people in different companies may be joint even if the contributions are not equal. The rights of joint owners of patents vary by country. In the US, each joint owner can exploit and license the invention to a third party without the consent of (or compensation to) the other joint owner. This is not the case in many other countries where the consent of the joint owner would be required to license a third party.

As a result of these differing rights, including situations where the rights of a joint owner make the patent rights essentially non-exclusive, it is crucial to determine how patent rights should be allocated in terms of ownership and licence rights in an agreement between the parties. Joint ownership may appear to be a reasonable compromise, but the results may be unpredictable and result in loss of valuable exclusivity over patent rights.

Rights in improvements

Rights in an invention that is an improvement to an underlying patent are owned by the inventors of that improvement (or their employer). Contractual provisions in licences which provide that improvements made by a licensee are to be owned by the licensor are subject in some countries to competition law scrutiny (the idea being that the original owner of a valuable technology should not be able to continue to dominate a field by having rights to all improvements). However, ownership rights in and licence rights to improvements and similar developments should be considered in any collaboration or licence.

Independent contractors

In general, an invention developed by an independent contractor is owned by that contractor, even if the contractor was retained specifically to do the development work. Agreements with third parties should cover ownership and provide an assignment of IP in writing. Time and again, often at the point of sale of a company, it becomes apparent that IP believed to belong to the company in fact belongs to a third-party contractor as a result of failure to have a written assignment of IP.

An independent contractor or a manufacturer or supplier that develops IP while working on a project will generally own that IP if there is no written agreement and assignment. There may be some type of implied licence to use the patent, but again this highlights the requirement for a written agreement covering ownership of IP rights. Some contract manufacturers own substantial IP portfolios, so it should not be assumed that they are not focused on IP issues.

Failure to tie up the issue of patent ownership when hiring independent contractors is one of the classic recurring errors in business relationships, along with failure to provide for ownership of software in software development agreements.

Patent ownership and universities

When contemplating an arrangement with a university or a university academic in any country, review the university's rules on IP ownership and conflicts of interest (these are often on the university's website). Determine whether the academic has third-party funding for his work that may affect rights to that work.

In the US, universities generally take the position that all inventions made on their premises or using their equipment or made by their employees during their work for the university are the property of the university. This is not necessarily the position elsewhere in the world, where a doctrine has existed, sometimes called the "professor's privilege", which allows academics to take title to their inventions. There are variations by country, including whether inventions automatically belong to the university as a matter of employment law, or whether the university has a right to acquire an invention, failing which it reverts to the academic.

Many universities have conflict of interest rules and procedures that must be followed before academics can enter into commercial collaborations. Academics often ignore these rules; they also sometimes get into tangles as a result of accepting various sources of funding with conflicting conditions. However, most universities actively pursue opportunities for technology transfer and establishment of start-up companies. For a business partnership to be successful, it is crucial to understand the rules-based approaches of most academic institutions and work within those rules.

Much work at universities is undertaken with government funding. In the US, a vast amount of funding comes through the National Institutes of Health (NIH) and the Department of Energy. Specific legislation covers ownership of patented intellectual property developed with government funding. The Bayh-Dole Act allows the university or laboratory to take title to patents, but without government consent that IP cannot be transferred to a third party. There are also certain rights and restrictions that may be attached to the patent and how it is licensed and exploited: for example, the right of the US government to use it anywhere in the world, rules providing a preference for licensing to a small company so long as it is as well able as others to exploit the technology, and a waivable preference for US manufacture of the patented item.

Keeping title records up to date

Title to patents is recorded by country in the country's patent office. In the US, title may be traced from the original inventors to the current owner and in other countries from the original owner onwards. This chain of title information is available online. Rules are pending in the US that will require disclosure of other parties with an interest in a patent.

Typically, a suit for infringement can be brought only by the current record owner (or its exclusive licensee) with the benefit of an unbroken chain of transfers of patents from the original inventors (in the US) or their employer (in many other countries). Accordingly, it is important when considering enforcement to ensure that this chain of title to the relevant patents has been properly updated. When title has not been updated in a timely fashion, trying to update it later can be difficult, as it may not be possible to trace the people who must sign the paperwork.

In some systems, where assignments are not recorded, there is a risk that the same patents could be sold again to a third party, which could rely on the failure of the patent office records to show the earlier assignment to establish its superior rights.

Encumbrances on title

As with other forms of property, patents can be mortgaged. To ensure that a patent being acquired has a clear title, a search should be carried out. In the US, the law is unclear on whether security interests (mortgages) should be recorded in the patent office or under state law, and it is necessary to check both the patent office and certain state recording offices (usually the secretary of state of the state of incorporation for US corporations) for "security interests" filed under the Uniform Commercial Code. Specialists carry out such searches.

Each country generally has an office where mortgages on patents can be recorded, and local law will dictate whether or not a failure to record will protect a purchaser from an undisclosed mortgage.

Trademarks

Ownership of trademarks is best established through registration. Particularly in the international context, an agreement over trademark ownership should be obtained with distributors and licensees and trademark filings made before allowing a third party to use the trademark. Use of personal names as trademarks may bring risks of disputes.

Registration

Disputes over ownership of trademarks are less common than those over patent inventorship or expectations that copyright created by a third party should be owned by the commissioning party. As noted in Chapter 3, trademark ownership rules in common law and civil code countries differ significantly. In general, in civil law countries, trademark rights are acquired by registration. In common law countries, trademarks are regarded as indications of a source of high-quality goods or services and ownership arises primarily through first use of the mark. However, registration provides significant advantages including a record of ownership.

International issues

Issues of trademark ownership may arise in international business where the trademark owner has not thought ahead and registered its trademark internationally so as to protect it in countries where it may do business. The risk is that a distributor in a foreign country may file for registration of the mark in that country. In some countries it may even be argued that the distributor of imported goods is in fact the first person to use the mark in that country. Thus trademark ownership should be addressed in contracts with distributors as well as through registration.

Personal and family names

Problems often occur either in family businesses where family members argue and one or more family members want to split off but trade under the family name, or where, for example, a designer trades under their own name, sells that business but later wants to start a new business using the same name. The latter situation can be addressed in advance, but problems in family businesses can be hard to predict. The law generally tries to strike a balance between trademark rights and the right of individuals to use their own name.

Joint ownership

Joint ownership of trademarks is permitted but may be problematic, especially if the joint owners split up. Joint ownership is comparatively unusual, given that trademarks generally indicate a single source of a trusted brand, although it is expressly catered for in Section 23 of the UK Trade Marks Act. When establishing a company or collaboration, joint ownership is likely to lead to future legal complexities because a trademark usually refers to a single source of goods or services. However, a jointly owned entity (such as a joint venture) could more easily own a trademark. The associated business questions of what would happen to the ownership of the trademark upon termination, including whether one of the co-owners may acquire exclusive rights to it, or whether the mark may be sold to a third party, would have to be addressed.

Recording ownership

Like patents, registered trademarks have a system of recorded ownership where the current recorded owner is the party that has the right to bring a suit. Also like patents, title to trademarks has to be updated to take account of corporate mergers, divestitures and so on. Failure to do so can bring later difficulties.

Encumbrances

As a form of property, trademarks can be mortgaged. In the US, as with patents, there is a debate over whether such third-party rights should be recorded at the trademark office or on a state level, so appropriate searches should be conducted to check whether a trademark is encumbered by a mortgage and appropriate filings made in both locations by the owner of a mortgage. In Europe, including in the UK, trademarks can also be used as security.

There are some complications in using US intent-to-use trademark applications as collateral for a loan because of legal restrictions on assignment of that type of application (see Chapter 13).

Copyright

The author is generally the original owner of copyright. An exception in many countries is when a work has been created by an employee in the course of his employment (see below).

Ownership of a tangible work versus ownership of the underlying copyright

As noted above, there is a difference between ownership of a work (a painting) and copyright in that work. Thus copyright will normally remain with the artist after the original artwork is sold. This is specifically covered in the US Copyright Act. A purchaser of an original painting should not be surprised that copies of it may be available for sale from the artist.

Employers and employees: works made for hire

Where a copyright work is created by an employee in the course of his employment, that work usually belongs as a matter of law to that person's employer. This is the rule in the UK. In the US, such a work is known as a "work made for hire", which is a work "prepared by an employee within the scope of his or her employment"; this has advantages for a business because the employer is considered to be the author and thus various protections for the actual author do not apply.

Joint ownership

Joint authorship, and therefore ownership, of a work may arise inadvertently: for example, when two companies are working together. In any joint artistic, literary or software project, rights should be spelled out in writing, including any rights to share in profits or royalties.

Joint ownership occurs where a work has two or more authors. Under US law, a joint work is one prepared by two or more authors with the "intention that their contributions be merged". In the UK, a "work of joint authorship" means "a work produced by the collaboration of two or more authors in which the contribution of each author is not distinct from that of the other author or authors". In some countries, joint works can arise by law, such as joint rights that result from broadcasts under English law. The issue with respect to joint ownership is the ability of each joint owner to exploit or license the work (or block that exploitation or licensing) and if money is received, whether it must be shared with the other co-owner. The rules vary significantly among countries, so it is important to have a written agreement in advance.

Derivative works and adaptations

Derivative works or modifications to or adaptations of a pre-existing work are generally subject to separate ownership from the underlying copyright work if they are themselves subject to copyright. The act of creating the derivative work or an adaptation would be an infringement of the underlying copyright in the absence of a licence, but a claim for infringement would not under most legal systems result in a transfer of ownership of the adaptation.

An example of a derivative work or adaptation is a translation of a literary work. The copyright in the original work and the copyright in the translation are required to publish the translated work. Without any written agreement to the contrary, a translator retained to translate a work will own copyright in that translation.

Independent contractors

As with patents, written agreements should be reached on ownership of copyright before retaining an independent consultant, contractor or staffing agency. In the absence of a written agreement, copyright in works created by independent contractors (commissioned works) will be owned by the contractor, contrary to the business expectations of the parties. This is often an issue when a company is being sold or needs to raise finance, and in the software industry when code has been written by contract employees. Where software is concerned, because there will be moral rights in some jurisdictions associated with the copyrights in the software, the written agreements should include an express waiver of these moral rights so that the developer is not in a position to impede commercialisation of the product.

If there is not an express agreement assigning ownership, there may be an implied licence in favour of the commissioning party, but the absence of an express agreement is always potentially problematical. Alternatively, the absence of a clear agreement may give rise to the work being considered a joint work, but with possibly unpredictable results in respect of sharing of revenue depending on the terms of the arrangement.

In the US, it may be possible to rescue the situation through the scope of what a work made for hire is. Employment in the context of work made for hire is based on common law principles of agency, so in some circumstances there may be so much control over contractors that they may be treated as employees for copyright purposes.

Universities

There may be similar concerns with copyright as noted above with patents. Many universities have developed policies on when they claim ownership of copyright works created by their employees. Often the question for university staff is whether a work is created in the course of the employment of the academic, such as teaching materials, as opposed to the results of independent academic research.

Recording ownership

Many countries have systems for recording claims to ownership or assignment of copyright that may help provide evidence of ownership. In the US there is a system of registration of copyright, and owners of copyright need to make sure that the registration document lodged with the copyright office specifically identifies the work and gives other relevant facts. However, the long duration of copyright means that ownership of works can become hard to find, and where it cannot be tracked down, the work is referred to as an "orphan work".

Encumbrances

Copyrights are a form of property that can be mortgaged. In the US, the general view is that a mortgage against a registered copyright must be recorded at the Copyright Office and a mortgage of an unregistered copyright is recorded at a state office, but most lenders will file in both offices if possible. Thus searches for encumbrances on title need to be conducted in both locations. In other countries, copyrights can be pledged or mortgaged according to local law. In some jurisdictions this may be through an assignment to the lender with a right to reconveyance on full payment of the loan.

Reversions

Transfers of copyrights in the US and certain other countries are subject to termination or reversion to authors or their heirs after a certain number of years. The rules relating to future reversions of copyright are complex and any acquisition of rights to an older work needs to be carefully reviewed (see Chapter 4).

Music, multimedia and dramatic works

Ownership of rights in music and entertainment works is complex. For example, there will be separate copyrights in a musical composition, the lyrics and the recording of a performance of that composition. A multimedia work may have a number of separate rights holders.

Rights of personality and publicity

In the US a right of publicity is a right to control exploitation of the identity of a person. In certain states, such as California, the right is part of a state statute:

> *Any person who knowingly uses another's name, voice, signature, photograph, or likeness, in any manner, on or in products, merchandise, or goods, or for purposes of advertising or selling, or soliciting purchases of, products, merchandise, goods or services, without such person's prior consent, or, in the case of a minor, the prior consent of his parent or legal guardian, shall be liable for any damages sustained by the person or persons injured as a result thereof.*

Rights of publicity are separate from copyright but may exist in the same work. For example, copyright in a photograph of a movie star may vest in the photographer, but the movie star may claim that he has separate rights in his image and that use in a commercial work would require his consent.

Rights of publicity need to be addressed when obtaining rights to content involving individuals. In the US, college athletes, whose likenesses were included in video games, sought compensation for that right, notwithstanding the existence of a licence between the video-game publisher and the sports league. Although English law does not have the equivalent right, in a case brought by Rihanna against Topshop about a T-shirt on which a photograph of her had been printed, Rihanna was able to rely successfully on a passing-off theory (see Chapter 3) that the T-shirts would be assumed to be authorised or approved by her, which they were not.

Design rights

For designs created after October 1st 2014, the rules on patents also apply to UK design rights. Previously, where a design was created in pursuance of a commission, the person commissioning the design was the first owner of any design right in it. This was different from the rule applicable to copyrights and the rules applicable in the US, where in the absence of agreement, ownership vests in the designer not the commissioning party. Under the new law, where ownership initially belongs to the designer, the rules are now consistent.

Trade secrets

More than one company may develop the same or a similar trade secret and each may have ownership rights. It is also the case that the law relating to joint ownership of trade secrets is not well developed. However, issues over ownership of trade secrets generally arise in the context of departing employees who move to a competitor or start a new company, or in situations where there has been a disclosure of trade secrets (for example, in connection with a business deal) and the party receiving the information later develops a product apparently based on the information disclosed. Most issues with trade secrets are best addressed through written agreements with employees and third parties governing use and protection of confidential information.

Corporate structure and taxation

Ownership of intellectual property within corporate groups may be complex and have significant tax consequences. As an initial point of reference, intellectual property would by default be owned by the entity employing the creators of that IP. So intellectual property created in the US by US employees would be owned by the US entity. If that intellectual property is to be used by a European affiliate, under tax rules typical of many countries the US entity would have to license, or would be deemed by the tax authorities to have licensed, the European entity to use the IP at a royalty rate equivalent to the arm's-length royalty that would be payable by a third party. The net result would be that income would flow back to the US and be taxed there.

Tax havens

Countries differ in their taxation of income associated with IP. Some countries are tax havens. Others have lower effective rates of tax applicable to IP income, often for policy reasons. For example, in April 2013 the UK established the Patent Box scheme, which allows a lower rate of corporation tax to be paid on income arising from certain patent rights where specified ownership and development conditions are met. The goals are to spur research and development and encourage IP ownership within the UK. These types of arrangements are, however, under review in the light of the focus on tax avoidance (see below) and the UK Patent Box is likely to be modified.

Multinational groups

Multinational groups set up IP holding structures designed to minimise their overall worldwide levels of taxation. Generally, transfer of ownership of pre-existing IP between affiliates in different countries may trigger a tax liability because transfer pricing taxation rules require the transaction to be for an arm's-length consideration (price), which is treated as the transferor's revenue and taken into account in calculating tax.

However, cost-sharing arrangements can be made to determine ownership of IP to be developed in the future for tax purposes through sharing of the costs of that development between affiliates. Where costs are shared with an offshore affiliate using a formula based on worldwide sales, that offshore affiliate may be entitled to receive and retain income from exploitation in countries outside the company's home jurisdiction. Using buy-in arrangements covering pre-existing IP and cost-sharing arrangements covering future IP, ownership of IP for tax purposes can be allocated between jurisdictions. For tax purposes, ownership of IP may be located in offshore jurisdictions through having entities in such jurisdictions contract for the development of that IP.

These types of arrangements resulting in low or no taxes being paid in certain jurisdictions have caused public and political consternation in both Europe and the US. For example, the European Commission is investigating whether certain tax arrangements in Ireland and Luxembourg amount to illegal state aid, and there have been tax-shaming political campaigns in the UK. However, as a headline in the *New York Times* in May 2013 stated: "One Response to Apple Tax Strategy May Be to Copy It."[1]

Practical and legal problems

Disconnects may occur between the finance department, which focuses on tax savings, and the legal personnel responsible for IP. On an administrative level, the financial rationale for which entities are supposed to own IP may not be clear and so IP filings are made in the name of the wrong entity and IP licences entered into which benefit the wrong affiliates. Furthermore, what constitutes ownership of an intangible asset for tax purposes may be different from what constitutes ownership for IP purposes, and confusion may arise over which IP rights (for example, the right to enforce) are owned by which entity. More substantively, legal considerations arise with holding-company structures in respect of patents and trademarks.

Regarding patents, consideration should be given under applicable law to whether a holding company would have the same rights to seek lost profits and an injunction as an operating entity. In some countries situations may arise where this is not the case.

As discussed in Chapter 12, licensing of trademarks in common law jurisdictions may require control over the quality of the goods or services licensed. Where an offshore IP holding entity is created, quality control may be difficult to achieve. Furthermore, in some countries, assignments of trademarks require the trademark to be assigned along with the goodwill of the company. This requirement also has to be observed in setting up holding structures.

Care should be taken to understand which entity within a group owns the IP necessary for a proposed transaction. A particular affiliate may simply not have the power to assign rights in or grant a licence for IP owned by another group company. Information may be available through public databases of registered IP rights, and reassurance may be obtained by requiring the party with which a contract is being made to provide a warranty that it owns the IP in question.

9 What IP costs to obtain, maintain and enforce

THIS CHAPTER OUTLINES what IP protection may cost. This is an integral part of (and limitation to) an intellectual property strategy.

It can cost a lot to protect your intellectual property. With the exception of copyrights (which in most countries do not require registration), substantial fees must be paid to file trademark registration or patent applications, prosecute those applications and maintain the registrations when issued in applicable markets. Furthermore, enforcement may be necessary to preserve the value of IP in the face of third-party uses. Enforcement of patents in the US, or defence of claims of infringement, may cost millions of dollars. Links to the schedules of fees of various patent and trademark offices are listed in Useful resources at the end of the book.

Patents

Patents are the most expensive form of IP. Costs associated with patents fall into three broad categories:

- fees payable to attorneys or agents for drafting the patent, fees paid for technical drawings, and fees paid for negotiating and corresponding with patent offices to obtain a patent;
- fees payable to the patent offices themselves;
- fees payable to attorneys, agents and experts to enforce patent rights.

For a quick summary of points to note and
strategic considerations, go to page 295

Internationally, costs include translation and notarisation (the stamping of documents by a public officer to authenticate the signatures) as well as the fees noted above for each country. Budgets broken down by category should be obtained to determine the cost and benefits of the proposed programme, domestically and internationally, because giving up halfway due to cost may put the invention into the public domain and lose any trade secret protection.

Search costs

Before a decision to file a patent application is made, a search should generally be undertaken to determine whether a patent can be obtained, and if so whether such a patent would be narrow or broad in scope. Generally, a patent cannot cover prior inventions, so if a field of technology is crowded with prior patents and publications only a narrow (or product-specific) patent may be obtained. Search costs range from near costless online searches conducted by an inventor to professional searches costing many thousands of dollars.

Initial professional fees and patent office fees

A patent requires the drafting of a technical specification and careful drafting of claims setting out the scope of the invention. Most patents require drawings of some sort. Attorney costs in the US for the drafting of a patent application range from $5,000 to $15,000 or more depending on the complexity and importance of the application.[1] And there will usually be an additional cost for professional drawings.

A decision may be taken to file a provisional application, which may preserve a priority date (an earlier date for filing, see Chapter 2) and cost much less than a full application. Such a strategy may enable rights to be preserved at lower cost while an invention is further developed and its commercial value better ascertained.

On filing a patent application, a filing fee is payable. In the US and Europe this is usually less than $1,000 for a simple patent, but it must be emphasised that this is just a small part of the overall cost. The US has also set up a fast patent application process (Track One), which allows applicants to bypass the backlog of pending patent applications, with a goal of obtaining a patent within one year. This costs an additional $4,140.

Continuing fees during the application process

The process of applying for a patent will take months and may take years. The technical term for this process is "prosecution". Patent office fees are paid upon filing, and may be paid at various points during the application process depending on the actions taken and on the granting of the patent. Each interaction with the patent office will generally require further work to be done on prosecuting the application, thus the more issues raised by the patent office the more expensive the patent will be.

Post-issue costs

In many countries there are post-grant opposition procedures where the patent may have to be defended against a third-party challenge to its validity. These proceedings, like litigation, may cumulatively involve substantial legal or patent agent fees.

International costs

Where an international filing programme is planned, costs will be incurred in translating the technical documents, filing and the application process in each country chosen. Some countries require certain documents to be notarised. There will also be issue and maintenance fees in individual countries and the costs of attorneys and agents in those countries. Costs may be both deferred and saved by filing under the Patent Cooperation Treaty (where economies are gained through a common search and examination), and in Europe by filing a European patent application (see Chapter 2). International costs are based on the number of countries in which patents are filed, and the driver, the need to cover major markets where infringement may be expected and the countries of likely manufacture.

Maintenance

Fees are payable to maintain a patent in force after its issue. In the US these are payable at $3\frac{1}{2}$, $7\frac{1}{2}$ and $11\frac{1}{2}$ years after the date of issue. In the EU, fees are not payable to the European Patent Office once a patent has been issued but rather to the national offices of the various member states.

Enforcement

Enforcement of patents is expensive. As well as lawyers, often experts are needed not only to explain or testify about technical issues but also to assist with the computation of damages. In the US especially, but also in the UK, patent litigation which goes to trial can cost millions. In civil law countries such as Germany, costs may be substantially lower because of procedural differences that limit the amount of evidence gathering and discovery of documents that can be associated with a case. Whether the truncated approach of a civil law proceeding or the full-blown approach of a common law proceeding is chosen will be an important strategic decision to be made at the beginning of any enforcement activities.

In the US, lawyers are permitted to take cases on a contingent basis, where they are paid only upon success, receiving a percentage of the proceeds. In certain countries, there is a growing market of "investors" who will finance litigation in return for a percentage of the proceeds. Patent assertion entities (PAEs) may also assist in enforcing patents. Thus mechanisms exist where third-party financing may be obtained to defray the large costs of litigation.

Personnel

Patenting also requires management time, with engineers, paralegal or legal personnel collecting information, communicating with outside patent personnel and maintaining records. Companies need to decide whether to use in-house resources or to outsource these functions.

Cost-benefit analysis

Patenting is an expensive undertaking. Costs and benefits should be reviewed in the context of overall available intellectual property protection. Searches may ensure that money is not wasted, and a comprehensive budget covering the full costs of an approach should be prepared before starting on a patent strategy. But it should be borne in mind that once a patent application has been published there is no going back. The technology will be in the public domain in countries where it is decided not to register the patent.

Patenting is just one form of IP. For example, as discussed in

Chapter 6, a choice may be made between patenting an invention or keeping it confidential, or making what is known as a defensive publication. In the software industry, patent protection is an additional form of protection beyond copyright, but the scope of eligibility for patent protection of software is unclear. A specialist patent attorney may give guidance on the incremental value of patent protection. A manufacturer could seek utility models in China (see Chapter 2). Design rights may also be available.

Using a decision tree approach to look at costs (see Figure 9.1), if the preliminary decision is to seek patent protection, a further choice will be to conduct a search to determine if a patent is likely be obtained, and if so of what scope. The next question would be whether to patent, and if so in which countries to patent. Considering major markets where infringement may occur and likely countries of manufacture would be one way of making that decision, taking into account that once a patent application is published, it is available for use in all countries where a patent is not registered. Particular

FIG 9.1 **Patent budget process**

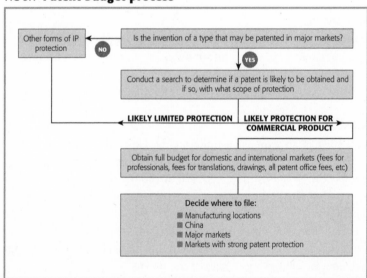

Source: Author

industries may drive particular strategies. For example, some companies sought patent protection for software only in the large US market, but changes in the US law in 2014 adversely affecting some types of software patent may change that strategy.

Trademarks

Expenses associated with trademarks include:

- initial brand selection and searches;
- fees for drafting the trademark application;
- fees for drawings where necessary;
- fees to the trademark office on filing, during the application process, on issue and thereafter to maintain the trademark;
- fees to agents or lawyers to prosecute the trademark;
- costs to enforce the trademark or defend challenges.

Internationally, fees include those set out above for each country. However, these costs are generally considerably below those for obtaining patents.

Trademark selection

Trademark searches are comparatively simple compared with patent searches, but it can be hard to find a trademark for a new product that has not already been taken (see Chapter 3). Initial costs may include use of brand consultants, designers for logos, search services and trademark counsel to advise if a proposed trademark is available.

Application

Trademarks cost significantly less than patents. Once a mark has been selected and a search undertaken, the process of applying for a trademark is comparatively simple, unless the mark is similar to one already registered. Expenses may increase if third parties file oppositions to registration. Fees, which depend on the number of goods and services covered, are due upon filing. Regarding international protection, advantage may be taken of the Community Trade Mark (CTM) and the Madrid Protocol, which is a treaty simplifying multiple country filings. Renewal fees are also payable. In common law countries, registration of a trademark is not required for protection, but in many civil law countries registration is a prerequisite for protection. As a result, where a trademarked brand is likely to be copied, there may be little choice but to register in significant markets.

As well as the costs of filing and maintaining trademark registrations, brand owners also incur costs in filing for their brand name and perhaps some derivations in the various primary top-level domain names, such as .com, .net, .eu, .jp and .cn, or any of the new category top-level domain names applicable in their industry (for example, .services or .bank).

Enforcement

Trademark litigation is generally less expensive than patent litigation because the issues are often less complicated and technical. However, in common law countries, survey evidence may be needed to show the strength of a mark or the likelihood that the public may be confused by an infringing product. Designing and carrying out surveys may be expensive. And repeated enforcement actions can become significantly expensive.

A trademark owner dealing with widespread knock-offs faces difficult decisions: how can a mark be effectively policed at a reasonable cost so as to preserve exclusive rights? A strategy should be developed using the range of options available, including government options. (See Chapters 7 and 16.)

In many countries, if a trademark is recorded, infringing imports can be stopped at the border by customs officials. Law-enforcement agencies may be interested in counterfeiters, particularly if they are associated with known criminals. Websites offering products for sale, such as auction sites, have take-down procedures for fake goods. Beyond these available remedies, decisions must be made on which infringers to sue, often based on the proximity of the competition. For example, a luxury-goods manufacturer is likely to sue a high-quality infringer before pursuing street vendors selling low-quality knock-offs.

Copyright

Copyright is virtually costless (with the exception of any purchase price) until enforcement is required. The difficulty is that copyright provides limited protection to technology.

Copyright is probably the lowest-cost form of IP protection. In most countries the right arises automatically on authorship of a work and there is no need to register copyrights. However, there may be local advantages to registering or recording ownership and advice should be obtained if a particular country is of interest. In the US, registration is required for enforcement for works by US authors and for any copyright owner to be entitled to certain enhanced remedies. It is also helpful in establishing title to a copyright work. Registration is a comparatively simple process and much guidance is available online from the US Copyright Office.

Enforcement

Copyright law is surprisingly complicated given the simplicity of the basic concept. Where copying is not slavish, proving infringement of protected copyright expression may be more complex (and thus often more expensive) than trademark litigation. However, copyright litigation is generally less expensive than patent litigation. A major difficulty with enforcement of copyright is the ease of copying and distributing digital content, including over the internet, as well as the protections given to internet service providers (see Chapter 7). A copyright owner must adopt business strategies that reduce incentives for copying and take advantage of the range of governmental, law-enforcement and civil remedies available. As with trademarks, a strategy is likely to be based first on stopping copying, which is the most competitively harmful.

Design protection

The shape and appearance of utilitarian objects is generally not protected by copyright. Protection may be available for such aspects through trade dress rights, but specific protection may be obtained under design rights. In the EU, Regulation 6/2002 on Community designs provides cost-free protection against copying for novel designs for three years after public release. There is no equivalent unregistered right in the US.

In the EU, a more extensive registered design right is available subject to payment of registration and renewal fees. National registered design rights protection is also available.

In the US, protection is available through the design patent, which is essentially a collection of professional drawings and formal documents. Legislation in the form of the Patent Law Treaties Implementation Act 2012 has been enacted bringing the Hague Agreement into effect in the US, and this may allow design patents to be filed much more simply and cheaply than is currently the case.

Enforcement

Litigation costs are comparable to trademark litigation, but significantly less than patent litigation. As well as the issue of whether the design has been copied, whether the design merits legal protection is often a cause of litigation.

Trade secrets

The costs incurred in maintaining trade secrets are the administrative costs associated with having written confidentiality agreements, maintaining secure premises and networks, and having policies that prevent disclosure by employees and contractors. Given cyber-security risks and the multiplicity of personal devices, these expenses are increasing but probably unavoidable.

Enforcement

Trade secret litigation requires proof of a number of things, including secrecy, misappropriation and damage, all of which may be factual. Thus litigation is not necessarily simple or inexpensive.

10 IP's role in protecting product sales

THIS CHAPTER DEALS WITH IP's role as a barrier to competing products, and as such an asset that enables new products to be created and sold by providing a return to an innovator, as well as a tradable asset that may be used to bargain with another company to obtain access to a market. It should be read in conjunction with Chapter 7, in particular the section on developing an internet strategy, and Chapter 16 on developing an overall IP strategy.

Intellectual property provides value for companies in at least three ways. First, patents, trademarks, copyrights, designs and trade secrets may provide strategic barriers to entry by competitors and so protect revenue gained from product sales. These barriers may be passive, in the sense that resources (such as trade secrets) are not available to the public, or active, in the sense that the legal rights owners of IP have may be actively enforced through litigation or other means when those rights are not respected. Second, IP, patents in the main, may be traded for other needed intellectual property, thus enabling products to be sold that would otherwise be blocked. Third, IP may be used as a revenue generator (see Chapter 11).

Patents as a barrier to entry

Patents may enable a patent owner to prevent sales of infringing products sold by a competitor through injunction. Although there are limits on when courts will grant an injunction, as described in

For a quick summary of points to note and
strategic considerations, go to page 296

Chapter 2, an injunction enforces the patent owner's rights to exclude infringing products from the market.

The classic role of patents in promoting innovation and protecting revenue can be seen in the pharmaceutical industry, which is characterised by the enormous costs of research and development, especially in establishing the safety and efficacy of a new product. Under the regulatory regimes of many countries, companies gathering clinical data for a new product are granted periods of regulatory exclusivity during which the same product copied by a competitor will not be approved for marketing by the applicable regulatory agency. However, such periods are short and patents are critical to enabling innovative pharmaceutical companies to capture a return on their investment by preventing copying by others after the period of regulatory exclusivity expires.

The distinguishing feature of pharmaceutical patents is that there are a small number of patents covering a particular product and perhaps only one covering the active ingredient. A pharmaceutical patent is obtained to act as a barrier to entry, to protect future sales of a particular product from competition.

In contrast, many thousands of technology patents may cover a device. Some of these may be licensed under FRAND obligations (see Chapter 2). Others may cover only a feature of a larger device or a particular way of carrying out a particular process that may also be carried out in other ways. The maker of, say, a mobile phone therefore has a choice of which patented features (available for licence) to include in the device and on which royalties will be payable to the IP owner.

In the technology industry, patents can be obtained for three main purposes. First, patents may be filed on features desirable to users of a device where the goal is to stop use of those features by competitors, and thus act as a barrier to others using that feature; second, other patents may be filed primarily as "currency" for negotiation and for defensive (counterclaim) purposes in litigation; third, yet other patents may be filed with the goal of "taxing" competitors by seeking a royalty which increases a rival's costs. In many cases the motive for filing or purchasing patents is a blend of all three.

In the phone wars (see below), Apple is using patents and design rights to try to block use of specific features attractive to consumers that it believes give it advantages in the marketplace. It is therefore trying to use patents in a traditional strategic manner as a barrier to entry. Other phone companies are using their patents as bargaining chips to obtain needed cross-licences. However, many patent owners simply seek to obtain "rent" or "tax" for use of their technology by often more successful participants in the market. Courts in the US are defining rules on whether and when an injunction may be granted preventing sale of an entire phone if only one feature infringes (see Chapter 2).

Look before you leap

Patent enforcement strategy needs careful planning and preparation. There is a long list of potential own goals when launching patent litigation against a competitor. In particular, there is the risk that a patent claim against a competitor brings a more threatening patent claim in return: the counterclaim risk. There is a scene in the film *Raiders of the Lost Ark*, known as the gun versus sword scene, where the hero, Indiana Jones, played by Harrison Ford, is threatened by a sword-wielding opponent. Ford takes his gun and promptly shoots the swordsman. No company wants to wave a weak patent sword only to be shot by a more powerful bullet.

In the US, the threat of an action for patent infringement may lead to a litigation being filed by the threatened party seeking a declaration that it does not infringe in a jurisdiction favourable to the defendant (see Chapter 11). In the UK, there are legal remedies against unjustified threats of action for patent infringement. Similar procedures exist in other European countries.

Larger companies considering suits against smaller competitors should bear in mind that damages are generally based on sales by the parties, and so paradoxically a smaller defendant that has a credible counterclaim against a larger plaintiff may stand to get a much larger sum in damages. Assuming equally strong claims by each party, a settlement should favour the smaller company.

There is also the possibility that a threat or filing of litigation may lead an accused infringer to seek to invalidate the patent. Although attention may be focused on the accused infringer, there may be other companies waiting in the wings to enter the market if a key patent is invalidated or revoked. Thus ill-considered actions may have significant consequences.

Use of patents against knock-offs

Patents are also used against what might be called knock-offs or cheap copies of a product, often imported, although less frequently than copyrights, design rights and trademarks. Copying of patented inventions occurs with consumer goods such as torches and toys. But patents are often too expensive and too slow to use as a tool to prevent copying in fast-moving markets, and it can be difficult to sue a company based in a foreign jurisdiction. Where there is widespread, large-scale copying of a patented product, in the US proceedings may be initiated through the International Trade Commission to block imports to overcome these jurisdictional issues.

With consumer goods, design rights, and in the US design patents, may be a more effective tool than utility (invention) patents because they are obtained more quickly and at lower cost, and because they may be less expensive to enforce through litigation. Where knock-offs of patented products are concerned, other IP rights should also be considered, such as copyright, trademark and trade dress rights. As with designs, more nimble litigation strategies may be available at a lower cost than are available for patents.

Patents as currency

As well as protecting revenue by creating barriers to entry, patents have an important role as the currency for negotiation of cross-licences permitting product sales growth where other companies have blocking patent positions. Defensive patent portfolios may be amassed either through internal development or through purchase for cross-licensing purposes, including in particular for defending against claims by a competitor through a counterclaim (see above). Cross-licensing may arise through a business negotiation or through settlement of litigation. However, the defensive patent "arms race" among technology companies amassing huge portfolios of patents has been derided as a "race to the bottom" because of a focus on quantity of patents rather than quality.[1]

The phone wars

The smartphone industry became involved in highly complex litigation as industry players sought to gain advantage through patents in a quickly evolving marketplace. In 2015 the litigation seemed to be winding down (though there were new eruptions in India and China), but it illustrates many aspects of IP litigation. There are new-entrant winners, such as Apple, over traditional handset manufacturers, such as Nokia, Motorola and Ericsson, and challengers to Apple, such as Google and Samsung. There are also powerful companies such as Microsoft trying to enter, influence or gain revenue from the marketplace.

The convergence of phone technologies to include cameras, data and video means that there are patent owners outside the industry, such as Kodak with its digital camera portfolio, that have sought to obtain revenue from the smartphone industry. Oracle is apparently seeking to challenge the Android-based ecosystem on the basis that the Android operating system infringes its proprietary rights based on the Java language and Oracle's Java Application Programming Interfaces. It claims that Google is fragmenting the otherwise compatible Java-based ecosystem through its creation of the incompatible Android operating system.

The litigation in the smartphone industry has been almost unprecedented in its scale and complexity. It has also been complicated by the fact that many patents involved are the subject of FRAND, and the exact legal position on what FRAND means is only now becoming clearer.

Older handset players have used litigation, possibly to slow the growth of new entrants but ultimately as a tool to establish the level of "tax" on those new entrants through royalties for use of the older participants' patent portfolios. Thus even as older participants' product sales fall in relative terms, they are still receiving significant revenue through royalties from the overall market.

Newer, innovative handset players such as Apple are seeking to prevent use of particular features by competitors as well as to reduce the royalties they may have to pay to those competitors.

There has been fierce competition concerning operating systems. Steve Jobs famously viewed the Google Android operating system as a "rip off" and stated that he intended to "destroy" Android by launching a "thermonuclear war".[2] And Microsoft was assumed to be seeking to obtain royalties on use of the "free" Google Android operating system (where Google seeks a return through advertising) both to level the playing field in favour of its Windows mobile operating system but also simply to obtain large licensing revenues. Microsoft has amply succeeded in that goal given the revelation in 2014 that it obtained more than $1 billion in Android-related royalties during 2013 from Samsung alone, the largest Android manufacturer but only one of many licensees of Microsoft.

In 2014 Microsoft acquired Nokia's handset business and thus its strategy may change as it enters the handset market as a participant as opposed to licensor. Indeed, Samsung claimed in litigation filed in 2014 that the Nokia deal undermined the basis of the licence and co-operation agreements with Microsoft that it signed in 2011.

The same may be said of Nokia as it exits handset manufacture. Competitors have expressed concern that Nokia will be more aggressive in enforcing its patents when it is not subject to the risk of a claim against its own handset business and have objected to the proposed Microsoft/Nokia deal. Competition law approval of the Nokia/Microsoft transaction in China was conditional on the parties agreeing to license their standard essential patents on FRAND terms and on Microsoft licensing certain patents to Chinese Android manufacturers on terms at least as favourable as its then current business terms. This may turn out to be a major tactical benefit for the rising stars of the Chinese telecoms market, Huawei and ZTE.

Major players including Google, Samsung and Ericsson have more recently bitten the bullet and entered into cross-licences, while Apple and Motorola settled their differences by withdrawing their claims against each other rather than entering into a cross-licence, as did Apple and Samsung to resolve their differences outside the US.

Lessons
The phone wars are a result of large amounts of money being at stake at a time when there was a lack of legal precedent on: how to value FRAND rights on a portfolio level in negotiations with powerful new entrants; whether and when injunctions were available on FRAND

patents; and how patents on features would be enforced. There were large economic incentives to litigate the individual patents that were asserted, given the chance that patents may be found invalid on many grounds or not infringed.

The lessons of the phone wars include the following:

- In an industry based on standards that require licensing on FRAND terms, it has turned out not to be possible for market incumbents in the phone industry in most circumstances to prevent entry into the market by new competitors. Thermonuclear war has not worked.

- Overall, the FRAND patent system seems to have functioned well to allow vigorous new competition in phone markets.

- At the start of the phone wars, there was little law setting out the rights of the owner of a FRAND patent, such as whether and when injunctive relief could be obtained. There was also little law establishing rules for calculating royalties on large patent portfolios, and at least in the US little law on when injunctions could be obtained on patents covering optional features of a phone not necessary for it to work under an industry standard.

- As happened in the phone industry, where there is a combination of new technology with great legal uncertainty and large sums of money at stake, litigation usually ensues. In addition, the convergence of many technologies on a smartphone beyond voice phone technology (for example, camera, data storage, data transmission, music and video) meant that many patent owners from inside and outside the industry had an interest in the field, thus increasing the overall number of patent litigations.

- However, it is now clear – as a result of the limits imposed on obtaining injunctions under FRAND patents, the initial damages awards in the US under FRAND patents and the fact that supposed standard essential patents have been found not infringed or invalid – that FRAND patents are not as valuable in litigation as many imagined.

- Arrays of patents covering individual features not required by industry standards have also generally not been effective in blocking new market entry, only enabling product differentiation among competitors.

- Portfolios of patents have been used as the basis for large royalty payments from competitors and as currency for needed cross-licences. Thus while not preventing market entry, patents have acted as a means of allocating royalty income among industry participants. They have also been used by patent owners outside the phone world to earn large sums in royalty payments from non-competitors.

- The massive international litigation in the phone industry has shown that courts faced with national versions of the same patent may reach differing conclusions, making simultaneous litigation in several countries extremely challenging.

- The strategic value of FRAND patents and patents on features in the phone wars may have disappointed their owners, but nevertheless brands, trademark rights and design rights have been surprisingly valuable. In the US, design and trademark rights have been important in Apple's litigation success and Apple retains its market position as a prestige product based in part on how "cool" its products are – the result of meticulous product design and branding.

Trademarks as a barrier to entry

Trademarks may act as barriers to entry. For example, an originally patented product may retain customer loyalty as a result of its brand even as unpatented competition comes onto the market. This occurs in the pharmaceutical industry where consumers may suspect that generic medicines are not as good as branded products. In many industries, a new brand may have to advertise more than the incumbent, or cut prices, to gain customers. An established brand may therefore be cheaper to produce and market than, or have a price-premium advantage over, a newcomer.

Many companies carefully build a brand identity with trademarks, typefaces, colours and designs to encourage consumer identification and loyalty. Distinctive design or branding features on websites, marketing materials, products and packaging may be subject to various forms of protection in many countries. These may include trademark rights, rights in distinctive features of product packaging or colouring protected by trade dress rights, design rights and copyright. As a result, brands are strongly recognised by consumers and have the benefit of associated legal rights.

Use of trademarks against knock-offs

Trademarks may be successfully used against legitimate competitors and identifiable copyists such as retail outlets. The internet has enabled widespread sales of knock-offs, and enforcement against fly-by-night defendants such as street sellers is difficult. Trademarks recorded with customs may prevent imports and law-enforcement agencies may be interested in counterfeiting carried out by criminal organisations. However, legal enforcement may have to be part of a larger strategy of brand management, customer education, supply chain management and trade association activity.

Copyright as a barrier to entry

Copyright works well to protect against substantial copying by direct competitors even when new technologies are involved.

There is a crucial difference between copyrights and patents when it comes to IP strategy: a patent may be filed on an invention that the patent owner does not intend to use but that may be used by competitors. Thus patents may be used to increase competitors' costs beyond the actual products created and sold by the patent owner. By contrast, copyrights protect works that have been created against copying and modification.

Copyright is legally created when a work of authorship is created. Thus it is in theory an automatic barrier to entry with virtually no additional cost in most countries. The strategic approach to be taken in relation to competitors will come from decisions about which material to claim copyright on and which copyrights to enforce. A company may use notices of copyright and copyright registrations to claim copyright in areas that may seem surprising (for example, decorative designs on snack food). The extent to which such things may be the subject of copyright may be open to question, but claiming copyright by notices and registration is inexpensive.

As noted in Chapter 4, copyright has its limitations. It protects neither ideas nor the purely utilitarian: it is about the protection of the expression of an idea. Therefore in considering copyright as a barrier to entry those limitations need to be kept in mind. For example, if a software company develops a program that sends invitations to meetings, copyright does not prevent a rival from independently creating a program that does the same thing, so long as no prohibited copying is involved. A patent may protect such an invention, but copyright does not.

Copyright is an effective barrier to entry where direct copying of, say, a distinctive fabric design is involved. In such circumstances, copyright provides powerful legal remedies to the copyright owner. The further a competitor moves from directly copying, the harder it becomes to enforce copyright, until the point is reached where a competitor has just used unprotected ideas.

New technologies that use copyright material often defend their use under the US doctrine of fair use. Although that doctrine is flexible, courts focus on how much material is used and how competitive the relationship is between the copyright owner and the infringer, and whether business is being diverted. A news aggregator that uses small pieces of text may be in a different position from one copying substantive sentences or paragraphs that provide the gist of an entire news story.

Use of copyright against pirated material

Copyright is a powerful weapon when the infringer can be identified and is in a jurisdiction where it is possible to take action. These two criteria have become harder to meet in the internet age. The huge proliferation of pirated material available through the internet has been coupled with a policy balance in favour of loose regulation that has protected legitimate ISPs from liability.

These issues are addressed in Chapters 7 and 16. In this context, IP strategy against pirated content has to be viewed as part of a broader series of barriers to entry and protection, such as developing international pricing and distribution strategies that do not encourage piracy, encouraging legitimate sales channels and using available technological measures to protect content.

Design rights as a barrier to entry

Design rights have features of both patents and copyright. Unregistered design rights where they exist are, like copyright, virtually costless (except for the price of the commissioned design) and similar business considerations apply (although the detailed legal tests for copying are different). Registered design rights and design patents require investment but may be infringed without proof of copying. Historically, design rights were not on the front line of IP protection. However, cases over the past few years indicate that where an original design that is attractive to the marketplace has been reproduced, design rights are a valuable part of an IP rights portfolio.

Trade secrets as a barrier to entry

A true secret covering a valuable process that is hard to replicate is itself a valuable barrier to entry. And it continues as long as there is no betrayal of the secret by anyone entrusted with it or theft of the secret. Unlike other forms of intellectual property, a trade secret is protected not just by the legal processes of litigation but also by the practical difficulty of replication.

Where a trade secret is truly hard to replicate, its value depends on taking the rigorous and consistent logical (information technology) and physical (building and other security) steps necessary to keep it secret (see Chapter 6). Some argue that trade secrets are becoming less valuable because of the pervasiveness of cybercrime and espionage on the internet and hacking into corporate networks, coupled with the difficulty of thwarting such attacks (see Chapter 7). In fields such as delayed-release formulations for drugs, it is also argued that the value of trade secrets has diminished in recent years as India and China have used an increasingly skilled workforce to replicate profitable products in legal ways.

However, once a secret has been divulged through reverse engineering or breaches of confidentiality, protection is over unless other forms of IP protect the product. For example, it may be that the loss of the uniqueness of the Coca-Cola formula would have little overall impact on the company, given the importance of the Coca-Cola brand to the success of its products.

11 IP as a revenue generator

THE PREVIOUS CHAPTER discussed IP's role in protecting revenue. This chapter examines IP as a revenue generator, when the IP owner is not using the IP in its own products or services in a particular line of business. It covers the licensing and sale of IP but focuses on use of patents as a financial asset. This is a 21st-century phenomenon which echoes the 19th-century market in patents, and which has brought a proliferation of patent assertion entities (PAEs). Chapter 12 addresses the mechanics of patent licences.

Historically, patent licensing was used by manufacturers as a way of obtaining revenue from foreign markets, though in home markets the view was sometimes taken to license patents to competitors in the belief that the additional revenue from royalties would outweigh any disadvantages of letting competitors use the patent. And cross-licensing (where each company licenses the other under its patents in a reciprocal arrangement) was used by big industry players to preserve freedom to operate with competitors of equal rank.

In 1983, the US government and courts adopted a pro-patent stance that lasted for around 20 years. Before that, patent litigation was an arcane and not necessarily effective remedy for patent infringement and often resulted in complaints of anti-competitive conduct. You had to have a strong case to succeed in patent litigation against third parties. However, in the early 1980s three things happened. First, at the end of 1982, a new appeals court, the Court of Appeals for the Federal Circuit,

For a quick summary of points to note and
strategic considerations, go to page 298

was established which unified US patent law. Second, patents began to be associated with the protection of US innovation. Third, patents began to be seen not as monopolies inconsistent with competition but as a legitimate form of property and a just reward for innovation.

Attention became focused on patents as a result of corporations such as Texas Instruments, IBM and Lucent (the former Bell Labs) earning significant revenue from patent royalties rather than manufacturing. Patents began to be perceived as a potential stand-alone generator of income. Large damages awards for patent infringement obtained by independent inventors showed that significant revenues could be obtained even without a business infrastructure. There was a growing sense that many companies had IP assets that they had not realised the potential value of (the thesis of Kevin Rivette and David Kline's book *Rembrandts in the Attic*, published in 2000), that failures to patent had cost certain companies huge potential revenues, and that money could be made out of patent assertions and licensing separate from manufacturing.[1]

Strategic management of patents

As a result of the influences described above, some companies view patents and patenting as a strategic activity. A company's patent portfolio may be developed and segregated for different purposes and the patents used in a wide range of monetisation strategies:

■ **Barriers to entry.** A company may decide not to license a patent in order to create a barrier to entry – for example, a patent covering a unique product or specific features of larger products that are believed to be important. The aim of any litigation under these patents would be to stop use of the infringing products through an injunction.

■ **Defensive use.** As discussed in the previous chapter, when patents are filed or purchased with a view to defensive use through a counterclaim if the company is sued by a competitor or otherwise as currency for cross-licensing and settlement of competitor claims.

■ **Revenue-generating licences.** When patents are licensed and asserted in litigation in order to raise revenue or "tax" a competitor's or a third party's products (see below), or where a business decides that it can gain more revenue from licensing a competitor than keeping a proprietary position.

■ **FRAND-encumbered patents.** When patents are licensed to industry members pursuant to obligations to license standard essential patents (see Chapter 2).

■ **Licences for new technology.** When patents underlying unused technologies are licensed to a third party or spun off into a new entity.

■ **Patent monetisation structures.** When patents can be spun off into an entity for purposes of assertion (see below).

■ **Divestitures.** When patents are sold to a third party for assertion against others subject to a licence back to the seller to avoid future infringement (see below).

Generating revenue by licensing

Although much patent licensing is in the form of a win-win business negotiation, patent assertion is by its nature somewhat contentious. The list above includes instances of revenue generation by licensing. However, corporate licensing has at least two different business approaches. The first may involve a potential licensee desiring to use new and attractive technology that it has not previously used. Such a process involves a generally cordial business negotiation under which both parties perceive they will gain.

Alternatively, the need for a licence may be based on an allegation that existing products of the potential licensee infringe the patents of the licensor. This type of negotiation may often involve the patent owner showing how the potential licensee's products infringe a patent of which the licensee was previously unaware. This type of licensing is usually tied to a litigation strategy and a licence may be entered into only through settlement after the litigation has begun (as discussed below, some negotiations may be started by the filing of a litigation without prior notice). The potential licensee may feel aggrieved by the claim of infringement, that it invented the technology in question, and that it is being accused of infringement of what was an unknown patent by sale of products already on the market, where it is locked in by prior investments and therefore is being held to ransom by the patent assertion.

Patent monetisation structures

Many patent owners that have patents they wish to assert against an infringer worry about the burden and cost of litigation, especially if it results in a counterclaim against them under the patents of the defendants. As a result, such patent owners may think twice about asserting their patents or consider divesting themselves of the patents in question in return for a cash payment.

However, where divestiture is considered, patent owners may wish to keep some control over the patents, possibly because they are important to the products of the patent owner and they do not want them falling into unknown hands, or because agreement on price is hard to reach, or there are other issues between the parties. Accordingly, structures have been created where patents are spun off into an entity in which the original owner maintains an interest and possibly has an option to reacquire the patents. Some of these types of structures are referred to as patent "privateers", and when used to bring suits against competitors of the original owner without the balancing threat of counterclaims against the original owner have been subject to antitrust and competition law scrutiny (see Figure 11.1).

In the US, a defendant sued under the patents held by such an entity may be able to challenge the arrangement for not transferring sufficient rights in the patents to the new entity, and therefore be able to claim that the entity does not have standing or the right to sue under the patents without involving the former owner. Thus while the risk of counterclaims and extensive involvement in litigation may be reduced by a spin-off, too much complexity and continued involvement by the seller may have unintended consequences.

Licensing back

A divestiture of patents covering the products of a seller would be a major mistake if the purchaser of the patents could turn round and

FIG 11.1 **Patent enforcement structure: a "privateer"**

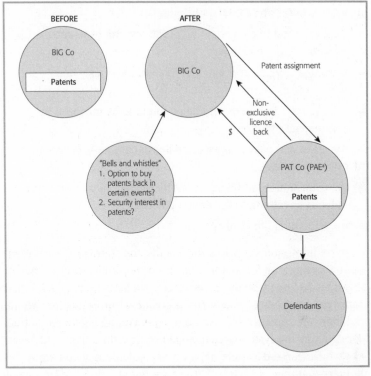

a Patent assertion entity.
Source: Author

sue the seller. A sale to an enforcement entity is usually coupled with a non-exclusive licence back to the seller. The risk of such a strategy is that depending on the applicable law, the licence could be subject to termination in the event of bankruptcy of the new patent owner (see Chapter 12).

The value of a patent as a litigation asset

The value of a patent as a litigation asset depends on many factors, including:

■ the history of the patent and its commercialisation;

- bars on past damages;
- prior licences and FRAND obligations;
- the likelihood of challenges to its validity and prior success in rebutting such challenges;
- the patent's scope and whether this has previously been determined;
- the likelihood of the patent being found to be infringed by commercial products;
- the estimated past and projected annual amounts of those infringing sales;
- the contribution of the patent to the product in question and industry royalty rates for similar patents;
- the remaining life of the patent.

In addition, market prices for patents and individual settlement amounts reflect the fact that the inefficiencies and risks of US patent litigation discussed below mean that infringement claims brought under certain types of patent cost a great deal of money to defend, and there are considerable risks to a defendant taking a case to trial. Hence, while the system is changing to combat this, historically even weak infringement claims have some settlement value from the moment that they are made. Experience has shown the amounts of settlements that typically may be obtained.

The factors above may be used both to establish a value for a patent as a litigation asset and to estimate the value of an individual claim against an alleged infringer.

Patent assertion entities

PAEs (see Chapter 2) have become a major force in US litigation, particularly in respect of software and business method patents. Non-US companies that do business in the US may be targets for enforcement claims by PAEs, and there is some evidence that non-US companies should be more worried about patent litigation than US ones, because of reported biases against them in the courts.[2] For this reason, and to understand the strengths and weaknesses of generating income through patent assertions, this chapter looks at how a PAE may typically assert a patent in the US and how a company may react. Although there is a feeling that the PAE party is over as a result of changes in the law, what has probably happened is that an era of mispriced IP assets is coming to an end, but strong patents will still be valuable litigation assets.

PAEs and the US litigation system

The law is clear: a patent is a property right and if a third party truly infringes a valid patent, the owner should be compensated. However, the difficulty is that US litigation, like any litigation, is a messy business and US patents, like other patents, are often imperfect instruments with unclear boundaries setting out the scope of products infringed by the patent. Therefore, because of the expense and uncertainties of US patent litigation, a patent claim has historically had some settlement value even if weak.

It is claimed that some PAEs seek to profit from the imperfections of the law and the litigation system by taking advantage of:

- the lack of clarity of the legal scope of many patents, especially software patents, and the time it may take and the expense involved in litigation before that scope is understood;
- the fact that in the US patent infringement may be entirely innocent – no copying is required;
- the related fact that an accusation of infringement is often made after a defendant has invested in a technology and will incur high costs shifting to an alternative (this is called lock-in);
- the high costs of defending even meritless patent lawsuits;
- even though many patents are of low quality and probably invalid, the fact that proving invalidity in court requires clear and convincing evidence on the part of the defendant;
- the usual rule in the US that a losing party does not pay the costs of the winning party;
- the uncertainties of litigation in front of juries, especially those in areas such as Texas where certain courts are regarded as favourable to PAEs;

- the potentially large amounts of damages that may be awarded, especially by juries;
- the immunity of PAEs from a risk of counterclaim (because they sell no products), the lower expenses they incur because they have few documents that need to be copied and produced in litigation, and the absence of reputational risk from industry participants and customers.

However, changes are occurring that proponents hope will level the playing field and neutralise some of these factors:

- A more rigorous economic analysis is being applied to establish the amount of damages that a patent plaintiff may obtain, especially where a patent covers, for example, only one feature of a mobile phone or other device also covered by thousands of other patents – and hence is of low value. Royalties are required to be tied to evidence of relevant licences or based on solid theories.
- Patent reform legislation (the America Invents Act) has increased the opportunities to challenge the validity of a patent in the patent office and outside the court system.
- Supreme Court decisions in 2014 indicate that in future it will be easier for a winning defendant in an IP dispute to obtain costs and fees than it was in the past, and for a defendant to invalidate patents because they are unclear, or because they cover methods or computer implementations that are not patentable.
- Given the distaste for PAEs that has been expressed at the highest level of government, it is likely either that further legislation will be passed to curtail litigation by such entities, or that the courts will continue to respond to limit unmeritorious suits brought by PAEs.

PAE tactics

PAE patent assertions are all about maximising financial returns: they are only about the money. Typically, PAEs are seeking to obtain licence fees under their patents from various targets. Their goal is to achieve some multiple of the investment they have made acquiring the patent that is being asserted. They target those who generate the most sales revenue from the infringing products and so may sue customers of a manufacturer of an allegedly infringing product rather than the manufacturer itself.

In the US, not all district courts are equal. PAEs choose favourable venues: those regarded as more plaintiff or patent friendly because cases go to jury trial quickly; or those where juries have been more likely to make large damages awards; or those where patent owners have had a higher-than-average chance of winning. Other courts, in contrast, may have advantages for a defendant when, for example, the defendant is a large local employer, or the judges are more willing to entertain motions for summary (early) judgment of patent invalidity, thus possibly favouring a defendant sued for infringement. PAEs search out the courts most favourable to them, indulging in what is referred to as forum shopping.

In recent years, much PAE litigation has been in small cities in Texas, where for various reasons judges have been hospitable to patent litigators and juries regarded as plaintiff friendly. Many suits are also brought in Delaware, which has a sophisticated patent court where PAEs have had good win rates. More recently, as the likelihood of obtaining an injunction in US district courts has decreased, PAEs have turned to litigation in the International Trade Commission.

To obtain the benefit of a favourable forum, a PAE serious about litigating may "sue first and talk later". Thus the first thing a defendant may learn about a patent is that it is being sued for infringement in Texas. This practice is popular because people who are threatened with litigation may take the initiative and seek from a court in a jurisdiction of their own choosing what is known as a "declaratory judgment" that they do not infringe the patent owned by the defendant. So, for example, a PAE that is threatening to take action against a Californian technology company runs the risk of being brought into court in California, which would be regarded as much more favourable to the technology company than a court in Texas. The PAE may sue first to ensure it can sue in Texas (although see below on the possibility of transferring a case to a more favourable venue).

Some PAEs send out letters to large numbers of potential

defendants, including customers as well as manufacturers. Depending on the PAE and the sophistication of the recipients, such letters may be threatening or seemingly innocuous. PAEs may try to avoid creating a situation in which a US court would have jurisdiction to issue a declaratory judgment by simply writing to ask if a company wants to license a patent owned by the PAE and offering to enter into licence discussions. Such a seemingly innocent offer, however, should be taken seriously as a potential prelude to litigation.

Dealing with a PAE

From a defendant's perspective, once litigation has been filed against it, money must be spent on defending the claim and there is the ultimate risk of having to pay a damages award at trial. Some of the steps that a defendant should take when sued or contacted by a PAE are outlined below.

Lawyers can help

A person threatened over a patent should generally contact a specialist IP lawyer in their local jurisdiction. If the letter is sent from a US address or refers to a US patent, the local lawyer will be well advised to consult a US lawyer as well. Even an innocuous "offer to license" letter should be taken seriously, although there is no reason to panic. A claim of infringement may require the recipient to initiate a "document hold", so that documents that may be required to be copied to the plaintiff in litigation are not destroyed. A lawyer can advise on issues such as preserving e-mails and suspending e-mail deletion cycles.

The recipient of a letter or claim should be aware that internal e-mails (or external e-mails to non-lawyers) discussing the patent (for example, "we have a big problem that has just come up") may be produced in litigation and later claimed to be some admission of wrongdoing. In general, no response should be made to a letter from a PAE without legal advice.

Check on insurance and indemnities

The next matters to look into are whether the costs of defending the allegations are covered by insurance and whether there is an indemnity from a third-party supplier that may be applicable. In either case, the insurer and the party that has given the indemnity must be contacted promptly.

Even if a third-party supplier has not provided an express indemnity it is possible that warranties of non-infringement may be implied under applicable law, or that if a patent claim affects many customers, the supplier may want to take control of the situation or at least offer assistance.

Assess the scope of the issue

Having hired a lawyer, the next step should be an initial attempt to size up the scope of the problem to see if the problem can be "put in a box", in terms of an estimate of seriousness, without a deep dive into legal analysis.

Who is the patent owner?

Find out who is asserting the patent and whether they are asserting it against others. Much information can be obtained quickly and inexpensively from the internet, public databases and the relevant patent office. Other industry players can be contacted to find out if they have been contacted and what they know. It is often a huge comfort to know that others have received an identical approach from the same plaintiff, suggesting that no one company has been singled out. Lawyers who defend PAE cases may have significant market knowledge. For example, the litigation history of the plaintiff may be known, including whether the plaintiff has sued other industry players, owns other patents and has ever taken cases to trial. A pattern of settling cases early in litigation may be apparent; or a pattern of taking cases to trial may be an indication of a serious litigant. The plaintiff's lawyers may be known for their trial skills or not.

Where did the patent come from?

A patent's history may limit its worth. Quickly reviewing the history of the patent through its assignment and other records at the relevant patent office together with internet searches can reveal a lot of information with minimal expense. It can show the circumstances of invention, and give indications of how the patent has previously been exploited, if at all. Searches may show whether the patent has been owned by a company that may have granted still-continuing licences to third parties, has been under FRAND obligations, or has been subject to patent marking obligations that if not followed may preclude past damages (see below and Chapter 2). The patent's expiry date may be determined; whether maintenance fees have been paid; whether it has been interpreted by a judge in prior litigation; and whether it has been subject to a patent office review of patentability, such as a re-examination proceeding or an inter-partes review. Much analysis may be devoted to these issues later in litigation, but significant initial insight may be gleaned from a quick and dirty review.

Weaknesses in the patent

- **Prior litigation.** Where litigation has previously defined the scope of the patent, this may be helpful in challenging a PAE's assertion. In the absence of such "official" definition, a PAE is likely to play hardball.

- **Invalidity.** The US Supreme Court cases on software and other patents described in Chapter 2 mean that some patents may be challenged as impermissibly covering only abstract ideas, not patentable technological inventions. Strong prior art may also be a potent weapon. One immediate question is whether any accused product was on sale before the patent was filed, thus suggesting invalidity because patents generally cannot cover something that was older and public. This is often an attractive argument to run depending on how long before the patent filing date the sales occurred. Contact may be made with other defendants and a joint effort undertaken to locate prior art; or commercial search or crowdsourced services can be used, some of which specialise in assembling prior art to counter claims by PAEs.

Estimating the financial case

Dealing with a PAE is all about the money. The case is based on the risk to the defendant of a damages award and the costs of defence. The aim of a defendant should be to show that the scope of products and the dollar value of sales that could possibly infringe are small. Therefore if the accused product can be identified (which unfortunately is not always easy), its past, current and future sales should be estimated. It would obviously be helpful to show that sales may be discontinued, or that sales will remain modest during the remaining term of the patent.

The big money in a patent case is often based on damages for infringing sales in the past. Yet there may be aspects of patent law that may prevent claims for damages on past sales: for example, allegations of inducing another to infringe a patent, or contributing to infringement by providing material or equipment for that purpose, require knowledge of the patent to be actionable in the US. Where a patent covers a product, marking of products sold by the predecessor patentee or its licensees with a patent number will have been a requirement before any claim for past damages can succeed (see Chapter 2).

Deciding a strategy

Based on the considerations described above, an initial assessment of perceived risk may be made. Key factors will include whether the amount of allegedly infringing past and future sales can be estimated, and if so what is the likely basis for calculating damages. Another key factor is whether the patent appears vulnerable to a validity attack.

If good prior art is located, or other weaknesses in a patent identified, a strategic decision may be taken on whether to rely on the weaknesses to try to force a settlement, to seek invalidity in litigation, or to seek to have the patent limited or invalidated in the relevant patent office. In the US this might include the procedures now available under the America Invents Act 2011, such as inter-partes patent review or the "covered business method" patent review. Although these procedures are new, the standard for patent invalidity is a preponderance of the evidence as opposed to the clear and convincing evidence required in court, and the procedures have been found effective for patent challengers.

The initial assessment of the perceived financial risk may determine a proposed approach. For example, in many cases, defendants form a joint defence group and sign a joint defence agreement (tailored to address US legal issues including antitrust compliance) where they can work together and share expenses on matters of common interest, such as seeking to invalidate the asserted patent by gathering prior art. A defendant sued over a product with low sales may decide to be a follower not a leader in any such litigation. A defendant with major product sales at risk, however, may want to defend the case vigorously and lead that defence.

Where just a letter offering a licence has been received, as opposed to the filing of a lawsuit, there may be a difference between internal and external responses. There are good reasons to investigate a patent when it has been brought to the attention of a company, even if that investigation may not be extensive. Simply doing nothing has been a partial basis for a finding of wilful infringement in the US (see Chapter 16). However, that does not necessarily mean that a response, and certainly not a substantive one, needs to be given to a letter from a PAE. It is better to discover first whether there are others who have received a similar letter. In essence, it is a tactical decision as to whether to respond or not, bearing in mind that by responding you may run a risk in some circumstances of drawing attention to your business.

When to take a stand

In certain circumstances, a claim by a PAE may be significant to a company because of the possibly high damages and importance of the product, or the low likelihood that the plaintiff will settle or for some other reason. In such circumstances, the company threatened by litigation may decide to file litigation seeking a declaratory judgment in a jurisdiction favourable to that party. Such an action would seek a declaration that the party does not infringe the patent under which it has been threatened. If a suit has already been filed, the defendant may seek to have the case transferred to a more friendly jurisdiction. There are limits and rules on when such steps can be taken, but they are part of the armoury of a potential or actual defendant.

A defendant may also want to establish that it is not a soft touch – that is, that it will always settle easily. In such circumstances, a defendant may decide to litigate aggressively including laying the groundwork to try to obtain fees from the PAE. Where a settlement demand is too high, there may be no alternative to litigation. Some companies, such as EMC Corporation, take a firm line on not settling with PAEs.

In other circumstances, the overall economics need to be considered, as well as whether money spent on litigation would be better spent on a quick settlement. Opinions differ, even among lawyers paid to fight, on whether fighting every claim by PAEs is a real disincentive to future PAE claims. Like many issues, it probably depends on the business and claims in question.

Settling litigation – assessing patent risk

Settling a case is not always easy. There is as yet no generally accepted model for quantifying the risk to each party in a dispute over a patent of the decision going against them – the risk of patent invalidity or non-infringement for the plaintiff or the risk of a large damages award against the defendant – and therefore no generally accepted methodology for valuing a specific patent assertion. Although most cases settle for small amounts, there are sometimes cases that result in a large damages award (for example, the $533 million award by a Texas jury against Apple in February 2015 in favour of a small company that, according to a Bloomberg Business report of February 2015, an Apple spokesperson claimed "makes no products, has no employees, creates no jobs, has no US presence, and is exploiting our patent system").[3] And although the risk in the US of a PAE getting an injunction is much reduced, it still exists. Hence there is still a tendency for litigation to be initiated or unduly prolonged, rather than a speedy and rational negotiation being conducted. The search continues for mechanisms whereby disputes can be resolved based on commonly accepted valuation and risk assessment measurements, or market mechanisms, more efficiently than by litigation.

Mechanically, a settlement of litigation will involve dismissal of the claims by the parties against each other and usually a licence to the patent that is the subject of the litigation. As a result of lack of trust between the parties, often the payment is a lump sum as opposed to a running royalty to avoid any future relationship with the plaintiff. However, difficulties may arise in negotiating the amount of a lump sum over what happens if the defendant merges with or becomes part of a larger group, because if the volume of sales covered by the licence increases, so should the size of the payment.

Patent aggregators have interests in certain fields and may become intermediaries for settling litigation (see Chapter 15) where their knowledge of market pricing, lack of emotional involvement and ability to assemble a group of potential licensees may enable a global settlement to be concluded. Defendants often try (but also often fail) to obtain a "never darken my door" settlement which includes other patents owned by the patent owner or its affiliates that have not yet been asserted. As a result of past poor behaviour by certain PAEs in hiding patents that were later asserted against the settling party, drafting settlements with PAEs to try to avoid later ambush has become quite an art.

Assistance from government

Where an industry-wide mailing of threatening letters has occurred, US-based defendants may be able to talk to their state attorney general, given the concern among many of them that PAEs may be pursuing unfair and misleading tactics. The US Federal Trade Commission has also become interested in misleading letter-writing campaigns by PAEs and has obtained at least one settlement barring a PAE from making deceptive representations when asserting patent rights.

Litigation outside the US

The preceding discussion about PAEs refers to the US legal system. As noted in Chapter 2, each country has its own procedural rules governing patent litigation, which may make it a more or less favourable location for the assertion of rights. For example, countries outside the US may be less favourable to enforcement activities by PAEs because, for example, contingent fee arrangements (where the lawyer finances the litigation and receives a percentage of recoveries) may not be available, a losing party may be required to pay a winning party's fees, decisions may be made by experienced specialist patent judges, patents may often be held invalid and, critically, damages awards may be lower. Paradoxically, lower litigation costs may also encourage a defendant to litigate rather than settle. Studies in the UK in 2012 and 2014 found two reasons for the low level of PAE lawsuits in the UK compared with the US: the high percentage of invalidity findings in the UK; and the potential liability for the defendant's costs.[4] However, the fact that a plaintiff in the UK may be a PAE is generally not relevant to the case itself. In a 2014 case where Vringo, a telecoms company, was suing ZTE under a patent bought from Nokia, Mr Justice Birss specifically stated that whether ZTE is right or wrong that Vringo is a "patent troll" it "is irrelevant and I will ignore these allegations".

The more ready availability of preliminary injunctions and the separation (and often slower pace and lower chances of success) of invalidity proceedings from infringement proceedings in Germany may indicate a forum favourable to a plaintiff; indeed, it has been a forum for troll activities. Infringement suits claiming millions have been filed in Germany by PAEs.

The EU unitary patent

Concerns have been expressed that the new pan-European patent (see Chapter 2), which may be enforced in a single proceeding across the EU, may lead to forum shopping and increased actions by PAEs seeking to enforce patents solely for money because of the huge market covered by such patents.

Trademark licensing

Trademark licensing was used historically to exploit foreign markets by licensing the trademarked product. This can be seen in the food and confectionary industries, where UK brands are often manufactured in the US by US companies. However, the modern concept of a brand, of which a trademark is a symbol, allows much broader licensing opportunities. As well as having brands that protect their core business, companies such as Virgin, Trump and Disney have broadened their business scope through licensing or joint ventures in areas far from the original core business.

From both a legal and a business perspective, maintaining the strength and cachet of the brand in these types of business requires stringent control over the choice of licensees, the use of the trademarks themselves, the nature and quality of the goods or services licensed, and the policing of unauthorised use. Licence provisions are discussed in the next chapter.

Copyright and revenue generation

As well as the obvious role of copyright in preventing copying, a role that technology has made ever more difficult, copyright has always had a licensing model, be it for sale of books in foreign markets and languages, for sheet music, or for playing music on the radio or in public places. (See Chapter 12 for licensing models.) Copyright is the primary form of intellectual property protection for software.

Software

Software is distributed through licences. Thus the entire software industry runs on a model of licensing copyright in return for revenue and reliance on copyright (and trade secret where software is distributed as source code) to prevent competitors and counterfeiters from copying the software programs.

Books

Book publishing runs on a similar model with the exception that licensing tends to occur internationally with sales in the publisher's home market being made through sales of physical (and now electronic) books. While a book may be resold, generally it may not be copied because of the protection of copyright law. However, with the advent of electronic books, publishing is moving towards the distribution of digital content through licensing.

Music

The music industry has a number of revenue models all based on copyright. Sheet music is reproduced and sold. Public performance of music requires a licence for public performance. Organisations exist to grant such rights and collect revenues. The creation of a record, CD or tape using music subject to the copyright of a third party requires a mechanical licence. The copying of a CD or tape for commercial purposes would require a licence to master rights.

The motion-picture industry is equally dependent on a copyright-based licensing model. Movies are, for example, distributed pursuant to licences to distributors. And rights to photographs may be repeatedly licensed for stock purposes.

New technologies

Where new technologies affect copyright, disputes arise until solutions are found. Much internet business involves some use of third-party content. Disputes have arisen in the context of news aggregation over how much use is too much use. Court decisions and legislation eventually lead to settlements of disputes and business solutions.

The music industry has begun to embrace an evolving online licensed and legal model, whereby music is either downloaded or streamed from licensed sites. This has set up convenient legal sources for internet users which result in more legitimate use and less piracy, but the royalties payable particularly to artists are considered by many to be too low, and the appropriate levels and models for royalties to rights holders are similarly subjects of review and dispute.

Copyright libraries

Copyright libraries may generate substantial repeat revenues for many years through multiple licence fees for repeat use of copyrights. As a result, as discussed in Chapter 15, copyright libraries have attracted the attention of investors.

12 Licensing transactions

THIS CHAPTER ADDRESSES the contractual terms of licence agreements. At its most basic, a licence is a grant of rights by the owner of IP to rights to use its IP in a way which without the licence would be unlawful. The scope of the rights granted forms the subject matter of the licence agreement. A licence is usually granted in return for payment. However, a licence may be granted in return for, say, a licence back of other IP (a cross-licence) or equity in the licensee. Licensing has evolved over the past 30 years from a series of one-off transactions into a significant business sector.

Unless a business has licensing as its business model (like a music publisher or software company), or is licensing IP not used in its own products, a decision to license is often based on a conclusion either that a non-exclusive business model will bring more revenue overall or that licensing will enable revenue to be obtained from markets that are otherwise unavailable. For example, more revenue may be gained from licensing to the dominant incumbent in a particular market than through unsuccessful competitive entry.

In many ways, a licence is like a lease of property, and like property, a licence may be granted for only particular parts of the property (fields of use), for a particular duration and a particular territory, with parts of the property reserved for the property owner. Some restrictions may, however, be subject to antitrust and competition law limitations discussed below. Each slice can be granted to one

For a quick summary of points to note and
strategic considerations, go to page 300

licensee exclusively or to many licensees non-exclusively.

An exclusive licence between a small biotechnology company and a large pharmaceutical company to develop a drug may be a highly complex strategic alliance. But non-exclusive licences of patents may be straightforward. The concerns of licensors vary across industries and according to the type of IP being licensed. A trademark licensor will be concerned that its brand will be used in an appropriate manner and on high-quality goods. The software licensor will want to ensure that its software is not copied or reverse engineered. However, most licences have some terms in common.

Crucial terms

The licensor

A licence transaction is not an acquisition of title, but due diligence is necessary to establish what rights are held by the licensor. Does the licensor own the IP or is it licensed from an affiliate or a third party? A classic example in biotechnology involves a licence to a large pharmaceutical company from a small biotechnology company of IP that it has developed and owns. So far, so good. However, it often turns out that the small company relies in turn on technology licensed from a university which has to be sublicensed to the large company. A similar situation may arise within a corporate group, where IP may be held not by the obvious operating company proposed as the licensor but by one or more IP holding entities. Again, a sublicence may need to be created. If a licence is like a lease of property, a sublicence is like a sublease, and it carries obligations and risks.

Generally, a sublicensee has to comply with all the applicable provisions of the head licence (the licence with the owner of the IP) to avoid its licensor being in breach. The head licence may not only restrict the terms of the proposed arrangement but also raise other risks. For example, what happens to the proposed sublicensee if the head licence is terminated? Will the sublicensee lose its rights? In many cases, the proposed sublicensee may need to seek a direct agreement from the owner of the IP to protect it if the licence from that owner to the intermediate licensor is terminated for breach or bankruptcy.

The licensee

When contemplating a licence, similar issues arise with regard to the licensee as for the licensor. Who is the proposed licensee and will that entity need to sublicense? Categories of sublicensee may include the following:

- **Affiliates,** so that an entire corporate group is covered by the licence. This is usually linked to the size of payments to be made to the licensor.

- **Service providers and contractors such as outsourced service providers,** so that they will have access to the licensed technology or software to perform their role. The issue here may be whether such service providers are competitors of the licensor.

- **Third parties,** so that a licensee may grant further licences. This raises a number of business questions for the licensor, including compensation to the licensor; whether undesirable sublicensees could be appointed; enforcement against sublicensees; excluding liability claims from such sublicensees; and determining what happens to the sublicensees if the head licence is terminated.

The rights being granted

Existing IP

Once the parties are established, the first term of a licence is the definition of the rights being licensed. Which patents, technology, copyrights, trademarks or other rights are being licensed? Licences may specify lists of patents, or the other IP rights that are the subject of the licence, and try to accurately limit and define the scope of unpatented technology.

Future IP

As well as existing IP, what rights are there in the future to improvements or new developments or versions by the licensor? The licensee will want to know that it has all the rights that it needs from the licensor and that it will have the benefit of future technology. However, from the licensor's perspective, the costs of developing new technology may not be recovered if it is automatically included in an existing licence. There may also be better partners for a new generation of technology.

Territory

As noted in Chapter 2, IP rights are generally territorial. Licences may be limited to a specific territory, such as a region of the world, a country or even part of a country. In the 19th century, one of the seminal US licensing cases involved the right to sell patented casket lids in Boston. In considering the territory to be granted, the impact of free-trade areas should be considered as well as the possibility of grey-market imports (see later). For example, if licences are granted exclusively to different licensees in different countries within the EU, there will not be true exclusivity because resellers can resell goods across national borders.

The products or fields of technology covered

Many patents and forms of technology or trademarks are applicable to different types of products or different styles of products. A licence may be granted to single or multiple fields of use or product types. Thus a trademark licence may be limited to T-shirts and not include other sports apparel, and a patent on automotive brakes may be licensed to one company for high-performance vehicles and to another company for commercial vehicles.

A licence to a process or method may be for use in a particular application, or a particular type of product. For example, a method used in plant breeding may be granted to one licensee for wheat and to another for corn.

In respect of copyrights, a recurring issue is the scope of media and technologies in which the copyright may be exploited. Does publishing include only book publishing or electronic publishing? Does a licence to broadcast a musical work include the right to broadcast over the internet? Careful drafting of the scope of rights being granted is crucial.

Customer scope

Competition law issues may have to be considered (see below), but a licence may be granted allowing a licensee to sell only to particular types of customers. For example, a licence could be granted to sell voice-recognition software to the educational market.

Duration

IP licences may be granted for limited terms or the life of the IP right. A licence of patents or technology for a fixed number of years less than the life of the IP right raises interesting issues of leverage or bargaining power. On the one hand, the licensee may believe that it can move on to a new product or that new technologies may be developed, so that by the time of a renegotiation it may be able to bargain for a lower royalty. On the other hand, a situation can arise where the licensee is locked into a technology by virtue of prior investments and thus may have to pay a higher royalty for the continued right to use that technology. Licences with a royalty duration longer than the life of the licensed IP are discussed below.

Exclusivity

Licences may be exclusive, meaning that only the licensee can exploit the IP; sole, where only the licensor and one licensee may exploit the IP; or non-exclusive, where there may be one or many licensees in addition to the licensor. Like all aspects of IP, exclusivity should be viewed from three perspectives: product scope or field of use, territory and duration. Exclusivity in a business sense can be affected by legal issues, such as the free movement of goods within free-trade areas, and by practical considerations, such as the impact on exclusive territorial rights of internet sales.

A licensee may demand exclusivity in order to protect its investment in developing a licensed product. However, in an exclusive licence with sales-based compensation to the licensor, the licensor will be entirely reliant for its income on the efforts of that one licensee to commercialise the IP. This can lead to what is usually a difficult negotiation on performance targets or minimum payments required for the licensee to maintain exclusivity, and can be a potential trigger for termination if those targets are not met.

A non-exclusive patent licence may be regarded as simply an agreement not to enforce the IP being licensed. By contrast, an exclusive licence is much more like a property right. In US copyright statute, an exclusive licence is treated like a transfer:

> A "*transfer of copyright ownership*" is an assignment, mortgage, exclusive license, or any other conveyance, alienation, or hypothecation of a copyright or of any of the exclusive rights comprised in a copyright, whether or not it is limited in time or place of effect, but not including a nonexclusive license.

An exclusive license of a patent may also be tantamount to an assignment, enabling a licensee to sue in its own name, but most exclusive patent licences require the patent owner to be a party to infringement litigation. To obtain the benefit of its exclusivity, the licensee will want to ensure that if necessary, the licensor will co-operate in litigation as needed by the licensee as well as maintain the licensed IP.

Payment

Monetary obligations in licences compensate the licensor for the value of the IP rights that are made available to the licensee as well as for any services provided by the licensor, such as technical assistance. The payment structure should in theory attempt to apportion the income of the licensee attributable to the exploitation of the IP between the licensor and the licensee, so that the licensee is fairly compensated for its risks and investments and the inputs to the product other than the licensed IP, and the licensor receives a fair return for the value of its IP (see Chapter 14).

Licences are also the vehicles through which many patent assertions are settled (see Chapter 11). Disagreements over price are usually overcome when licensing occurs in a business context such as developing a new technology, but as discussed in Chapter 11, the lack of commonly accepted valuation methodologies means that when an issue of patent infringement arises, the parties often resort to litigation rather than negotiation until the strengths of their respective positions become clear. Where licences of large patent portfolios are concerned, although recent cases have provided guidance, there remain big differences in approach to valuation. This can make business discussions difficult and again may lead to litigation. For example, companies argue over whether the sheer number of patents in a portfolio is of importance as opposed to whether the focus should be on a limited number of important patents.

Fixed payments

In the context of settlement of litigation, often a single lump-sum payment is made. Such a fee is the entire consideration for a licence, which is called a paid-up licence. Licences may also be granted in consideration of a series of fixed payments. However, licences typically have payment structures including an upfront, advance or signing fee, together with future running royalties based on sales by the licensee. In this case, initial payments may or may not be set off against future running royalties as a matter of business negotiation.

Royalties

Licences are usually paid for through royalties. A royalty is simply a payment of a fixed fee per item sold ($5 per television sold), or a percentage of the licensee's list price for each item, or a percentage of the licensee's receipts from sales (for the reason that the licensee may be selling to a retailer at a large discount on the list price). The term "net sales or receipts" is often used, allowing certain items such as credits, tax, insurance and shipping to be deducted from the licensee's receipts from sales.

Sales-based royalties have two aspects: the royalty rate (the percentage applied to the sales in question) and the royalty base (the scope of the products or services on which the royalty will be charged). The effective payment is a combination of both the royalty rate and the royalty base, and it does not generally make sense to discuss one without the other. In some cases, charging royalties on products not covered by the IP of the licensor may have competition law implications (see below).

Royalty rates may increase or decrease in steps depending on such things as time, annual sales levels or cumulative sales targets. These mechanisms are designed to fine tune allocation of income between the licensor and the licensee.

Royalties may continue for the life of the IP being licensed (and cut short in the event that the IP is invalidated), or become paid up after a certain number of years or once a set amount has been paid. There are competition law and enforceability implications where royalties on patented technology are required to be paid beyond the expiry date of a licensed patent, although this law is subject to challenge. Alternatively, as noted, a licence may be fully paid up in return for an initial lump sum or a series of annual payments not dependent on use.

Payment structures

Payment structures allocate not only income but also risk between the licensor and the licensee. Lump-sum payments mean that a licensor will receive payment (albeit a capped one) even if the licensee never successfully exploits the licensed IP. By contrast, a licence based solely on royalties puts all the risk of exploitation on the licensor. Payment structures may also be affected by the market knowledge of the two parties. A licensee expecting high sales may bargain for a fixed-fee transaction if its market estimates exceed those of the licensor.

Resolving price issues

Disagreements on royalty rates in negotiations may be resolved in a number of ways, including minimum royalties, royalties that are capped annually or totally, and royalty rates that increase or decrease as annual or cumulative sales hit certain thresholds. Milestones may also enable a licensee to pay more to the licensor as development risks decrease or annual sales targets are met, thus validating the value of the licensed IP.

Particularly in the pharmaceutical industry, where a product is being developed, payments may become due to the licensor when specified milestones are met, such as the successful completion of clinical development stages and safety testing. As each milestone is met, the future of the product becomes more certain and the rights to the product more valuable.

Sublicensees

One important issue to be addressed is royalties on sales by sublicensees if sublicensing is permitted under the licence agreement. Both the licensor and licensee will want to benefit from sales made by sublicensees. One commonly adopted structure to deal with this is for the licensor to receive a percentage of revenues received by the licensee from its sublicensees, with that percentage of revenue being usually higher than the basic royalty percentage on net sales by the licensee (because the licensor will be receiving not a percentage of sales but a percentage of a royalty on sales).

Costs

Costs and potential costs are also allocated between the licensor and the licensee. As well as product-related costs, these allocations may include costs of prosecuting and maintaining the licensed IP, costs of enforcement of that IP against infringers, and costs of defending the IP against challenges and settlements of such claims.

Stacking royalties

Royalty structures may take into account royalties on the licensed product payable by the licensee to third-party owners of technology as well as to the licensor where that third-party technology is also needed to practise the originally licensed technology. These are called stacking royalties. This may arise when multiple patents belonging to multiple parties are needed to make and sell a product.

These royalties may be reflected in the original royalty rate, so a lower rate than would otherwise apply is agreed. Alternatively, royalties payable to third parties that are not known at the time of signing may be offset in future against the original royalty payable to the original licensor. This should, however, be subject to negotiated caps so that the original royalty is not too diminished. A partial offset of a percentage of the royalties payable to the third party, subject to a maximum overall offset, ensures that a licensee has "skin in the game" and will not just agree to future royalties knowing that they are simply a full offset against the original royalty.

Royalty offsets

"Back of the licence" provisions may transfer significant value from one party to another. Often, companies will negotiate headline milestone and royalty rates, which typically come at the front of an agreement and focus less on deductions of costs and liabilities that occur in later sections of the agreement dealing with IP issues. However, ill-thought-out or poorly drafted provisions, such as allowing offsets against the royalties owed to the licensor of stacking royalties, or costs of applying for registration of IP, or legal fees for asserting or defending licensed IP, may cost that licensor significant sums. For example, if all legal fees defending a patent can be deducted from royalties, this is essentially a blank cheque for a licensee to use the amount of royalties to pay its lawyers on litigation, which may ultimately be more harmful to the licensor as it could result in a finding of invalidity of the patent in question.

Mechanics of payment

The provisions a royalty system needs to take into account include:

- royalty base;
- royalty rate;
- timing of payments (for example, a certain number of days after each quarter);
- royalty reports showing calculation and deductions;
- audit rights to confirm amounts payable;
- currency and manner and place of payment;
- currency conversion and exchange rates;
- any mandatory withholding of tax by the licensee and evidence required to enable the licensor to obtain tax credit (or an additional amount to compensate the licensor for required tax withholding if the licensor is unable to use tax credits).

Termination

Many companies do not pay enough attention to licence termination provisions, only to regret it when things do not work out. Often a licensee makes material investments in and around the licensed technology and will try to avoid easy, hair-trigger termination of its licence for fear of losing that investment.

However, if an exclusive licence has been granted and the licensee is not performing, the licensor will wish to claw back and relicense the IP because its returns on the IP depend entirely on the licensee.

Termination provisions have three aspects:

■ the events that will lead to termination of the licence;

■ what happens to the rights of each party upon termination (which can be complex);

■ what happens if there is a dispute over termination.

Typical events enabling termination by the licensor include:

■ material breach of the licence by the licensee which the licensee has not remedied within a certain number of days;

■ in exclusive licences, failure to meet performance targets or other milestones;

■ bankruptcy of the licensee (see below);

■ change in ownership of the licensee (possibly).

Typically, licensees are not interested in termination of their rights to use the licensed IP, but in some situations they may want to terminate a licence to pursue a different technology, or to abandon an unpromising project that has onerous performance obligations attached. A licensee may bargain for termination for convenience, with the licensor bargaining in return for a substantial period of prior notice.

The consequences of termination of a licence should be spelled out, including when the right to use the licensed IP stops. Some of the questions that may arise on termination are as follows:

■ For how long, if at all, and in what circumstances may the licensee be permitted to continue to use the licensed IP?

■ Is there a sell-off period during which a licensee can sell off licensed inventory?

■ What happens to sublicensees? Are their rights terminated, or may they be taken over by the licensor?

- Are there any payment obligations?
- What does the licensor need from the licensee if the licensor is to relicense the IP or exploit the licensed IP itself? This is an issue in the pharmaceutical industry where the licensor may need access to data and IP of the original licensee. Termination provisions in some pharmaceutical and biotechnology licences run for many pages.

Disputes

Differences between the parties over the grounds for termination, such as failure to meet performance targets, may be resolved through building dispute resolution procedures into the licence agreement. These could include mediation or occasionally binding arbitration.

Assignability

Non-assignability of a licence may affect the ability of the licensee to sell its business or a product line. In essence, the more assignable a licence is the more valuable it is to the licensee. Counter-intuitively, at least under US law, if a licence agreement is silent regarding the right of the licensee to transfer the licence to a third party, often the licence is not assignable. This is not the case for all licences, nor is it the case in Europe or Australia. It is therefore best to provide that a particular licence is, or is not, capable of assignment as part of the negotiations between the licensor and licensee.

One reason licences are often not assignable without the consent of the licensor is that for commercial and reputation reasons, a licensor may have a strong interest in the identity of its licensee. Furthermore, where a licence is granted for a fixed fee based on assumptions about the licensee's sales, an assignment to a larger licensee will result in the licensor earning less than if it had licensed directly to the larger company.

However, except where the licensor has responsibility for product development or where the licensee is concerned that the licence may be transferred to a competitor, a licensee should have fewer concerns about assignment by the licensor, so long as the licence and the applicable IP owned by the licensor that is the subject of the licence are assigned together.

Issues specific to particular types of licence

Patent licences

Identification of IP
Typically, patents and patent applications are identified by number, filing date and country.

The grant
Patent licences grant some or all of the rights of a patent holder under the patent statute of the country in question, principally the rights to make, use and sell an invention. As noted above, non-exclusive patent licences are essentially permissions to use IP and are generally comparatively simple. In each case, the grant may be limited by field, product, type of customer and territory, subject to antitrust and competition law review.

Specific provisions
In an exclusive licence, the licensor has important obligations relating to the IP being licensed to ensure that the licensee receives the benefit of that IP. These include:

- pursuing patent applications;
- defence of oppositions and other validity challenges;
- payment of maintenance fees;
- co-operation between the parties in enforcement, including being a party to litigation.

Patent licences also raise important questions about who owns improvements to the licensed technology made by the licensee. A licensor may require at least non-exclusive rights to such improvements to avoid being blocked in certain fields. This may raise commercial and possibly competition law concerns, as discussed below.

As noted in Chapter 2, an obligation to mark products with patent numbers may be required to preserve the right to sue infringers for past damages.

Other obligations

Where patent applications are licensed, their subject matter should be kept confidential until publication of the patent application (see Chapter 2).

A patent licence will often include separate confidential know-how and technical assistance. This type of licence is discussed below, but where rights to differing kinds of IP, such as patents and know-how, are licensed under the same licence, co-ordination is required to cover what happens when one form of IP expires or comes into the public domain, such as when the licensed patents expire.

Financially, separate royalties may allow continued receipt of royalties for the IP that is still proprietary. However, patent and know-how licences are often proposed on the basis that they terminate upon expiration of the licensed patents. If this is the case, does the licence to know-how continue but become paid up at that point? Should the royalties continue at a lower level? Or does the right to use the know-how terminate?

Technology and trade secret licences

Identification of IP

A licence should ideally describe specifically what is being licensed. In the case of confidential information, this can be difficult. Documents such as contracts ideally should not be confidential because they may need to be disclosed to third parties or used in litigation. However, if a non-confidential description will not suffice, a separate confidential document may be needed.

The grant

The grant under a licence of confidential information will specify how that information may be used and may be limited as desired by the licensor.

Specific provisions

The principal provisions with regard to valuable confidential information will revolve around the protection needed to keep the information confidential and what to do if there is a breach of that confidentiality.

Other obligations

Licensors of technology may take on a number of obligations. The most important may be related to the technology itself: to develop it further, to provide technical assistance and technology transfer. These obligations raise issues of scope, duration (how long the technology will be supported) and payment (will the sometimes fixed payments from the licensee cover the licensor's obligations?).

Risk allocation issues are discussed below.

Trademark licences

Identification of IP

Trademark licences typically identify the trademarks with reference to registrations, numbers and countries. Unregistered material may also be licensed and scheduled.

The grant

A trademark licence typically grants the right, which may be narrowly tailored, to use the trademark on specified goods or services.

Registration and enforcement

The licensor of a trademark is usually required to (and wants to) register, maintain and enforce the licensed trademarks, and maintain the personnel and infrastructure needed for effective quality control of trademark use and licensee operations.

A trademark licence will address registration of the mark in the licensor's name and co-operation by the licensee in that process. Similar provisions will cover enforcement of the trademark.

Control of trademark use and quality control

The basic requirement of trademark licences is that the quality of the goods and services of the licensee be subject to control by the licensor (see Chapter 3). A licence for a valuable trademark generally imposes extensive obligations on the licensee, including: how the trademark is used (its form, its colour and how it is applied); on which specified products and services it can be used; how it is to be used in marketing and advertising; provisions for prior approval of products or services to be branded, marketing, advertising and other collateral material; and in manufacturing arrangements, the ability to inspect manufacturing facilities and provision and approval of samples.

Regulation

In some cases, a licensor will provide much more than just a bare trademark licence. For example, an entire industry exists in which licensees receive franchises that may include a business format, supplies provided by or on behalf of the licensor and other support. In a number of countries including the US, regulations on franchises and dealerships require detailed disclosure about the company and the law provides protection for the distributor, franchisee or licensee against termination. Specialist franchise lawyers should be consulted when establishing a franchise system. Indeed, in the US there can be tricky legal issues surrounding what are called unintentional franchises, where a licence or distribution agreement is caught by state or federal franchise regulation with unexpected resulting obligations on the licensor.

Copyright licences

Identification of IP

Typically, a licence of a work will identify what is being licensed by title, author and other identifiers.

The grant

Copyright licences may grant some or all of the rights of an owner of copyright under the copyright statute of the country in question. These rights are often spelled out in detail, and rights reserved to the copyright owner also clearly delineated. As discussed above, it is important to define the forms of technology that may be exploited and clarify what is and is not covered (for example, print versus e-books), reserving to the copyright owner all rights not specified.

Specific provisions

Responsibility for pursuing infringers is usually agreed between the licensor and licensee.

Other obligations

Obligations in the agreement depend on the type of copyright licensed. For example, a book-publishing licence will list the respective responsibilities of the author and publisher.

Software licences

Identification of IP

A software licence will identify a program by name, version and other identifiers.

A crucial aspect of a software licence is the form of software provided to the licensee. The software's source code is generally readable by humans and reveals the details of the software. It is normally treated as a highly valuable trade secret and rarely provided to third parties or licensees. Source code may sometimes be put into escrow and, for example, made available only if the licensor fails to maintain the software and keep it operational. If it is provided, there will be strict conditions regarding its confidentiality and use. Most software licences are to object code: the type of software that is read by machines, not humans.

The grant

Software licences are for a copyright work: the software and associated documentation. Some licences also include trade secrets. Against the background of the statutory scope of copyright, a software licence specifies in great detail how a program may be used. Most of the restrictions are to avoid the price of the software being too low for the volume of use by the licensee, to avoid unlicensed software proliferating, or to prevent the licensee competing with the licensor.

Use of the software may be limited to a single machine, and copying may be limited to one back-up copy. Licences usually restrict transfer of the software, sublicensing, or use of the software to provide services for third parties. Licences of object code typically prohibit reverse engineering or any attempt by the licensee to access the underlying source code.

Permissible licence terms may be governed by applicable national law, which may limit such restrictions. For example, in the EU, software protection is governed by the Software Directive, which provides for protection of computer programs but also puts limits on the rights of the software owner. In particular, it provides that reverse engineering is permissible in certain circumstances. These provisions were inserted at a time when IBM was still the dominant force in computing, and the legislation was intended to allow others to engineer systems that would work with IBM's. In practice, the computing market developed in wholly unforeseen ways and the provisions were of little use. This is a good example of the risks of over-prescriptive legislation aimed at solving perceived market imbalances.

Other obligations

Software licences have some features that are like a sale of goods, even though they are characterised as licences. Software is delivered and installed and tested. If it does not work, usually the licensor will replace it.

Possibly in a separate maintenance agreement, a software licensor will agree to fix problems, provide technical support and so on. These obligations raise business issues of scope, duration (how long the software will be supported) and payment (will the often fixed payments from the licensee cover the licensor's obligations?).

Liability

The licensor

Crucial in most licences is the potential liability of the licensor for the risk of claims arising from the licensing and exploitation of the IP. From a licensor's perspective, the return on the licensed IP may be capped in terms of the royalty or fees received. However, use of licensed technology or software may lead to large IP infringement, personal injury and business loss liabilities. In the case of a trademark licence, in particular, the licensor may be held liable for acts of the licensee that have nothing to do with the licensor. For example, the owner of a franchised fast-food trademark can expect to be involved in a claim for personal injury brought by a customer against a franchisee.

Risk allocation provisions in software licences often include the following, subject to limitation through consumer protection or other applicable laws. These types of protection are useful in other licences as well:

- **Limited express warranty.** The licensor will warrant that the product will work according to certain specifications but disclaim any other warranties implied by law as to quality, fitness for purpose or non-infringement.

- **Limited express remedies.** The licensor will agree to certain remedies if the express and limited warranty is broken, for example to fix the problem or to refund all or part of the licence fee if it cannot be fixed.

- **Exclusion of consequential damages.** The licensor will disclaim any liability for consequential damages to a licensee's company (for example, a licensed accounting system crashes and a company loses money and reputation).

- **Limited indemnity for IP infringement.** The licensor may agree to indemnify for certain types of IP infringement. For example, infringement of copyright and misuse of trade secrets may be regarded as the fault of the licensor, as would any claim of infringement relating to a licensed trademark. Infringement of patents is much more difficult, as noted above. It may be entirely innocent. Moreover, it may be hard to allocate responsibility when the licensed technology or software is part of a larger system or product assembled by the licensee, which is accused of infringement. However, subject to exceptions for such combinations, modifications or other actions by the licensee, a licensor may agree to indemnify for patent infringement, often with the proviso that if an injunction is threatened, it may modify the software, or terminate the licence and provide a refund of all or part of the fee.

- **Overall cap on licensor liability.** The licensor may seek to cap its overall liability to fees received from the licensee. This is often the most difficult term to negotiate. From the perspective of the licensor it makes sense – why do a deal that will cost you money? However, as noted above, a licensee may say that without the licensor, it would not have incurred the liability in the first place. This negotiation is more difficult regarding IP infringement because insurance cover may not be available as it is for other losses, such as general liability or business interruption.

- **Prohibition on certain uses of licensed technology.** Use of the licensed technology or software for hazardous activities may be prohibited.
- **Indemnity from licensee and legal compliance by licensee.** Applicable laws may make it hard to avoid liability for personal injury caused by the licensor, but especially in respect of trademark licences a licensor may be brought into a claim against a licensee when it is not the licensor's fault. A licensor may therefore seek indemnity from the licensee for this type of claim. A licensor may also require a licensee to comply with all applicable laws and regulations, carry adequate insurance, provide proof of that insurance and add the licensor as an additional insured under the licensee's insurance policy.

The licensee

A licensee will be concerned that the licence will not cause claims against it. The licensee will therefore seek assurances that the licensor owns the technology and has the right to grant the licence, and will seek indemnity for claims of infringement caused by use of the licensor's IP.

Bankruptcy

Since the dotcom bubble burst in 2001, bankruptcy has become an ever more important part of IP strategy and risk assessment. This is because licences may be terminated when either the licensor or the licensee goes bankrupt – which happens not only to smaller technology companies, as a result of failure to raise needed capital, but also to multinational companies such as Nortel Networks in Canada (see Chapter 13) and Qimonda in Germany, each of which had large patent portfolios and numerous licensees.

Licensor bankruptcy

Generally, a licensee of IP is in a difficult position when its licensor goes bankrupt. Under the laws of some countries, the bankrupt licensor may terminate the licence, leaving the licensee without needed IP rights, or the licensed IP may be sold in a bankruptcy auction or similar proceeding free of the contractual rights of the licensee.

When entering into a licence or other IP-based transaction that is crucial to its business, the licensee should consider the creditworthiness of the licensor and whether protection may be obtained against the licensor's bankruptcy or proceedings by a lender to the licensor enforcing its security. The law in this respect is complex and discussions about a licensor's solvency may be sensitive. Accordingly, what needs to be determined is how critical the IP is to the licensee. Are there readily available substitutes for the licensed technology and at what cost, including any necessary adaptation costs? A licensed trademark may have no substitute, however.

Protective structures

Where a transaction is sufficiently important, protection in the event of bankruptcy should be considered. This will depend primarily on the laws of the countries of the licensor and licensee.

Commonly used in the software industry is an escrow arrangement, which may also be useful where licensed technology has documented aspects or physical embodiments. In an escrow arrangement, a third-party escrow agent holds the source code to the software or other critical embodiments of the technology on condition that they are released to the licensee in the event of bankruptcy, or preferably the licensor failing to support or maintain the software. In this case, the licensee will in theory have possession of what it may need to continue to use the licensed technology. In practice, the licensee will also need access to the individuals who originally developed the software or technology in order to use it effectively. Thus provision should be made for hiring the relevant staff of the bankrupt entity if this proves feasible.

Other forms of protection may include:

- investigating whether the licensor has borrowing secured against the IP and obtaining a non-disturbance agreement from the secured lender should the lender gain possession of the licensed IP as a result of a default by its borrower (in some countries, the law may require the IP to be sold in a public auction, which means that the secured lender may not take possession if the IP is sold to a third party at the auction, thus making this device less useful);

- in territories where it will be advantageous, filing a copy of a licence agreement with the applicable patent office so that third parties are on notice, and/or making other filings in offices used to record encumbrances against property;

- taking a security interest (mortgage) in the underlying IP so that claims in bankruptcy for breach of the licence are secured rather than unsecured;

- moving the licensed IP to a more creditworthy entity that acts as licensor (possibly a "bankruptcy remote" structure that is shielded legally and operationally from the credit risks of the underlying business – see Chapter 15).

US protections

There are special protections for licensees of IP under the US Bankruptcy Code, but these may be no more than "half a loaf". The normal rule in a US bankruptcy is that a trustee of a bankrupt company can reject a continuing contract (an executory contract). This amounts to a form of termination. Section 365(n) of the Bankruptcy Code protects a licensee of some IP from rejection of its licence in the event of the bankruptcy of the licensor.

These protections allow a licensee to keep its licence and permit access to material held in a third-party escrow arrangement. However, although the licensee is required to continue paying royalties, the licensor is not obliged to perform under the agreement. This type of bare licence may work well for non-exclusive licensees operating under simple patent licences, but it is not as helpful in preserving rights in more complex situations, particularly in exclusive licences where a licensee needs the licensor to do more than just passively license rights, or where the licensee relies on services from the licensor as in many cloud or "software as a service" arrangements.

Importantly, most cases hold that the protection of Section 365(n) does not expressly apply to trademarks (although similar protection of trademark licensees may occur under new case law), and some question whether it applies to IP outside the US. Obtaining the protection of Section 365(n) requires a licensee to monitor a bankruptcy proceeding and exercise its rights promptly. And although not common, it is possible for a secured lender to sell a borrower's assets without a bankruptcy occurring or for licences to be sold separately from the underlying IP in a bankruptcy. In such circumstances, a licensee may be faced with a purchaser claiming that it has bought the patents but not assumed the licence agreement, and that, if at all, it is bound only not to sue the licensee, not to honour any other obligations.

In most other countries, an equivalent to even the limited protections of Section 365(n) of the US Bankruptcy Code may not be available. Thus where a licensor is being liquidated, there may be a real risk of a total loss of licence rights.

Licensee bankruptcy

In the event of the bankruptcy of a licensee, questions arise about what happens to the bankrupt company's licences from third parties. In particular, can those licences be terminated by the licensor? Or can they be sold and assigned if the bankrupt company is liquidated?

Termination

Licences often expressly permit the licensor to terminate the licence in the event of the licensee going bankrupt or suffering a similar process such as receivership. The business logic behind such a provision is that a bankrupt licensee is unlikely to be effective in exploiting the licensed technology.

Under the laws of many countries, these contract provisions mean what they say: that the licence can be terminated, potentially leaving a company without needed IP. In the US, the position is complex. The Bankruptcy Code is protective of the bankrupt company and generally makes such events as termination purely because of bankruptcy unenforceable. However, the complexities of the interaction of IP law and bankruptcy law mean that in the US, termination of a non-assignable IP licence may sometimes be possible in the event of a licensee going bankrupt.

Such termination provisions may therefore represent a real loss of value for the licensee (because the IP may no longer be available) and so should not be accepted lightly in negotiations. A compromise negotiation position could be based on termination for non-performance, whether or not the licensee was bankrupt.

Assignability

For the licensor, crucial to control of licences is to make them terminable in the event of the bankruptcy of the licensee, and non-assignable by the licensee to a third party in any circumstances. This is because the licensor will not want the IP transferred to a licensee that it does not find desirable. The opposite is true for the licensee, which for business flexibility reasons, if nothing else, wants its licences to be freely assignable. This is because such strict non-assignability may prevent the licences from being sold to a third party in a liquidation of assets (or, indeed, in any other business transaction, including the sale of the business of the licensee).

Legal limitations on licence terms

The terms that may be included in a licence agreement are generally open to business negotiation, but there are legal limitations. These include provisions that are either unenforceable or ineffective under applicable IP law; provisions that violate prohibitions on exports of technology for national security reasons; restrictions on licence terms as a result of government funding or because of the tax status of the licensor; and, most importantly, limitations required by competition and antitrust law.

Limitations on territorial exclusivity

International licensing, pricing and distribution strategies have to take into account the ease of import and export, especially through the internet.

Competition law considerations, especially in the EU, may prohibit clauses in a licence that prevents, for example, a licensee in France from filling an order placed by a customer in Germany. However, anywhere in the world there are limitations under IP law on how watertight territorial exclusivity can be. This is a result of the doctrine of exhaustion of IP rights and the potential for grey-market imports.

Grey-market products can be distinguished from infringing products in that they have been put on the market legally in one part of the world by the IP owner or its licensee, but then exported to another country. Whether that sale is legal depends on whether that country regards the original sale in the other country as having exhausted the IP rights.

Countries are free to adopt an international, regional (for example, depending on free-trade areas) or national theory of exhaustion under Article 6 of the Agreement on Trade-Related Aspects of Intellectual Property Rights (TRIPS), which states that "nothing in this Agreement shall be used to address the issue of the exhaustion of intellectual property rights".

In the US, the rules differ depending on whether the imports are of patented, trademarked or copyright goods. In the EU, the general rule is that imports from elsewhere within the EU cannot be prevented, but imports from outside can be prevented. The main point in the EU is that if licences are granted to individual countries, those licensees are to a certain extent in competition with each other.

Prohibitions on export to rogue states

Many countries have export control restrictions on goods, services and technology destined for states that operate outside the normal bounds of international comity, such as North Korea and Syria. Exports of certain types of technology (for example, encryption and nuclear technology) to certain destinations may also be prohibited from licensing either absolutely or subject to prior approval because of national security or policy. Export control is a complex area and there can be substantial penalties for non-compliance, so it is imperative that advice is taken before any transaction involving sensitive technology, or where a licensee may be connected with a controlled destination country.

US government funding and universities

The government funding enjoyed by many US universities may bring with it mandatory licensing terms under the Bayh-Dole Act. And certain types of transaction may be difficult for universities because of their status as charities or because their facilities are funded by certain types of bond. Again, this is a complex area and advice should be sought.

Competition and antitrust laws

In the late 1970s, the exploitation of patents was subject to intense scrutiny throughout the world because there was a perceived conflict between the rights granted under a patent to exclude others and the freedom of trade promoted by competition or antitrust laws. The US Department of Justice had a list of nine no-nos prohibiting various licensing practices; the EU had restrictive guidelines on what forms of licence were appropriate; and throughout the rest of the world most inbound licences were subject to some form of government scrutiny, largely under the supposition that a local licensee may be subject to unfair exploitation by the foreign licensor. And patents were often assumed to have the type of market power that is problematic in competition law.

Throughout the 1980s and 1990s (and generally continuing to the present day), the view was taken that patents were a form of property like any other and a just reward for innovation, and that technology licensing was generally pro-competitive. Hence any challenge to licensing should be based on economics as opposed to a desire to protect the licensee, formalistic rules, unwarranted assumptions, or suspicion of IP in itself.

Many countries had concerns not only about competition law but also about industrial policy and foreign-exchange control. Vestiges of these concerns remain throughout the world. For example, in Brazil, all technology licences must be registered with the INPI (National Institute of Intellectual Property) to allow payments outside Brazil.

Non-compliance with competition and antitrust laws may result in civil and criminal penalties as well as more practical business issues over enforceability of the licences that a company enters into, with contracting parties in the EU sometimes raising a "Euro defence" to enforcement of an agreement. Hence seeking legal advice at an early stage pays dividends. Companies dealing with the US should be aware that a broad swathe of e-mails and internal documents may be reviewed in litigation challenging the legality of a transaction. In the EU, the European Commission has power to raid premises and review and remove documents.

Agreements with competitors

With IP licensing, there are often legitimate reasons for a competitor wishing to license another. However, in general, transactions among actual or potential competitors are subject to much greater competition law scrutiny than those where there is no actual or potential competitive relationship. The competition authorities are concerned that a licence (and especially a cross-licence) may be used to divide territories or product markets, to restrict output, or to set the price at which products covered by the licence are sold to the public. Any proposed business arrangement with a competitor with these types of features is a "red flag" and therefore legal advice should be sought at an early stage.

US case law

Government enforcement: antitrust guidelines

In the US, the legality of licensing arrangements has been developed under case law and precedent. The enforcement intentions of the Federal Trade Commission and the Department of Justice (the government departments charged with protecting competition) are periodically set out in guidelines. There have been more recent guidelines on specific IP topics, but the latest general guide is the Antitrust Guidelines for the Licensing of Intellectual Property, issued in April 1995.

Mandatory reporting of transactions

As well as the case law governing particular restrictions in a licence, under US law exclusive licences or sales of IP exceeding certain monetary thresholds and a range of transactions transferring rights in the pharmaceutical industry may be subject to reporting under the Hart-Scott-Rodino Antitrust Improvements Act before the licence or transfer can become effective. Failure to notify potentially carries significant fines. In addition, certain agreements relating to pharmaceuticals are also required to be filed under the Medicare Prescription Drug, Improvement and Modernisation Act.

Patent and copyright misuse

One confusing aspect of US law is that the public antitrust enforcement position of the government may be more lenient than the applicable case law. Separate from but closely linked to the antitrust laws, certain types of licence terms may render a patent unenforceable in litigation and are known as "patent misuse". These generally cover situations where the power of the patent is used to control products or services outside the scope or duration of the patent rights. Classic examples of patent misuse include requiring the use of unpatented goods purchased from the patent owner as a condition in a licence to use the patent, which is called tying, and seeking royalties for use of a patent after its expiration or for unpatented goods. The doctrine is also found in copyright licensing, where, for example, restrictions on the use or development of competing products may not be permissible.

Red flag provisions

As well as the types of agreements noted above between competitors (affecting price or output, market division, and so on), US case law suggests caution (and obtaining legal advice) on proposed licences or other agreements including the following terms:

- restrictions on how the licensed products are to be priced;
- restrictions on activities of the licensee beyond the scope of the IP being licensed, including exclusive dealing arrangements that may prevent a licensee from researching, developing, dealing in, or using competing technologies;
- royalties that continue beyond the duration of the IP rights being licensed, or are based on goods or services not covered by the IP being licensed, or where a royalty is charged at more than one level of the distribution chain;
- tying arrangements where a licensee is required to purchase goods or services not covered by the IP being licensed;
- grant-backs that require a licensee to assign improvement technology to the licensor;
- restrictions on dealing with particular customers, or other restrictions regulating competition between the licensor and the licensee, or among licensees;

■ acquisitions of IP by a business with a significant position in the applicable market.

EU Technology Transfer Block Exemption and blacklist

In some ways, the competition law governing licence agreements is more accessible in the EU than in the US. This is because unlike the US, the European Commission has the ability to exempt certain classes of agreement from the competition law prohibition under Article 101 of the EU treaty, where those agreements either do not restrict competition or where the benefits to competition outweigh the burdens. It has done so for many years in respect of technology licensing, or what it terms "technology transfer agreements", by issuing regulations known as "block exemptions" and accompanying guidelines. A company can look at the block exemption and determine whether a proposed agreement contains "hardcore" prohibited provisions that will always be a problem under EU law, or certain other restrictions that are called out as being potentially subject to challenge in the particular circumstances. A new Technology Transfer Block Exemption (TTBE) has been adopted and was announced on March 21st 2014.

The EU takes the position that most technology licensing is pro-competitive, but its primary concerns can be seen in the list of hardcore and other restrictions to which the block exemption does not automatically apply:

■ agreements on price;

■ limitations on output (which as a matter of economics lead to higher prices), subject to exceptions;

■ allocations of markets or customers within the common market (geographic restrictions being in general a greater concern in the EU than in the US because of the focus on the creation of a single market);

■ restrictions on a licensee's ability to exploit its own technology or carry out R&D;

■ obligations on a licensee to grant exclusive rights or ownership to the licensor of improvements made by it to the licensed technology;

- obligations on a licensee not to challenge the validity of the IP licensed.

Abuse of a dominant position

In certain circumstances, conduct related to IP by an individual company may give rise to claims of monopolisation, unfair competition or abuse of dominant position. In broad terms, conduct potentially subject to legal review may include certain types of refusal to license or provide access to needed IP; acquisitions of IP (which may be subject to compulsory notification to competition authorities if certain monetary thresholds are met); certain baseless assertions of IP; and use of IP to restrict competition beyond the scope of the IP.

In general, an abuse of dominant position may be found more readily in the EU than a finding of monopolisation in the US, which is comparatively rare. And it is fair to say that although the US law is protective of the process of free competition, the EU law may be more protective of smaller companies that are perceived to have been damaged by the conduct of larger companies.

Beyond the US and the EU

The opening up of markets over the past 30 years or so has led to an increased focus on competition laws to regulate market conduct. As a result, such laws have proliferated throughout the world. Most major trading countries now have effective competition laws that need to be understood and followed. Countries within the EU will have both national and EU regulation.

China in particular now has active competition law enforcement, and as noted above set conditions on the sale of Nokia's handset business to Microsoft. It has also investigated Qualcomm's licensing practices.

For a licensor based in Europe or the US, as well as the risk of fines from authorities, there is a risk that agreements may not be enforceable. For example, failure to comply with competition laws in a lower-cost market may enable a licensee in that market to use those laws as a defence when, for example, the licensor seeks to enforce an export prohibition.

Administrative requirements relating to licences

When agreeing an international licence, each party should check that there are no administrative requirements in the other party's country.

A number of mandatory administrative requirements may apply to licence agreements. Advantages may also be gained from voluntary procedures under local law. These may include:

- recording the licence in the appropriate IP or other office, which may be necessary for its effectiveness in general or against third parties;
- consent to payment of royalties outside the country from a central bank or other body;
- stamp duty or other tax on the transaction;
- filing with or review by competition law or other government authorities.

13 The market for IP: how IP rights are bought and sold

THIS CHAPTER ADDRESSES buying and selling IP separately from buying or selling a business. Traditionally, IP has been bought and sold as part of many mergers and acquisitions (M&A). Any acquisition of a company will almost invariably include IP, even if it is only the name of the company, a website, or the company's IT systems and data. In many acquisitions of consumer brand and technology-based companies, the primary asset may well be IP because manufacturing and many other functions are outsourced. Historically, however, outside the M&A or brand acquisition context, high-value, stand-alone transfers of IP were comparatively unusual.

Patents

New business models have resulted in new markets in IP, especially patents, and transactions are occurring more frequently where IP is transferred separately from an underlying business for substantial sums of money.

The sale of its patents by Nortel Networks is an example of the new marketplace at work. Nortel was a Canadian telecommunications company that went bankrupt in 2009. Among its most valuable assets was its patent portfolio. The patents were sold through an auction process. Google emerged as a leading bidder, offering $900 million for the portfolio in order to bolster its position in phones using the Android operating system. Other bidders included RPX Corporation (a

For a quick summary of points to note and
strategic considerations, go to page 302

defensive patent aggregator, see below), which was seeking to acquire the patents to prevent them falling into the hands of patent assertion entities (PAEs) that would sue its member companies. However, in 2011 the patents were acquired for $4.5 billion by Rockstar, a consortium of technology companies comprising Apple, Microsoft, Ericsson, Sony and Research in Motion (BlackBerry).

Some 2,000 of the patents were transferred to members of the consortium. Yet others were to be monetised through licensing and enforcement actions, and on October 31st 2013, Rockstar launched a series of litigations against Google and other manufacturers of Android-based smartphones under patents purchased from Nortel.

In 2012 Google in turn purchased Motorola Mobility for $12.5 billion, in large part for its portfolio of patents (estimates of the size of the portfolio range between 17,000 and 24,500, see Chapter 14). The rationale for the purchase was to "help protect the Android ecosystem".[1] In January 2014, Google announced the sale of Motorola to Lenovo, while retaining ownership of most of the patents it acquired, stating that Lenovo would acquire "over 2,000 patent assets".[2]

A further variant in patent strategy was seen in the 2013 sale of Nokia's handset business to Microsoft, where Nokia sold the physical assets of its handset business but retained the patents, using the transaction to establish a licensing value for the portfolio of €1.65 billion: Microsoft announced that it would pay €3.79 billion to purchase Nokia's devices and services business, and €1.65 billion to license the patents.

The Rockstar and Motorola Mobility acquisitions, however, reflected the intensity of the phone wars, especially with regard to the Android operating system. The market for patents appears to have settled down since, and in December 2014 it was announced that an affiliate of RPX Corporation had purchased the patent assets of Rockstar for $900 million, with all litigation brought by Rockstar including that against Google being settled and RPX receiving licence payments from over 30 companies and agreeing to make the patents available on FRAND terms.

As well as the big technology companies, there are other participants in the marketplace for patents including defensive patent aggregators such as RPX.

Patent aggregators

Patent aggregators acquire portfolios of patents with a view to generating income primarily through licensing. Standing alone in terms of its age, size, scope and resources is Intellectual Ventures (IV), which was founded by Nathan Myhrvold of Microsoft, who was joined by Peter Detkin formerly of Intel. IV has amassed a huge patent portfolio through acquisition and some internal inventive activity, raising money from technology companies that are also its licensees, as well as institutional investors. Over $5 billion is reported to have been raised, involving over 40,000 patents.

Patent assertion entities

PAEs acquire patents with a view to profiting from assertion of those patents, usually through litigation (see Chapters 2 and 11). In terms of their impact on the market, PAEs come in various sizes and flavours. At one end of the spectrum are small shell entities that may be established by a patent lawyer or an investor and acquire a single or small number of patents. Many of these are established in Texas and sue alleged infringers in the Texas courts. At the other end is Acacia Research Corporation, a publicly quoted company with a market capitalisation of approximately $600 million.

Defensive buyers

Some buyers seek to prevent a patent from being enforced by a competitor or a PAE. They may be either strategic buyers such as operating companies or defensive patent aggregators.

Defensive patent aggregators are entities or consortia that have been set up to avoid patents falling into the hands of PAEs. A defensive aggregator will typically be funded by membership or subscription fees and will acquire patents that pose threats to its members, hold them for a period of time, license them to its members and then sell them back to the market. The members are thus protected (because the licence survives the sale). Non-members, however, remain at risk of litigation under the patent. Examples include RPX Corporation, which is publicly quoted in the US with a market capitalisation of approximately $800 million, and Allied Security Trust, which is a consortium of technology companies often sued by PAEs.

Strategic buyers

Some companies acquire IP that has strategic value to their business, such as providing intellectual property needed for a new product line; or, as noted in Chapter 10, for defensive purposes to use as the basis for counterclaims if sued by competitors with stronger patent portfolios or as currency for negotiating a cross-licence of needed patents owned by competitors. Patents may also be purchased as the basis of a licensing programme and to remove them from the market so that they do not fall into the hands of PAEs. For example, ARM Holdings, a UK chip manufacturer, was a leading member of a consortium formed with Allied Security Trust, a defensive patent aggregator, that acquired the majority of the patents of MIPS Technologies, a rival chip manufacturer. According to ARM's press release, "a collective approach with other major industry players" neutralised any potential infringement risk.[3]

Examples of patent acquisitions by operating companies include Facebook, which acquired portfolios of patents from IBM and Microsoft in 2012, and Twitter, which in 2013 acquired a patent portfolio from IBM. Both these companies had comparatively small home-grown portfolios. These acquisitions were assumed to have been made to bolster the patent portfolios of the companies for defensive purposes.

For many operating companies, acquiring patents poses significant difficulties. It may be hard to spot patents that are a real threat, given the biases of the company's engineers. Attempts to buy patents may lead to those patents being asserted against the potential buyer (see the Google example above). As noted in Chapter 16, knowledge of patents has liability risks. Hence operating companies often team up with intermediaries and other market participants to achieve their goals.

Sovereign patent funds

In recent years, a number of countries have established national patent and technology funds. These include France Brevets in France, Intellectual Discovery in South Korea and Innovation Network Corporation in Japan. They have a number of different functions, including venture-capital investment, acting as an IP commercialisation business on a national level (much like university technology transfer offices that promote licensing of university technology), encouraging collaborations, and so on.

However, some of these entities also purchase patents and at least one has enforced them. For example, France Brevets acquired patents from a French operating company and asserted them in Texas.

Sellers

As discussed in Chapter 11, a divestiture of IP may "monetise" an otherwise unproductive or undervalued asset of an operating company. Some operating companies now routinely dispose of excess patents to offset the costs of their patent functions among other reasons. Thus despite their objections to PAEs, operating companies are active as sellers.

As a result of the business risks associated with high technology, sales of IP by bankrupt companies have also become fairly common. Individual inventors or small companies unable to enforce their patents may choose to sell their patents, often to a PAE.

Sellers also include patent aggregators that have acquired patents that they have licensed to their investors and are now selling the patents subject to those licences.

Intermediaries

Intermediaries have emerged to serve the patent market. These include patent and IP brokers, specialist lawyers, auction services, restructuring firms, small banks focused on IP transactions, specialist groups within larger banks and firms that put together consortia to acquire patents.

In conclusion, the patent market has changed hugely in the past two decades. In some countries, including the US, an active transactional market has developed in the technology industry. However, it remains a market of individual mainly private transactions.

Trademarks

Divestitures and acquisitions of brand-based companies are nothing new. However, as the outsourcing of business functions has increased, often what is transferred is nothing more than a set of intangible rights. Moreover, companies have been created to acquire groups of brands with a view to licensing them to third parties. Thus a company may acquire a number of fashion or other brands and license them for different products and in different market niches.

Such companies have fewer operating risks and require little capital compared with a manufacturing company. An example is Iconix Brands, based in the US, which purchased the Umbro brand clothing and footwear business from Nike for $225 million in 2012 and in 2010 acquired rights to the Peanuts cartoon brand for $175 million.

Copyright

Copyright covers a vast range of different types of property, from software to images to music catalogues. One common feature is that valuable copyrights tend to be used repeatedly by many users, thus generating cash flows. Where a large library is involved, such properties have caught the attention of financial investors attracted by steady cash flows that can be used to service debt or distributed to investors. Private equity investors are particularly interested in music and image catalogues.

Transferring IP rights

Ownership of intellectual property is usually transferred through a written document called an assignment, which together with any associated documents should cover crucial matters such as:

- the price;
- the IP rights being transferred;
- the countries covered;
- any prior licences and rights that encumber the IP;
- the rights the assignee has to past and future damages and income;
- the future co-operation the assignor has to give the assignee;
- the rights to use any other IP of the assignor that is necessary to use the assigned IP;
- warranties to protect the buyer should assertions made by the

seller turn out to be untrue – for example, if a patent owner wrongfully states that a patent has not previously been licensed when it has, a legal remedy should be available.

On a technical level, the formal and legal requirements of an assignment vary by country and by type of IP. Some assignments of registered intellectual property require greater formality, including, for example, notarisation of execution and for foreign use, apostilles (ribbons and seals) affixed by a government authority. If an international portfolio of IP is being purchased, numerous individual country assignments will have to be executed. This can take time and be costly. Updating title to IP is therefore often neglected, leading to later problems when companies go through multiple changes of ownership.

Recording title

Patents and trademarks generally have some form of recorded title in each country, and transfers of such IP generally will not be valid against third parties unless and until properly recorded within the correct time period. In some countries similar procedures may apply to copyrights as well.

Taxation

Stamp duties or other taxes may be payable on the value of an IP assignment. Where IP is transferred among affiliated companies, the tax authorities may assess income tax on the basis of income associated with the IP but transferred to ownership in another country (see Chapter 8).

Patent assignments

Make sure all necessary rights are assigned

The principal attribute of a patent is the right to enforce it. As a result, patent assignments usually include the right to sue for past, present and future infringement. If they do not, the new owner may not be able to bring a suit for infringement without the involvement of the prior owner. Complex assignment structures can sometimes be created where rights are reserved to the prior owner – for example, rights to a particular field, or a right of reversion to take the patent back in the future, or rights to control or benefit from enforcement of the patent. This can lead to situations where the assignee tries to enforce the patent but the accused defendant takes the position that the new owner does not have sufficient ownership rights to enforce the patent (a lack of standing to sue).

The importance of acquiring the entire patent family

Individual patents are often part of larger families of patents that are related to each other by claiming some common patent application as a parent. Complicated issues with obtaining and enforcing patents may arise where the new owner does not acquire all the family members; and incomplete patent families may be hard to sell.

Watch out for implied rights and continuing relationships

Patent assignments are subject to complexities where broad language about assignment of inventions may result in patents being assigned by implication, contrary to the intent of the assignor. Assignments in the context of continuing relationships, such as employment or independent contractor relationships, require specific language providing for a present assignment of rights to defeat a future patent assignment to a third party.

Trademark assignments

Trademark assignments, at least in common law countries, have legal technicalities associated with ensuring maintenance of brand quality and avoiding customer confusion. Complexities arise where marks are assigned to different owners in different geographies or for different products in the same country, or closely allied marks are sold to different owners.

Goodwill

At least in the US, there is a requirement that trademarks be assigned with the goodwill of the company associated with the trademark. This has both formal, in terms of the language of the assignment document, and legal aspects. (See Chapter 3.)

Geography

It is legally acceptable for a trademark to have different owners in different countries so long as it has only a local reputation in each country, but a proposed sale of a trademark along geographic lines should be reviewed carefully given the international nature of the internet. Such an assignment may have to be accompanied by contractual procedures to avoid confusion between the companies that will own the trademark and especially their online presences.

Related marks and product splits

Difficulties may arise when trying to split ownership of related marks for related products. In common law countries, it would be because the public would assume that the products come from the same source because of their related nature, and putting the marks into separate ownership would result in them losing their distinctiveness and therefore their legal protection as a trademark. In civil code countries, issues may arise because of the ability of one owner to block registration by the other owner. There may also be concerns about internet confusion.

Where an assignment of a trademark is not possible, a licence may be considered. However, a licence may be terminable in the event of the bankruptcy of the licensor; or there may be the issue of involvement by the licensor in the business of the licensee to maintain quality control, coupled with potential liability of the licensor for the business of the licensee (see Chapter 12).

Copyright assignments

Limited duration or limited rights

As noted in Chapter 4, assignments of copyright in the US and some other countries may be subject to a right of termination or reversion. Thus an assignment may not be a transfer of ownership forever but only for a period determined by statute.

In some civil law countries, copyrights may be so associated with the human author that assignment of all rights may not be possible. In such circumstances, licence rights may be obtained.

Conveyance of separate rights

As with patents, exclusive rights in copyright may be conveyed separately under English and US law. However, care must be taken to ensure that a partial assignment gives the assignee the intended right to exploit and enforce the copyright, with standing to sue infringers, within the agreed field of exploitation of the copyright.

Waiver of moral rights

In European and other civil law countries it is necessary to ensure that a written waiver of the moral rights of the author of the work is obtained as part of the assignment of copyright.

Due diligence

The value of IP may be significantly affected by ownership or other legal challenges, validity issues, or weaknesses arising from how that IP has been commercialised or enforced in the past. The apparent value of intellectual property may be deceptive. When acquiring IP rights or a company dependent on IP rights, a number of business and legal investigations should be carried out. This process is called due diligence, and it involves examination of the target's website, public filings and internal documents, and interviews with its staff. Far from being a boring formality, due diligence usually unearths material facts that apply directly to the value of the IP.

Due diligence helps determine the following:

- What the IP is exactly.
- The scope of rights under the IP.
- The duration of the IP.
- The history of the IP (prior commercialisation, prior licences and (for patents) commitments including FRAND obligations, prior litigation and validity challenges).
- Who owns the IP.
- The IP's legal quality and how that affects its value and projected life.
- The risks of third-party claims relating to the IP.
- Other important facts that affect the IP's value.

The first step in due diligence is to determine what IP is important. The information can then be used to prioritise further due diligence. Initial due diligence will identify the main patents, trademarks, copyrights and other IP under consideration for purchase, that is, those that account for or protect significant sources of revenue. During the identification process, it should become apparent how the IP is used in the business and how it protects or creates current or future revenue. Is it a barrier to entry? Does it protect valuable product features? Is it identifiable as the basis of licensing revenue?

Due diligence will also identify which IP the target believes it owns and which IP that it uses is licensed from third parties.

Acquiring IP rights

Patents

When one or more patents have been identified as being valuable, the following investigations should be undertaken:

■ What rights exist? How long is it before the patents expire? In which countries do they exist? Have all fees been paid to keep the patents in force? This requires detailed checking of records and databases and creating country-by-country schedules of patents.

■ Is title to the patents up to date with a complete chain from the inventors to the current owner? This involves checking record title and patent office files against transactions transferring title.

■ Are there encumbrances on title such as mortgages? This involves checking with patent and other applicable filing offices.

■ What is the scope of the patents (ie, what products or methods infringe the patents)? This is open to interpretation, but if the patents have been litigated, some findings are likely to have been made as to their scope.

■ What are the actual and projected sales of the patented products? How much may demand for the products be affected by technology developments?

■ Have the patents been licensed and on what terms?

- Are there potential infringers who may have defences to a claim for infringement? These may include acquiring products from a licensee or a being a licensee as a result of a prior business transaction, defences available under FRAND obligations or defences by reason of delay in enforcement. Some countries require that products be marked, and a history of sales without patent marking may preclude claims for back damages for past infringement before notice of the patent. In the US, claims for contributory or induced infringement of a patent require knowledge of the patent by the alleged infringer.

- How likely are the patents to be valid and enforceable? Have these issues been tested in previous litigation, or been the subject of an opposition or re-examination procedure? The validity of a patent may be challenged on the basis of prior art discovered during extensive patent searches, but there may be "own goals" that can be more easily and quickly ascertained from the files of the seller. For example, are there public uses, disclosures or sales prior to the filing of a patent that would be a statutory bar to obtaining a patent? Have there been changes in the law on patentability that may affect validity? Is there prior art of which the sellers are aware? One common example is where the patent application process or contested proceedings (such as an opposition proceeding) in one country reveal prior art not disclosed to or found by the patent office in another country. Where searches are undertaken, they may be targeted by looking for products that were on the market before the priority date of the patents covering those products.

- Was the process of applying for the patent carried out diligently? To an experienced patent lawyer, this may be apparent from, for example, the amount of technical disclosure; the number of patent claims and whether there are both broad and narrow (more specific) claims; what prior art may be disclosed or recited (in general, a strong patent is obtained notwithstanding prior art); how much prior art was disclosed to the patent office, and how many times the patent has been cited in future patents. Basically, it is possible to tell how much time and care were involved in obtaining the patent and how important it is in a particular field.

■ Does using the patent require use of third-party rights? The importance of this question depends on how the acquired patent is to be used. If the patent is being acquired to provide protection to a product, it is very important. If it is being acquired to enforce against others, this may be a secondary value and price consideration (a potential licensee may be willing to pay less if it has to pay stacking royalties to third parties). Where it is important, a lawyer will review the past claims of infringement received by the seller as well as the seller's procedures for identifying and mitigating risks. Where the seller does not conduct freedom to operate searches, or otherwise have knowledge of third-party patents, targeted searches may be undertaken (for example, patents of close competitors), subject to the legal issues and strategies discussed in Chapter 16. It should also be noted that the infringement risk profile of a product may change if, for example, ownership passes from a business with a large portfolio that may deter claims by competitors to a new owner with few patents.

Trademarks

Similar questions can be asked about a valuable trademark or brand that has been identified for acquisition:

■ What trademark rights exist? Due diligence on acquisition of a trademark or brand focuses initially at a legal level on the mechanical task of reviewing registrations for the trademarks by country and geography for payment of renewal fees, for the classes of goods and services covered by the registrations (their scope), and for correspondence of the registrations to the marks as actually used (ie, do the registrations cover the mark as it is currently used?). Trademark rights, unlike patent and copyright rights, may continue indefinitely so long as renewal fees are paid and the mark remains in use. Due diligence may include determining that for each country the necessary use has continued to support the registrations. Ownership of domain names associated with the trademarks is also reviewed.

■ Is title up to date? Title should be reviewed to determine whether the trademarks are owned by the entities using them, and to check that the history of assignment of the marks is complete. Searches may also be undertaken for liens and mortgages. In common law countries such as in the US, where the law requires, assignments are reviewed to determine whether goodwill was assigned together with the trademarks.

■ Have the trademarks been licensed? Licences and all other transactions with the trademarks should be reviewed to ensure that necessary quality control by the owner over uses of the marks by third parties has occurred.

■ Have the trademarks been subject to litigation or contested? Often questions arise regarding the scope of the trademarks being acquired or the ability to license those marks to others for related or new fields. Settlements of infringement claims by or against third parties or trademark opposition proceedings may result in acknowledgements that the trademark rights are limited and that certain uses do not infringe. Alternatively, the marks may have been found to be strong and infringed.

■ Do the trademarks infringe third-party rights? The files of the target company may be reviewed to uncover issues with third-party rights. Issues with third parties that may be using the same word trademark may also be uncovered by searching for the mark in a particular trademark office, on the internet or through a specialist trademark search service. Often conflicts arise where two companies adopt the same mark in different geographic or product areas. Thus where international expansion is a basis for acquisition, international searches should be carried out.

■ Are other rights needed? As well as acquiring rights to trademarks alone, rights may be required to other forms of IP, such as copyrights and trade dress rights in packaging and other branding and advertising elements, website collateral, and even formulas and quality-control specifications for products. The elements of the entire brand should be reviewed to determine the scope of assets to be acquired.

Copyright

Similar questions can be asked about material copyright, although tracing copyright ownership and title is much more difficult than with patents and trademarks. The longevity of copyright means that assignments of rights and other agreements may be hard to track down due to loss of knowledge, and rapidly changing technologies and the evolution of copyright laws may make older agreements difficult to apply to current business models.

- What copyrights exist, who was the author, who owns them now and what is their duration?

- Is title up to date? With patents and trademarks, there are clean records and official title registries, but this is often not the case for copyrights. Determining rights can involve review of old documents.

- Who owns or licenses the copyrights? With the passage of time, it can be difficult, or even impossible, to find the owners of copyright. The application of new technologies to old agreements may result in disputes regarding the ownership of rights because the wording does not address the new technologies or uses clearly. The same person may not hold all the rights that are needed. In respect of software, there can be ownership issues with recently created works as a result of failure to execute agreements. In large software programs where millions of lines of code may be involved, it is highly likely that some of the work has been done by independent consultants or contractors rather than employees. As explained in Chapter 8, the work product of the consultants or contractors would not generally, without an express written agreement, vest in the commissioning company. However, often the actual coders may be tracked down and, for a small consideration, necessary assignments obtained. The ability to be able to take the position that the company has full, unencumbered rights to the program may be necessary both if litigation is ever needed against

infringers and to use the software as collateral (security) for a
loan, so the effort involved is well worthwhile.

■ Is the work an adaptation, derivative work or infringement of an
earlier work? A work may infringe the rights of a third party if
used without a licence or beyond the scope of a licence.

■ Have the copyrights been licensed?

■ Have the copyrights been subject to litigation?

■ Has open-source software been used in the development of a
software product? A particular issue when acquiring software
is whether elements of open-source code have been used in its
development, with the result that distribution of the work would
require the source code to be put into the public domain.

14 Valuing IP

THIS CHAPTER ADDRESSES the valuation and accounting treatment of intellectual property, which has in many ways lagged behind the real business value of IP.

The implied value of the intangible assets of publicly quoted companies, such as those in the S&P index, is immense, but under US accounting rules internally developed IP is generally not valued as an asset, not even at its cost. Thus for investment and other purposes, the value of a company's IP may be hard to determine. Under most accounting rules, there is no collection of balance-sheet entries that identifies and provides a valuation on any specific basis of the complete range of intangible assets of a company. Given the gap between the net asset values of companies and their market values, this is hardly satisfactory.

However, accounting for and valuing IP, especially patents, is complex. In the case of a patent it requires analysis of: the size, growth and profitability of the underlying product market covered by the patent; the significance of the patent as a contributor to the commercial success of offerings in the underlying product market (relative to the contribution of other elements); how much of the market has been already licensed and at what royalty rates; the duration of the IP; the susceptibility of the IP to legal challenge (which may affect duration); and the quality of the IP from an enforcement perspective.

IP is difficult to understand and value in the financial context.

For a quick summary of points to note and
strategic considerations, go to page 303

Perhaps the biggest issue is that there is not yet a fluid and transparent market. Much thinking in respect of IP focuses on trying to solve this problem and create markets. Market mechanisms are developing in the technology field (Chapter 13), but in most circumstances valuation models other than pure market comparisons have to be used. Closely allied to valuation is the concept of patent risk: the risk to the patent owner that its patent may be invalidated or found not infringed, and the risk to an alleged infringer that it may be found liable for infringement. As a result of lack of commonly accepted approaches, many disputes over IP value are resolved through the expensive and inefficient means of litigation.

There are other reasons for the difficulty in valuing IP apart from the lack of a fluid market, including the following:

- IP is a derivative in the sense that its value depends on what it covers and the volume of those sales.

- It is hard to separate the value of IP from the value of other assets used to commercialise that IP.

- Much IP has a limited life, and patents especially are subject to legal challenges that may be fatal.

- A patent may be worth more to one company than another, depending on whether the company owns proprietary complementary technology necessary to exploit the patented invention, so a concept of "value" may depend on the context.

- Use of a patent may infringe the rights of another, and enforcing a patent can cost a lot of money.

- It is hard to generalise from one patent to another and average values do not make much sense. Academic studies, for example, show that the value of a population of patents is extremely skewed, with most patents being worth very little while just a few are worth a king's ransom.

- IP is a purely legal asset (a right to exclude others), and thus its value is affected by the quality of the asset, the legal remedies of the IP owner and applicable law affecting those remedies. Separate from the quality of the asset itself, as these permitted remedies change, such as the ability to obtain an injunction, so the value of the patent changes.

Determination of a patent's worth even under a seemingly precise standard such as "fair value" according to US accounting standards is a challenging exercise. The Financial Accounting Standards Board's ASC 820 (formerly SFAS 157) requires consideration of the "Principal (or Most Advantageous) Market" and the "Highest and Best Use" for the subject IP asset irrespective of the type of transaction contemplated and the actual or anticipated use of the asset by its current or prospective owner. The valuation analyst is, therefore, faced with the challenge of identifying and "modelling" the principal market and the highest and best use for the subject IP asset – hardly clear-cut aspects in many instances.

Notwithstanding these difficulties, the valuation of IP is important in a number of contexts. The IP acquired by a business in an acquisition has to be valued for financial reporting purposes. Valuation may be required for taxation where transfers of IP occur between related parties in an international context. The calculation of damages in litigation over patent or other IP infringement is a form of valuation. Although often driven by market factors, the pricing of licensing or IP purchase and sale transactions may also require a valuation analysis. Valuation may be required to establish the value of collateral for a loan or for litigation financing, or a company may wish to value its IP as a management or compliance tool or to provide information to investors.

Accounting treatment of intellectual property

Current accounting standards do not require the identification and valuation of all IP. The accounting treatment of IP varies between generally accepted accounting principles (GAAP) used in the US and the International Financial Reporting Standards (IFRS) used locally throughout the world. In most systems, IP may be treated differently depending on whether it is acquired or developed internally, leading to paradoxical results where more information is available on acquired IP than on a company's own basic brands or technology.

The main difference between US GAAP and IFRS is the treatment of internally developed IP, in particular the cost of research and development (R&D). Under US GAAP all internal costs are expensed as incurred. This is a reflection of the perceived uncertainty of future benefit from such expenditures. By contrast, under International Accounting Standard (IAS) 38, under certain circumstances, development expenses are recognised as creating an intangible asset, which may be recognised when it is probable that future economic benefits will flow to the owner that are attributable to the asset, and the cost of the asset may be measured accurately.

Where intellectual property is acquired, specific rules apply to how that IP is accounted for. Under US GAAP, ASC 805 requires that where intangible assets are acquired, the purchase price be allocated in a specified manner and values attributed to the various categories of asset. ASC 350 then requires that those assets be tested annually for possible value impairment. Under IAS 38, there must be a similar accounting for acquired assets. In the case of countries that have a stamp duty tax on the transfer of IP, it is often the case that differing IP rights will be listed in a schedule to an asset purchase agreement with values attributed. Hence in the case of acquired IP, far more information is available than for home-grown IP.

Valuation methodologies

Where IP is valued for tax or other purposes, various valuation models are used, including the cost approach, the market approach and the income approach. Sophisticated valuations should take into account not only financial and market information related to IP but also the strength of the IP itself on a qualitative, legal basis. This will influence the amount of revenue that the IP will generate, but there is also the chance that the IP will be invalidated and the revenue stream will cease, and hence the likely duration of the income stream.

The cost approach

Cost-based theories are based on the actual cost to create, or the estimated cost to recreate or substitute for the IP in question. Cost is not an ideal way of valuing IP because it may have little connection to the economic or business value of an asset. For example, the market value of a house may be more or less than the cost to rebuild it. However, given the uncertainties over the value of IP, it does at least provide a point of reference. The cost basis calculated may be historical and include R&D and associated capital investments, patents, registrations and other IP protection costs, and other related costs; or it may be an estimate of how much it would cost to replace the IP with new IP of similar effect in the marketplace (for example, historical advertising expenditures could be considered in the case of trademarks) and the amount of profits forgone during the period of recreation.

The market approach

Market approaches attempt to determine value based on comparable transactions. However, individual items of IP vary hugely in their characteristics and application.

The market approach is the method by which real estate is often valued, with comparisons made with similar properties and allowances made for differences. With IP, the difficulty lies in finding comparable transactions with public pricing information and then reconciling the differences between the transaction terms, the applicable markets and the IP involved in the transactions.

Databases are available but these are often skewed in containing only publicly related transactions. In some fields markets are developing: for example, a brokered market for US patents, usually in software and technology, which are acquired for the purposes of assertion, often by patent assertion entities (PAEs).

The values of patents sold for assertion are based on expected litigation recoveries. The values of patents acquired for strategic purposes may be higher. Transactions involving portfolios of technology patents have led to calculation of average prices per patent, even though patents usually have widely differing values. When patents are counted, it is often not clear whether the same measures are used for supposedly comparable transactions. For example, are patent applications counted? Is one patent a single patent in a single country, or a single patent throughout a region or the world, or a patent family in a single country, or a patent family throughout a region or the world? What about patents that have continuation patents based on the same technical disclosure (a more complex patent family)?

The usefulness of per patent average figures was further undermined by a 2013 judicial decision establishing FRAND royalties, which was based on a finding that the top 10% of electronics patents account for 84% of the value of all electronics patents.[1]

Despite these complications, there are some interesting high-level examples. In August 2011, in an article entitled "Doing the maths", *The Economist* looked at the price per patent paid in Google's acquisition of Motorola Mobility for $12.5 billion, reportedly including 24,500 patents, and Novell's sale of its patent portfolio for $450 million, coming up in each case with the same average price of $510,204.08 per patent. Interestingly, Google itself attributed a value of $5.5 billion to the acquired patents and developed technology in its September 2012 Securities and Exchange Commission (SEC) filing, and using the figure of 17,000 patents that has been circulating more recently, a figure of around $323,000 per patent may be calculated.

The price per patent paid in 2012 by the Rockstar consortium for the patents of the bankrupt Nortel Networks reportedly equated to $750,000 per patent (although in late 2014 at a time when the phone wars were winding down, 4,000 of the less valuable Nortel patents were resold for a price of $225,000 per patent).

In 2013 Kodak managed to obtain only $527 million for the sale to a consortium of 1,700 patents and 655 applications covering its imaging and printing portfolio, as well as multiple licences to the consortium members to its remaining patents. Of the $527 million, $94 million was, according to a court filing, allocated to the patent purchase, which would equate to around $40,000 per patent – a tiny fraction of the value estimated by some.

The sale of Kodak's patent portfolio has its own peculiarities, including the fact that a super consortium of buyers was the sole bidder and some of the patents had been widely licensed before the sale, but it does show that as with any other asset, IP values are driven by supply and demand as much as their inherent merit.

The income approach

Income approaches attempt to calculate the value of the future income stream attributable to the IP. An income-based valuation depends on accurate identification of the IP and the income that should be allocated to it. Where a total value is being calculated as opposed to a periodic royalty, the duration of the IP's income flow and the risks of termination or diminution of that income flow will also be important in order to calculate the present value of future income – with the concept that the riskier the income flow, the lower the value attributed to future years.

The income approach has a number of variants. These include excess earnings or premium profit methods, where an attempt is made to attribute to IP a portion of earnings that would not be earned without the IP; methods that allocate income to IP from the overall income from a product or a company after a return is first attributed to all other assets used in the particular company or product; relief from royalty, where a calculation is made of the royalty that a party would be willing to pay to a third party for the IP; allocations of profit to the IP and to other assets based on their relative estimated contributions; and cost savings, which estimates the savings from use of the IP.

The relief from royalty method is similar to the approach in US patent litigation, where the value of IP may be established for damages purposes under a "reasonable royalty" theory, which would be the royalty that a willing licensee would be willing to pay to a willing licensor. However, in litigation the assumption is that the patent is valid and infringed, whereas such certainties will not be the case in a business negotiation (see Chapter 2). It should be noted that the relief from royalty method may lead to an understated valuation of IP when the royalty rate selected for the analysis is drawn from licensing agreements for "comparable" assets (or even from licences for the very same asset being valued). The reason for this is that, in most instances, full ownership of all rights associated with an IP asset is more valuable than the partial rights granted in a licence. Hence, a negotiated royalty is likely to represent only a portion of the total earning power and "optionality" value of ownership.

The difficulty of the income method is fundamental: how to separate the income attributable to the IP from other contributors to the profitability of a product or company. As an initial step, income is calculated based on an accounting analysis of the products embodying the IP. However, once that income has been calculated, the value attributable to the IP as opposed to other drivers of value must be assessed. This is hard to do, so in many situations a default is made to a comparable royalty rate (with all the difficulties described above in finding a true equivalent), or a rule-of-thumb profit split such as the 25% rule, which can be used as the starting point for a valuation exercise.

The 25% rule is based on empirical work that established that a royalty for patented IP was often around 25% of the pre-tax profit of a licensee of a patent. However, this rule has been criticised for not taking into account the actual value of a patent (as in a device such as a mobile phone, which may be covered by thousands of patents). In litigation, the rule has been heavily criticised in the US for not relating to the specific facts of the case. In other words, the rule is merely a rule of thumb and may be completely inappropriate in a specific case. The courts now require substantial evidence to support damages calculations, including looking for the particular contribution of the particular patent. Chapter 11 discusses the valuation of a patent as a litigation asset.

Valuing early-stage technologies

In addition to the difficulties of establishing the value of intellectual property where the profitability of a product is known, many licensing transactions take place years before a product appears on the market. This is often the case in life sciences, where the valuation process must take into account a series of risks, such as the safety profile of the product, the risk of not obtaining regulatory approval, the size of the future market and the market penetration of the proposed product. These can be modelled based on a series of single assumptions, but a probabilistic model such as the Monte Carlo method can be used. In this case, ranges of assumptions are analysed to come up with a distribution of net present value calculations.

Valuing brands

In the context of valuing IP, brands require particular discussion because of their often great value and the fact that they are a major asset of many companies. Unlike patents, what you see tends to be what you get – there are far fewer hidden legal complexities and a strong brand from a business perspective is usually a strong brand legally. However, just as for patents, under standard financial reporting rules, the economic value of brands is not reflected on corporate balance sheets unless they have been acquired from a third party. Thus some of the most valuable home-grown brands such as Apple or Google do not add anything to their owner's reported assets value on the balance sheet. And, while it is possible for companies to disclose valuations voluntarily to assist investors, few do.

Brand consultancies each year disclose their estimates of the value of the world's top brands. They look at factors such as the revenues and profits of the branded business lines, the portion of those profits attributable to the brand, and in some cases other, more subjective or research-based factors. However, in the case of a couple of top brands, in 2014 Google was valued by Interbrand at approximately $107 billion and by BrandZ at approximately $159 billion, while Apple was valued by Interbrand at approximately $119 billion and by BrandZ at approximately $148 billion.

These are differences of tens of billions of dollars. It may well be that the absence of universally agreed valuation methodologies is what makes businesses hesitant to report the value of self-developed brands except when required by accounting rules to do so.

This is a striking example of how intangible assets exist in a financial and accounting fog, where the value of even the most important of such assets remains open to wide interpretation.

15   Using IP to raise finance

THIS CHAPTER ADDRESSES the role of intellectual property as a basis for raising money through financing. For owners of valuable IP, Chapter 11 described how that IP could be monetised through sale or licensing. These strategies involve some reduction in the utility of the IP to a company because it is sold and therefore no longer available, or because it is subject to a licence that may limit its further use or reduce its strategic value as a barrier to entry. An alternative strategy would be to keep the IP and not license it, but use its value as collateral (security) for a loan or use it as a basis for raising equity.

Despite the great value attributed in theory to intangible assets by balance-sheet calculations, IP and other such assets have not historically been regarded as valuable collateral for loans when standing alone. It is not unusual and routine for IP to be used as collateral for a loan as part of a larger financing transaction where many different types of assets are secured. However, IP has historically rarely been given significant separate value from the value of the company as a whole. There are a number of reasons for this:

■ **Valuation difficulties.** As noted in the previous chapter, valuation methods for IP in general were and remain somewhat uncertain, partly because of the lack of comparable transactions. Until recently, there were no liquid markets of any type for IP, especially patents. However, that situation is changing as

For a quick summary of points to note and strategic considerations, go to page 305

portfolios of patents and individual patents are bought and sold, establishing possibly comparable transactions that may be used for valuation. Furthermore, the knowledge gained from litigation involving patent assertion entities (PAEs) enables estimates to be made of what revenue a patent may bring if asserted and a basis for valuation in the market for litigation assets.

- **The separateness of its value.** There may be doubt about whether the IP is separable from the underlying assets: that is, whether the IP could be sold off in a foreclosure or other sale separately from the underlying assets of the company as a going concern without losing significant value. In other words, there is doubt about the IP having value other than as a barrier to entry for the particular company owning it. For example, patents may be sufficiently narrow in scope that they have application only to the products or services of the company and non-infringing alternatives to those products and services are available. This is really a question of the scope of the patents and what they cover, which requires expertise to establish. With respect to copyrights covering software, a similar concern may be whether the software is valuable without the developers of the software being available to work on it and fix bugs and other recurring problems.

- **Accounting rules.** The accounting rules for IP have not been favourable, at least in the US, to using IP as collateral. In the US, internally developed IP is not treated for accounting purposes as an asset of a company in the same way as real estate or other tangible assets. There is usually no immediately applicable balance-sheet entry indicating the value of such IP.

- **Dependency.** IP assets may not be stand-alone in the sense that third-party IP may be needed to use and exploit them without infringement. Those third-party licences may be terminated or not available in a foreclosure (see below). A buyer of patents for assertion may not be bothered if a licensee also infringes other IP. However, a strategic buyer of IP may want to acquire a package of patents and licences.

- **Lack of expertise.** Sophisticated lenders understand that certain IP, especially a patent, is a complex asset that may be subject to invalidity challenges that could shorten its life. However, the expertise to evaluate those risks is often not available to the lender.

Notwithstanding these overall issues, there have been historical exceptions in specific industries and as noted a nascent lending market appears to be developing in the US with regard to technology patents. It is likely that as the value of IP becomes more broadly appreciated and markets for IP mature further, secured lending on the basis of IP assets will continue to develop. Furthermore, governments seem anxious to promote lending based on using IP as collateral.

Legal process and technicalities

Due diligence

Where IP is a significant and material portion of the collateral underlying a loan or other form of financing, a lender will carry out significant due diligence focused on title (ownership) and value of IP. Lenders considering IP as collateral generally investigate the following and borrowers should anticipate this:

- **Title to IP.** Including a clean chain of title from the inventor/ author to the current owner.
- **Encumbrances.** Whether there are any prior liens, charges or mortgages against the IP. These may have to be released and cleared from the title to the IP.
- **Existing borrowing.** Whether there is existing borrowing that will not be paid off at closing. If so, inter-creditor arrangements may have to be negotiated with the other lenders. These can be lengthy and complex.
- **Duration.** The expiry dates of the IP and whether renewal or maintenance fees have been paid. If such fees have not been paid the IP may have expired early and thus be valueless.
- **Scope.** What products the IP covers.

- **Freedom to operate.** Whether third-party IP is required to exploit that IP. And where the IP needed for freedom to operate has been licensed, the terms of the licences including royalties, termination and assignability.

- **Existing licences.** Whether the IP owned by the target has been licensed to third parties and on what terms, with a particular focus on exclusive licences (which prevent future licensing and exploitation) and the terms of those licences including termination rights.

- **Importance of IP to licensees.** Whether the IP is essential to the licensees of the target. If it is not, licensees may terminate or possibly challenge the licensed IP to avoid paying royalties.

- **Revenue.** Whether revenue is generated by the IP, with what duration and with what offsets. A top-line licence royalty may be significantly diminished by offsets of licensee expenses allowed under the licence, including royalties paid to third parties, litigation or settlement expenses, costs of maintaining IP and tax withholding.

- **Payment enforceability.** Whether there are licence enforceability issues caused by provisions in the licence that are not permissible under applicable competition or patent law (a classic issue in the US is that royalties under a pure patent licence are generally not payable after expiration of the patent, although this rule is subject to a Supreme Court challenge).

- **Unlicensed sales.** Whether there are potential third-party licensees or infringers of the IP. This would be a primary focus of a lender that may have the expertise to enforce patents itself (see Chapter 11).

- **Past litigation.** Whether the IP has been involved in litigation and with what results.

- **Validity.** Whether there are or have been any third-party challenges anywhere in the world.

Covenants

As well requiring security or other documents to allow it to foreclose on the IP and its proceeds in the event of a default under the financing (see below), a lender will usually lay down terms controlling how the IP is exploited or enforced during the term of the loan and to prevent its disposal, so as to ensure its value as collateral is not diminished. A lender may also bargain to share in benefits from any such exploitation, enforcement or disposal. These restrictions may limit the future freedom of action of the company and so will be negotiated to reach mutually acceptable compromises.

However, terms demanded by lenders may be hard to square with IP monetisation. For example, in August 2014, Alcatel-Lucent, a telecoms company, announced the early repayment of a $1.75 billion loan secured on its patents and IP noting:[1]

> We have also been able to regain control of our own destiny, in particular, the release of intellectual property, giving us now the freedom and flexibility to leverage these assets as and how we see beneficial for Alcatel-Lucent's future.

Filings

In most countries, IP can be mortgaged or made subject to a charge or lien in the same way that other forms of property can be mortgaged. A lender will record its security interest in the IP as required under local law to put third parties on notice of that interest. This may require filings in the registry for mortgages of property generally as well as in the applicable patent, trademark or copyright office as required under local law. In the US, it is now a common practice to file at both state and federal levels.

In some countries a trademark may be secured by way of an assignment to the lender. However, in common law countries this can be problematic if the lender does not exercise the necessary quality control over the business of the borrower, which is, because of the assignment, the licensee of the lender. Other forms of mortgage structure are therefore preferred.

Scope of security

A lender will seek not only a security interest in the IP itself but also to secure proceeds from enforcement or sale or license of the IP and associated licences. However, certain types of collateral may be excluded from the scope of assets over which a lender may take security interests. In the US, for technical reasons, there may be difficulties in taking security over pending intent-to-use trademark applications. It may also, arguably, be a breach of a non-assignable licence for the borrower to grant a security interest in that licence. US state law, however, has protections for lenders in the case of non-assignable licences to enable their use as collateral (see below).

Termination risk

Understanding what may happen to IP and IP licences in the event of insolvency or bankruptcy is crucial to understanding the value of IP collateral. Lenders may be concerned about the risk that valuable licences may be terminated in bankruptcy. IP lender risks are illustrated in Figure 15.1.

Certain lenders may be interested just in taking security over patents and not worried by associated licences. Others may wish to preserve the value of a package of IP and associated licences to the target company, and revenue-bearing licences granted by the target company receiving finance. Taking an effective and valuable security interest in licences of needed IP from third parties to the target, as well as licences by the target to royalty-paying licensees, may be complex, particularly where there are restrictions on assignment of those licences to third parties.

As noted in the previous chapter, issues with IP and bankruptcy largely arise from the interaction between bankruptcy law and licences of IP. Most companies rely on licences of third-party IP in addition to their own IP, and those licences are potentially subject to termination in the event of bankruptcy, which might significantly affect the ability of the company to continue and would, until a new licence is obtained, affect the value of its own IP.

FIG 15.1 **IP lender risks**

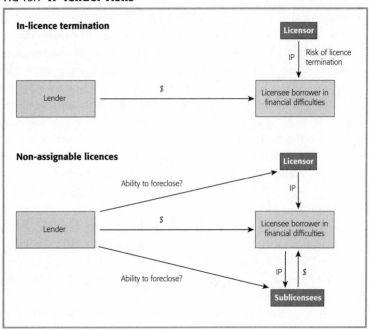

Source: Author

Asserting rights to non-assignable licences

Although US law generally allows the granting of a security interest in a non-assignable licence, it does not permit the secured party to operate under or assume that licence without the consent of the other party.

Consents

Indeed, lenders may require a company seeking to use IP as collateral to obtain all consents or rights necessary under applicable law from its licensors of material IP critical to the value of the borrower to enable those lenders to maintain those licences and transfer them along with the IP of the borrower.

FIG 15.2 **Bankruptcy remote structure**

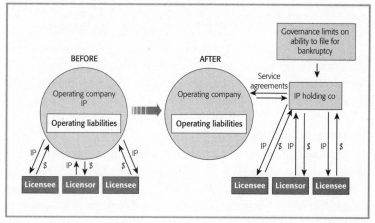

Source: Author

Bankruptcy remote structure holding IP

Alternatively, a "bankruptcy remote" structure may be created where the material in-licences, owned IP and out-licences are transferred to an entity that is shielded legally and operationally from the credit risks of the underlying business (see Figure 15.2). A lender may take security in the shares or other ownership rights of the entity itself, which holds the package of IP rights and licences. Such structures are not foolproof, but they may significantly improve the position of a secured lender.

Where IP is used as collateral

Technology patents

As the market for technology patents has developed, hedge funds and specialist lenders have begun to look at patents as potentially useful collateral. This is because the value of similar patents may be subject to estimation based on comparable transactions or the finance provider's experience in enforcing or buying, selling or licensing such patents.

Litigation finance

Patents may be used as the basis for financing in the area of funding for litigation. Specialist lenders and hedge funds may provide funding to pay for the legal fees of a patent owner in pursuing infringement litigation. An example of a publicly quoted litigation finance house is Burford Capital. Some but not all sources of litigation financing take a security interest in the underlying patents.

Pharmaceutical industry

In the pharmaceutical and biotechnology industries, finance has been available for two decades or more through acquisition by investors of streams of royalties payable to a company by a third-party licensee under IP licences. These transaction structures originated in situations where a university, hospital or company had licensed a patent covering a pharmaceutical product that had achieved significant success and was receiving a royalty on sales by the licensee.

Finance from investors in a royalty stream

In these situations the IP owner is usually receiving a significant income stream, but there is the risk that it may diminish or even stop. A finance provider, such as a private equity or hedge fund, puts up a lump-sum investment in return for the rights to the stream of future royalties for a fixed period. Thus the fund takes the upside on the royalties together with the risk of product failure, and the licensor has a fixed return on a net present value basis. A simple structure is shown in Figure 15.3.

In these structures, the finance provider normally takes a security interest in the IP as collateral. Depending on the structure and terms, the finance provider may acquire the royalty stream as a property right. In another variant of the structure, the royalties from a licence may be used not to repay a fund but rather to pay bonds issued to the public.

Revenue-based financing

More recent structures are known as revenue-based financings. In these transactions, a royalty payable to the financing source is created

FIG 15.3 **Simple royalty financing**

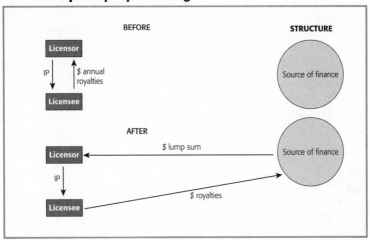

Source: Author

by the borrower based on sales of a product sold by the borrower. Again, the finance provider may take a security interest in the underlying IP as collateral.

Mitigation of collateral risks

As discussed in Chapter 2, pharmaceutical products may be covered by only one or two or at most a small portfolio of patents. Given the risks of invalidity of any individual patent, and the risk that a non-infringing product may be developed, how are such investments made without the investors assuming disproportionate risks? Of course, any negotiated transaction may allocate risks between the seller and the buyer. However, there are market factors that may mitigate those risks.

Identifiable patents, often of high quality

When the US market is under consideration, the patents protecting a product are often easy to identify because they have to be listed in the Food and Drug Administration's Approved Drug Products with Therapeutic Equivalence Evaluations, called the Orange Book. Patents are listed to allow the company selling the drug product to obtain certain procedural and other protections relating to patent challenges. The patents are thus known and can be examined in detail. Patents on new previously unknown drugs are often of high quality and withstand validity attacks. In contrast, patents on new formulations of old drugs may be more open to validity challenge, but in every case it is a matter of the particular facts.

Due diligence will include a review of the history of the invention, because that is the focus of any future validity challenge, as well as an investigation of any statutory bars to patentability (for example, any prior impermissible publications).

Predictable timetable

Historically, under the US Hatch Waxman Act, a predictable timetable for potential market entry would occur when a potential generic medicine entrant challenged an innovative new product. Thus future income streams could be modelled based on various outcomes to a patent challenge. However, the new patent challenge procedures under the America Invents Act may affect how this type of litigation evolves.

Other barriers to entry

Patents are not the only barriers to entry. There are certain exclusivities granted as part of the regulatory regime governing pharmaceutical product approval in many countries that may prevent another product coming onto the market. These "data exclusivities" are a reward for the huge expenses undertaken to obtain regulatory approvals to market pharmaceuticals. In the US, for a pharmaceutical that is a new chemical entity (that is, one not approved previously), a five-year period of market exclusivity from the time of regulatory approval may be granted. Other practical barriers to entry may also exist. For example, certain products may be extremely difficult to manufacture.

Transaction structures that allocate risk

Over the life of these structures, considerable creativity has emerged, with income streams being split into different tranches with different risk profiles, which are allocated to the finance provider and the IP owner. Risks are further allocated between the IP owner and the finance provider by means of representations, warranties and indemnities, and sometimes by events under which the relationship is terminated and the financing repaid.

Securitisation

Copyright securitisations

Under the structures described above, a single or a small number of royalty streams are sold to a single finance provider or used to finance a bond. A securitisation usually involves multiple sources of income which are bundled together and used to pay the principal and interest payments on bonds that are issued to investors. These structures are common outside the IP area, where the bundled assets may be mortgages or car loans or similar financial obligations.

Securitisations based on intellectual property royalties have occurred in the music industry for a number of years (they are often called Bowie Bonds, after the pioneering issue in 1997 based on David Bowie's music catalogue) and also in the film industry, where they are funded by receipts from a portfolio of films.

Brand-based securitisations

More recently, whole company securitisations have occurred in the fast-food industry, where the IP collateral underlying the structure is the restaurant brand. This market was badly hit by the credit crunch in 2009, but it has rebounded in the current low interest-rate environment.

In countries that have bankruptcy laws protective of debtors, securitisations are usually complex legal structures because of the desire to protect the brand and other underlying income-producing IP supporting payment on the bonds from the credit risks of the underlying business. This usually requires the brands to be transferred to a bankruptcy remote entity (see above).

In the US, such structures have to take into account the two primary rules of US trademark transactions: that the trademarks are assigned together with the applicable goodwill of the company; and that the owner of the trademarks exercises quality control.

International developments

In 2013 the UK Intellectual Property Office issued a report, *Banking on IP? The role of intellectual property and intangible assets in facilitating business finance*, with the aim of trying to encourage IP-based finance.

This trend can also be seen in Asia. In China, statistics issued by the Chinese Patent Office in 2014 show that pledges of patents have grown at 70% a year for five years and now amount to 40 billion yuan. In Singapore, in April 2013, the government announced its IP Hub Master Plan, with the aim of making Singapore a hub for IP filing, licensing, management and dispute resolution. The government is encouraging lending on the basis of IP, stating that it will partially underwrite the value of patents used as collateral to encourage banks to recognise IP as an asset class; and it is creating a new Centre of Excellence for IP Valuation. Malaysia has also announced initiatives to encourage use of IP as collateral and establish valuation methodologies.

IP and raising equity

It can be hard to raise initial venture-capital funding for a start-up in some industries, such as biotechnology, without some patent position, even though the technology may develop so rapidly that the initial patents soon become irrelevant. In this situation, patents are almost an imprimatur of innovation.

In rapidly moving fields such as consumer-facing internet technology, patents are often less important early in a company's history because the application process in the patent office can be too slow for the product development cycle, and because the interactive development process with users may result in patentable inventions being disclosed to the public before applications can even be drafted and filed.

In the technology world, however, having a patent portfolio may be regarded as an indication of strength, and patent-light companies may acquire patents around the time of an initial public offering (IPO), both for their profile and for defensive purposes. This is because an IPO is sometimes a trigger for litigation by patent owners who hope that the pressure to resolve a public dispute clouding an offering of stock will lead to a quick and favourable settlement.

16 Developing an IP strategy

THIS CHAPTER PROVIDES GUIDANCE on how to develop an overall IP strategy. Most companies have some form of ad-hoc intellectual property strategy even if management has not consciously thought about this. For example, patents may be filed when engineers or inventors think they have an important new invention. Trademarks may be filed for new brands. Appropriate notices of copyright may be applied to published works. Internet domain names may be obtained. Those who visit or work with the company may be asked to sign a non-disclosure agreement. Legal action may be taken from time to time, and every so often a third party may sue the company. Over the years, IP may have been generally ignored, or may have grown into a major cost centre with an entrenched bureaucracy. It may be regarded negatively as a source of risk and expense and not as a useful asset.

The broad goals of an IP strategy should be to bring order to an ad-hoc process, including at an operational level, putting in place efficient administration across the company's operations of such matters as:

- filing for registrations and trademark, domain name and licence renewals;
- establishing ownership of the IP developed by or for a business and avoiding unintentional loss of that IP, which itself mitigates many risks;

For a quick summary of points to note and
strategic considerations, go to page 306

- addressing other IP risks;
- developing a systematic and cost-effective approach to IP protection and enforcement;
- determining how the IP owned or licensed by a business will be exploited.

Exploitation may include:

- offensive or strategic use against competitors, such as creating barriers to entry or other advantages over competitors;
- defensive use, such as assembling a portfolio of patents, so that if there is a claim by a competitor against the company, there is currency to trade or offensive claims that may be made in return;
- use of IP to generate income independent of product sales by either licensing or sale of such IP.

Each of these three purposes should be viewed globally in respect of current and future geographic and product markets and tested by a cost-benefit analysis. The purposes may also change over time.

Lastly, consideration should be given to how IP can support the overall business strategy and plans, and how IP and related functions such as IT and security should be integrated into corporate governance and co-ordinated with other management functions.

However, not all businesses, even those in technology, need to have an intense and expensive IP focus. For example, and possibly surprisingly, many medium-sized software companies focus primarily on marketing and brands. Although policy and practice on such matters as ownership of IP developed by third parties (especially ownership of the code base), open-source software policies, compliance with licensing terms and maintenance of confidentiality are important (particularly to potential lenders and business partners), IP issues may be rare and patents may only become an issue because of claims by PAEs, as opposed to being regarded as valuable assets. Opportunities might be being lost and some risks might not be being mitigated – what matters is that a cost-benefit analysis should always be undertaken. Figure 16.1 illustrates a simple set of priorities for developing an IP strategy.

FIG 16.1 **Focus of IP strategy**

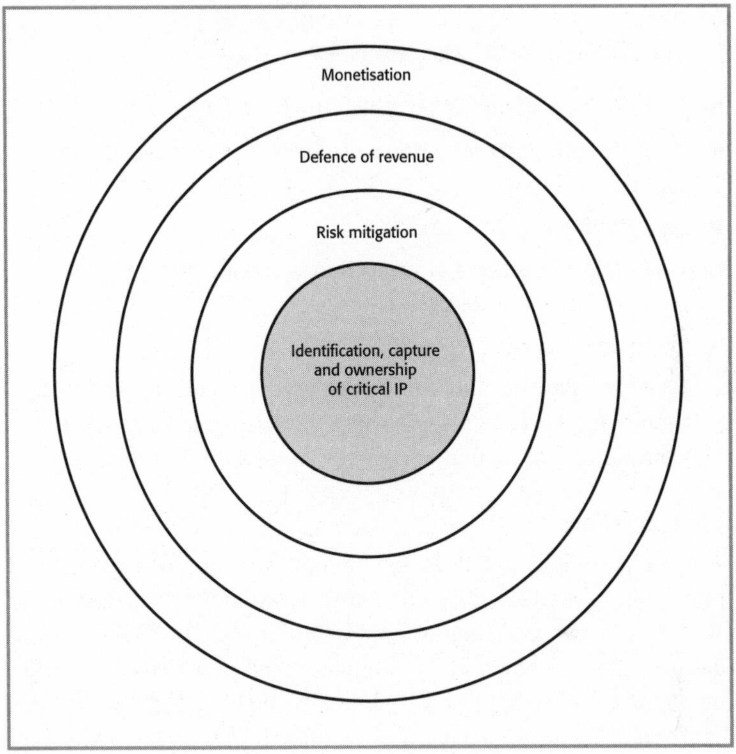

Monetisation

Defence of revenue

Risk mitigation

Identification, capture and ownership of critical IP

Source: Author

IP audit and establishing ownership

Scope

An IP strategy for an existing business should start with a well-planned and focused audit. The goals of an IP audit are usually to determine what IP assets a company has, how those assets are generated, and how they are identified and protected within the confines of the available budget. Such an audit should address asset identification as well as risk identification and mitigation. This is similar to the due diligence that is undertaken by an investor or purchaser when looking at IP assets (see Chapter 13), where the main question is: what IP does the company own and use, and with what risks? However, the approach is forward looking and focused on opportunities for value creation.

The questions to be asked include:

- What is the material IP on which the company relies?
- Does the company own or otherwise have the rights to use that IP?
- Has that IP been protected?
- How does the process of protection work, including confidentiality and security?
- What does the process cost?
- What IP risks exist and what steps have been taken to mitigate them with regard to disputes over ownership, infringement claims and termination of rights to needed third-party IP?

Identification

The audit initially involves the identification of the types of IP purported to be owned by the company, starting with registered IP such as patents, trademarks, copyrights (in certain countries) and design rights, and internet domain names, all of which can be listed by country, by territory and by title (ownership), and checked and confirmed. The audit may then identify forms of IP used in the company that are not registered, such as unregistered trademarks, product designs and packaging, copyrights (including software and website content), databases, manuals, know-how and trade secrets.

Applicability

Registered IP should be reviewed to determine what applicability it has to the company's products and services. Patents that have been filed may not protect the latest products and may no longer be relevant. Trademarks may have been filed only sporadically, and the registered trademarks may not correspond to the form of the marks in use. On a geographic level, filings may not have been made in markets that are now important from either a sales or manufacturing perspective.

Ownership

A review of ownership of IP usually reveals that best practices are not being followed. For each type of IP, it should be determined who owns it and whether it has been protected. For example, is the IP owned by the company or by a third party, such as an employee, a customer, a consultant or contractor, a supplier or licensor? This entails a review of the agreements relating to IP made by the company. Is confidential information protected by appropriate agreements with employees and others and by appropriate physical and network security to guard against cyber-attacks and other forms of misappropriation? Is IP developed by employees and contractors assigned to the company? Do customers own IP that the company uses (not uncommon where customers pay for product modifications)? Are employees under non-compete obligations, or can IP "walk out of the door"?

At its most basic, answering these questions should enable plans to be developed to ensure ownership of IP developed by or for the company and necessary confidentiality and security. These steps should provide for copyright protection by virtue of its automatic application once owned and for trade secret protection by virtue of the procedures and agreements implemented.

Capture

Processes to capture and register IP are often haphazard, and so an audit should examine what they are, including:

- IP ownership provisions in agreements with employees, consultants and third parties;
- how brands are chosen, cleared by way of search and protected, and in which markets;
- how patentable inventions are identified – in particular whether this is a bottom-up process where engineers suggest patents that may be obtained or whether there is a managed process for reviewing engineering work for patentable inventions – and where a decision is taken to file a patent, in which markets is this undertaken;
- how designs are protected and in which markets;

- whether initially secret developments are protected;
- whether the different functions of the business (technology, design, marketing and legal) are working in a co-ordinated manner to maximise available IP protection.

The basic question is whether valuable IP is being lost through a failure to protect. If the answer appears to be yes, the next step is to try to estimate the costs and benefits of improving systems to capture that IP. The process should be examined to determine whether the captured IP protects the company's current and future products or not, whether it can be better focused and whether there are opportunities for obtaining IP for strategic purposes (see below).

During the audit, it should also be determined whether there are valuable inventions, trademarks and designs that have not been protected but still could be through registration, taking into account applicable deadlines for filing.

Risk mitigation

Infringement of third-party rights or failure to protect IP assets may be costly, and risk mitigation may pay for itself through the avoidance of a single litigation. An audit should review the systems in place to guard against IP risks.

The audit stages discussed above may, for example, reveal risks that need to be addressed and mitigated, such as IP that the company believes it owns but for which ownership is not documented; IP that is owned by third parties but used by the company under unwritten, short duration or terminable arrangements; or agreements that do not protect IP through non-disclosure and limited-use obligations.

Risk mitigation may be addressed on many levels, such as:

- filing for and obtaining registered IP rights, thus recording and demonstrating ownership and limiting the ability of others to claim or assert that IP;
- employee policies and agreements establishing IP ownership – including mitigating the risk that employees bring in third-party IP or leave with the company's IP;

- consultant policies – essentially the same as for employees;
- contracts with third parties – clearly defining the permitted use of IP and IP ownership, ensuring confidentiality, assessment of the impact of bankruptcy of a business partner on the availability of critical licensed IP, identifying alternative IP if necessary, monitoring that licensed IP is used within the permitted scope and that needed licences are long term or renewed as needed, and, importantly, seeking indemnity from the third party if licensed IP is the cause of an infringement claim;
- supply and distribution chains – avoiding creating grey-market or counterfeiting problems;
- physical, network, cloud and internet security and privacy – ensuring best practices are followed;
- cyber-liability insurance protecting against data breach and loss and other internet and network losses;
- proper treatment of the personal data of employees and customers – ensuring legal compliance and compliance with a company's privacy policy and applicable data protection laws;
- clearance of brands from a legal perspective and appropriate registration;
- in the areas of copyright text, artwork and photographs, obtaining necessary rights to commissioned work and permissions for stock works and compliance with those permissions;
- searches (but see patent search implications below) and monitoring of competitor and PAE IP strategies, including who is suing and being sued within an industry, and consideration of use of opposition, post-grant patent and other patent challenge procedures to address problematic patents (see below);
- consideration of sole or consortium acquisition of problematic patents and working with patent aggregators;
- IP insurance and indemnities from suppliers where available;

- in software and e-commerce, purchase of third-party components that may bring with them an IP indemnity as opposed to a do-it-yourself solution undertaken without a freedom to operate search;
- open-source software compliance policies (see Chapter 4);
- if commercially possible, limiting liability to customers for third-party infringement claims.

Patent searches

Various patent-related risks may be mitigated through searches: the risk of investing in a product that may not be patentable, or where only a weak or narrow patent may be obtained; and the risk of infringement of third-party patents through targeted freedom to operate patent searches. However, great care should be taken over written and e-mail communications about third-party US patents.

Legal advice should be sought on the risks and benefits of a search for US patents including ease of interpretation of patents in the particular technology; the risk implications of gaining knowledge of third-party patents compared with the likely useful knowledge gained, and likely strategies for dealing with patents identified; the strategy for the search so that it will produce relevant patents; and possible mechanisms for reducing the risks of knowledge of patents being imputed to the company.

Essentially, where a problematic US patent is uncovered, it is generally risky to ignore the issue.

Careless commentary on US patents

Allowing staff the freedom to undertake searches and surveys of competitor patents can give rise to problems in the US. Whatever the strengths of a third-party patent that may be uncovered, in US patent litigation "careless words cost lives". The scope of documents that must be copied and produced to the plaintiff in US litigation is extremely broad. A hastily written e-mail can become a "smoking gun" that has a disproportionate effect on a jury in litigation.

Communications with US lawyers about US patents should generally be privileged and should not need to be produced in litigation (although there are exceptions). However, depending on the facts, other correspondence, including that with patent agents outside the US, may not be so privileged.

Knowledge of US patents, wilfulness and indirect infringement

Because of the way the US patent system operates, in some industries, assessing the risk of infringement of third-party patents through freedom to operate searches was regarded as risky in itself, and some lawyers advocated an ostrich-like approach of ignoring third-party patent risk until it materialised. The reasons for the concern included:

- **Indirect infringement.** Although direct infringement of a patent may occur without knowledge of the patent, in the US there is also liability for inducing another to infringe a patent or contributing to infringement. This type of liability generally depends on knowledge of the patent and intent to cause infringement. As a result, when a potential defendant develops the necessary knowledge and intent related to a patent through its own actions, it may be increasing its exposure to past damages.

- **Wilful infringement.** In the US, there is a unique aspect to patent infringement – the possibility of the court awarding up to treble damages (and attorneys' fees) against an infringer who is considered to be wilful at trial. This essentially makes a bad outcome much worse if a case goes to trial. Before trial, a credible allegation of wilfulness may make a case more expensive to settle. Under more recent law, to establish wilful infringement, a patent owner must show that the infringer acted despite an objectively high likelihood that its actions constituted infringement of a valid patent and that this risk was known, or should have been known, to the defendant. This is more pro-defendant than the previous law, but a company may still be at risk if it takes no action following patent searches which reveal a third-party patent that a product may infringe.

- **Lack of clarity.** In areas such as software, even reasonable people can differ over the scope of a US patent before – and even after – a decision is made by a judge. Hence there is a concern that the result of a search may just be to create uncertainty over essentially unknowable outcomes with the disadvantage of having gained knowledge of a possibly troublesome patent.

■ **Lack of useful solutions.** In the past, it was felt that when problematic patents were identified, there were no good ways to solve the problem. For example, there were no effective methods for invalidating weak patents and courts had high standards for avoiding claims of wilful infringement.

The current law is more favourable, especially where there is no evidence of copying. There are also more effective ways of invalidating a patent than in the past. The inter-partes review established under the 2011 America Invents Act has been found effective as a means for challenging patents on the basis of invalidity (see Chapter 2). There is a market for buying patents. Law firms and possibly other intermediaries may be used to carry out searches and provide only limited results that do not identify specific patents, and to undertake anonymous patent acquisitions.

However, recent cases show that even under the newer law, a company is still in a worse situation if it identifies a problem US patent but does nothing about it and has no credible defence. If problematic patents are discovered, steps should be taken to deal with them, for example by confirming non-infringement or invalidity through legal means such as obtaining an opinion; redesigning the product so that it does not infringe (a "design around"); seeking a licence or to purchase the patent alone or with others (this needs careful consideration because such actions may invite a claim or make a patent owner realise it has something of value); or seeking to challenge the third-party patent in a patent office proceeding or otherwise.

Legitimately copying competitors' products
The patent system is built on the premise of a bargain with the public whereby exclusive rights are granted to a patent owner in return for educating the public on the invention. In theory, there is nothing wrong with learning from third-party patents and reverse engineering a competitor's products. Although copyright protects expression of ideas, ideas should be free for use unless they are confidential or subject to a patent.

However, caution is needed. Many products are sold under contracts that may prohibit reverse engineering. Courts also take a dim view of subterfuge. "Designing around" a patent is legitimate. Copying is not, and the line between the two may not be clear. Courts are also dubious about claims of lack of knowledge of patents where a patented machine or device is copied.

Insurance

Cyber-liability insurance for data losses and other internet or network risks is now readily available, but cover for IP claims is not. However, whenever a claim is made or sustained, insurance policies should be checked to see if they provide cover. At the same time, contractual indemnities from suppliers should be reviewed.

For many of the reasons that make IP hard to value or hard to use as collateral, such as lack of agreed methodologies to assess and quantify risks, insurance related to IP is generally undeveloped, particularly in relation to patents. The various types of risk need to be analysed and applied to each form of IP. There are three main types of losses related to IP: infringement or misappropriation by third parties of intellectual property owned by an organisation; infringement by an organisation of third-party IP; and loss of income resulting from invalidity or other defects in an organisation's own IP. Each may be separately insurable. Other related forms of insurance include media liability covering an organisation's publications and cyber-liability covering data breach and certain other network and internet losses. These types of policies often exclude patent infringement liability.

The availability of IP insurance differs enormously throughout the world and should be investigated locally. Most traditional commercial liability policies only narrowly address intellectual property issues. Advertising injury is often covered, but depending on the policy wording, this usually applies only to advertising activity and may expressly exclude patent infringement liability.

Specialist advice should be sought on the forms of insurance available. Cover for patent infringement risk is starting to become more widely available at a reasonable price. As well as insurance, some protection against claims by PAEs in the US may be obtained by joining a defensive patent aggregator (a business that acquires problematic patents that may otherwise be bought by PAEs, see Chapter 13) if one exists in the applicable industry.

Protecting a company's products

The history of a company's IP enforcement and infringement claims should be reviewed to determine the effectiveness and potential weaknesses of its IP strategy compared with competitors. On the defensive side, a history of claims against the company may indicate a failure to mitigate the risks of third-party claims, although it can be hard to prevent claims by PAEs. On the offensive side, the enforcement actions that have been undertaken should be reviewed, together with their associated costs, and whether any such enforcement has been effective in preventing copying or achieving other strategic goals. In particular, are there circumstances where the company's products or services are being copied but it has no effective IP remedy?

A basic standard of effectiveness is whether the current IP practices and processes protect the company's core technology and brands. First, is the technology and are the brands protected from infringement by competitors? Second, and much more of a challenge, is the technology and are the brands protected from infringement by counterfeiters or copyists?

Regarding relations with competitors, a company's strategic position and flexibility depends on both its offensive patent strength and its defensive weakness. Even if it has patents that protect its products, an attempt to protect a product through an infringement lawsuit may be met by a claim or claims for infringement from that competitor, possibly in an unrelated area (see Chapter 11).

Large technology companies may use third parties to carry out "patent landscaping" to create a picture of the relative strengths and weaknesses of a company's patent portfolio compared with those of its competitors across all areas where they compete. This may lead to decisions to develop or acquire patents in particular fields. Basically, however, if a company has materially fewer patents than its main competitors, it may be in a position of relative weakness.

Piracy

When dealing with piracy, a first step is to determine whether the business model can be changed to reduce incentives for piracy or limit sources of supply. But protection against copying by illegitimate third parties such as pirates is a much harder proposition than dealing with competitors, partly because of the geographic location of the copyists, their fly-by-night nature and the limitations of legal remedies available.

As noted in Chapter 7, some people think that piracy problems in the copyright world may be partly the result of the failure of the IP owner to satisfy market demand at a reasonable price. Alternatively, or in addition, a company may not be policing its own supply chain through exclusive supply contracts and supplier audits to prevent the creation of grey markets. Suppliers and customers may instead be brought into the IP protection process and be used as sources of information about piracy. These aspects of the company's activities and strategies should be reviewed and necessary changes made.

Cost-effectiveness

As noted above, the most cost-effective method of enforcing IP may be to use the procedures that stop goods at the border. Certain areas of counterfeiting may be of interest to law-enforcement agencies, and criminal actions may involve lower costs and be more effective for the aggrieved party than a civil action. For example, periodically there are co-ordinated international efforts by law-enforcement agencies to seize domain names used to traffic counterfeit products. Governments and law-enforcement agencies are increasingly interested in finding more effective ways to identify and stop counterfeits. Infringements may be ranked by business and brand impact, with those closest to the core business being pursued first.

If a company's problems are international, it should obtain the underlying IP protections necessary to enforce rights internationally, including in countries of manufacture. Some jurisdictions may be more favourable to a plaintiff; for example, France may be more favourable to plaintiffs in the fashion industry, partly because of the Comité Colbert, an association comprising French luxury brands. The UK has procedural mechanisms such as asset freezing orders and *ex parte* search and seizure orders. Germany may offer preliminary injunctions.

To save costs, reviews of internet sites and issuing take-down notices to remove infringing content can be done by appropriately trained staff or third-party services, as opposed to lawyers. In certain circumstances, some companies use automated procedures. Where problems are endemic in an industry, trade associations – and on a political level the government – can be used to marshal resources and co-ordinate persuasive efforts with particular internet service providers that are used by infringers.

Lastly, there may be technological measures that a company can take to reduce piracy by avoiding copying in the first place, such as encryption, password protection and licence keys to activate software. Such measures may be much quicker and more cost-effective than taking legal action.

Strategic IP management

Forms of IP protection

An IP strategy should determine which of the available forms of IP protection a company should obtain (see Figure 16.2). In many circumstances, the primary decision is between patents and trade secrets (see Chapter 6). Ideally, IP protection should be viewed holistically, meaning that the available forms of IP are assessed not just for technology or trademarks separately, but also for product design and packaging and the overall image and brand of the business or product line.

The importance of brands and branding

Much of the discussion above has addressed patents. However, even for many technology businesses, branding is crucial – and brands may be as valuable as any technology. As a result, the development of distinctive brand elements and protection of those elements should be a priority for many businesses.

FIG 16.2 **What are you trying to protect?**

Potential IP	Ideas invention	Information	Music, literature, art	Software	Process	Industrial material	Device	Branding	Cell culture	Plant
Patent	✔			✔	✔	✔	✔		✔	✔
Trade secret	✔	✔		✔	✔	✔	P		✔	P
Copyright		Selection/creativity	✔	✔			P	✔		
Design rights				GUI			✔	✔		
Database rights		✔								
Trademark							P	✔		
Trade dress/unfair competition							P	✔		
Domain name								✔		
Plant variety										✔
Plant patent										✔

Note: P = possibly
GUI = graphical user interface
Source: Author

IP portfolio management

IP may be captured, developed, purchased or licensed in order to gain broader competitive advantages beyond just being a barrier to entry benefiting the current products of a business. As discussed in Chapters 10 and 11, a company may acquire patents for the purposes of bolstering its defences in the event of a claim by a competitor, for offensive purposes, or as the basis for a licensing business. It may also buy patents that come onto the market to prevent them falling into the hands of hostile third parties. More fundamentally, a company may acquire or license IP to support innovation that it is undertaking.

Unworthwhile IP

Some registered IP may not be worth the expense of maintaining it. Registered IP that is no longer needed can be sold, but companies can also save money by abandoning no longer relevant IP through non-payment of maintenance fees. Such decisions may be more easily

FIG 16.3 **Patent portfolio analysis**

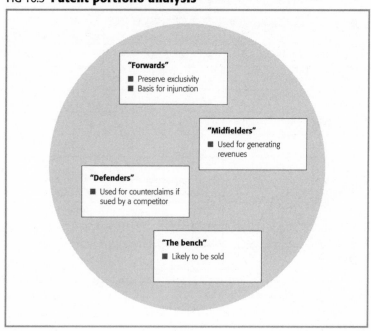

Source: Author

taken for patents than for trademarks, which could end up being used by a third party. However, many consumer-goods groups would benefit from a hard-nosed review of their trademark portfolio. They may well find that they are wasting substantial amounts of money in maintaining global registrations for brands that have purely historical value. Unilever is an example of a business that has carried out a major cull of its trademark portfolio.

Figure 16.3 is a simple analogy of a patent portfolio to a soccer team.

IP as a driver of the business strategy

IP strategies can be used to pave the way for a company's products. For example, although it may be a complex decision with legal obligations, a company may seek to have its IP embodied in industry standards and gain advantages through receipt of royalties, or sale of components to competitors, or lower costs. A brand and an associated suite of design elements may be developed with a view to future expansion and licensing opportunities, and trademarks may be applied for long before a product comes to market. A patent acquisition strategy may be developed in advance to facilitate entry into a new product sector by having patents to cross-license with industry incumbents.

China

China needs to be part of any IP strategy. It is both a potential place of manufacture and a huge consumer market. It is also a source of potential commercial partners and purchasers for a business. Chinese businesses are prolific filers of IP rights and the government is active in IP policy. Companies that have no connection with China may suddenly find themselves negotiating with a Chinese business, potentially at a disadvantage through a failure to file for rights in China.

Governance

The security of systems, particularly the security and privacy of customers' personal, health and financial data, is crucial, and legislation around the world requires board-level attention to this. The US Securities and Exchange Commission has become focused on cyber-security. It is also becoming more common in the US for companies that suffer material losses in IP litigation to be subject to litigation from shareholders. All this, as well as the increasing importance of intangible assets, means that IP and IT management should be integrated with and part of mainstream corporate governance and risk management procedures, with the role and responsibilities of the board of directors clearly defined.

IP strategy checklist

Some questions that managers may ask when trying to develop an IP strategy are as follows:

- What is the IP budget? Who works on IP matters?
- Do the people responsible for the various types of IP (patent, trade secret, trademark, copyright and design) work as a team?
- How is the overall IP function co-ordinated with management generally (business development, marketing, technology, legal and financial functions)?
- What is the material IP on which the company relies – patents, trademarks, copyrights (including software, manuals, publications and website collateral), designs, trade secrets, databases, know-how, etc?
- Does the company own the IP, or does it have a long-term, documented right to use it?
- How reliant is the company on third-party IP and are those rights secure from counterparty risk (termination and insolvency, etc)?
- Do the patents and registered rights owned by the company cover its current and planned products?
- How does the company ensure that it owns the IP it develops or pays for (from employees, contractors and customers)?
- How does the company decide whether to obtain patents or registered rights? What is the process of identifying and protecting IP? In what countries does the company have IP protection and how does the internet affect that protection?
- What forms of IP protection are available for the company and its products or services? Which are used?
- Does the company protect its confidential information and data through agreements? Can the IP "walk out of the door"?
- What are the company's physical and network security measures? Does it have a plan for dealing with and reporting a data breach?
- How does the company mitigate its IP risks – loss of IP, ownership disputes, third-party claims, loss of licences, security clearance procedures?

- If the company is developing software, does the company have an open-source software strategy?
- Are third parties copying the company's products at home or abroad? Are its enforcement efforts effective against competitors and pirates?
- Are the current strategies likely to be effective against future competition?
- How do the company's strategy and IP position compare with those of its competitors?
- Is the company changing so that new IP approaches are required?
- Does the company take advantage of the most cost-effective means of protecting its IP?
- If the company has significant piracy problems, how does it prioritise enforcement and budget? Are there technological solutions to piracy? Is the company exacerbating piracy problems through marketing or pricing strategies or supply chain issues?
- Can the company's IP be used to generate new sources of revenue (monetisation)? Are there patents that could be sold or licensed?
- Is there IP that could be abandoned to save money?
- Are there reasons to acquire IP from third parties?
- What is the history of claims against the company?
- If a competitor sues the company, does the company have IP rights that can be used as a counterclaim against that competitor?
- Are PAEs active in the industry? What strategy will be taken to resist them?
- Does the company offer IP indemnities?
- Does the company obtain IP indemnities from suppliers?
- Does the company have any applicable IP and cyber-liability insurance?

Executive summary

1 An introduction to intellectual property
Points to note

■ Intellectual property (IP) assets underpin the value and competitive advantage of many companies.

■ Given the large proportion of the market value of listed companies attributable to intangible assets, shareholders are by default investing in IP.

■ Multibillion-dollar transactions have revealed the high prices that businesses are willing to pay for IP.

■ In recent years, drawn by large damages awards, companies have been investing in IP (notably patents) simply for the income that can be generated through licensing and litigation against sellers of "infringing" products, highlighting that what is an asset for one business may be a risk for another.

■ IP is often subject to legal challenges, and changes in the law, which affect its value.

■ New technologies may devalue IP through enabling copying and sale of pirated products or legitimate new distribution methods not protected by the law.

■ IP is hard to value from an accounting perspective, and is subject to accounting rules that do not treat it equally to tangible assets.

■ Internationally, the principles governing IP are broadly similar. However, IP rights are largely national and the way they are applied and enforced can, for historical, political and economic reasons, vary significantly from country to country.

- There are five main types of IP:
  - Patents, the most complex, fragile and expensive form of IP, protect inventions by giving the owner a legal right to prevent others from using the invention without the owner's permission. A "utility model" is a lesser form of patent available in some countries and important in China.
  - Copyrights protect creative expression from being copied.
  - Design rights protect the appearance of useful objects.
  - Trademark law protects ways that a company or product may be recognised and also protects a business from third parties that create a false association with it. A trademark is often associated with a broader brand recognised by consumers. Related to trademarks are internet domain names.
  - Trade secret law protects confidential information.
- There are other forms of intangible assets that may be valuable but are not strictly IP, such as information about consumers.

Strategic considerations

- A single product can have multiple forms of IP protection, and co-ordinated use of all available forms of IP will create a stronger position.
- The different forms of IP may be used together to protect all the elements of a brand, often the most valuable IP owned by a business.
- A strategy can be created internationally given the overall uniformity of IP; China should be part of that strategy.
- A business strategy based on IP needs to take into account IP's legal strengths and weaknesses as well as its practical limitations; for example, the law is unlikely to plug the holes in a strategy that encourages international piracy.

2 Patents

Points to note

■ Patents, the most complex, fragile and expensive form of IP, protect inventions by giving the owner a legal right to prevent others from using the invention without the owner's permission.

■ Patents provide an incentive to innovate in return for making the invention publicly known and enable commercialisation of inventions.

■ Patents do not give an owner a right to do anything, but do provide a right to take legal action to stop others from commercialising the invention; they thus create a barrier to competitors.

■ An invention has to be new and sufficiently inventive to be patentable, and in most countries it must not have been publicly disclosed before the patent application is made.

■ Some patents are hugely valuable; most are not. And around 50% are allowed to lapse.

■ A US patent on average has only a somewhat better than even chance of surviving a fully litigated challenge to its validity; and the owner of a US patent on average has around a 26% chance of prevailing in a fully litigated case against an infringer.

■ Awards of damages for patent infringement are often made by juries in the US and may be large.

■ Given the risks and expenses for both sides in all countries, the majority of patent litigations are settled by agreement before trial.

■ A product such as a mobile phone may involve thousands of patents, but a billion-dollar pharmaceutical may be covered by only one or two.

■ The most valuable patents are those that cover bestselling products and are unlikely to face legal challenge because of their inventiveness and the thoroughness of the owner in the application process.

- Certain types of invention are not patentable – there is much argument over genes and "laws of nature", stem cells, software and business methods, and standards vary between countries.

- Patents are time limited (usually 20 years from filing) and lapse early within that term unless renewed upon payment of the requisite "maintenance" fees.

- Patents are granted and enforceable only in countries where they are filed.

- Strict national time limits apply for filing a patent internationally after an initial filing in one patent office. However, filing under an international treaty may be used to meet the deadlines.

- Patents owned by participants in industry technical standards are subject to special rules, such as an obligation to license them to competitors under fair, reasonable and non-discriminatory (FRAND) terms.

- When a patent is infringed the usual remedies are an injunction (a court order prohibiting further infringement) and damages. The principles used to award injunctions and assess damages vary from country to country, and are in constant flux.

- Patent litigation is expensive and complex because every aspect of a patent will be argued – what it means, whether there has been infringement or not, and whether the patent is valid.

- The legislative and judicial trend in strengthening the rights of patent owners in the developed world now seems to be reversing.

Strategic considerations

- Not every invention is worth patenting – the process is expensive and time-consuming; even when granted a patent is expensive to enforce and may well be challenged; it may be more cost-effective to rely on other forms of protection such as design rights or trade secrets.

- Searches of older patents and publications can help determine whether a strong patent can be obtained (but knowledge of third-party patents has legal implications, especially in the US).

■ The "scope" of a patent is an important determinant of value, in that it determines the range of products that a patent owner may prevent from being sold. A patent rarely covers all products in a category and usually only ones with specific features; what range of products infringe the patent owner's rights is often litigated.

■ The law governing what can be patented is in flux, especially in the US, largely because of the political fall-out from the activities of patent assertion entities (PAEs, sometimes called "patent trolls"). This creates uncertainty, though the way the law is changing is likely to cause more problems with existing patents rather than those sought in future, as patent lawyers will be able to take the changes into account when drafting future patent applications. However, whether the patents that can be obtained are of sufficient scope to protect investments in areas such as diagnosing disease remains to be seen.

■ Think hard about where to file patents. Do not be too local in approach because what is patentable varies by country, and it may not be possible to file a patent later in a market that has become important but was considered too marginal to include when the patent was first filed. Do not neglect China, including the ability to obtain utility models there.

■ As discussed in Chapters 10, 11 and 16, patents can be used as a barrier to competitors, to generate income from licences, and defensively in a counter-suit if sued by a competitor. It is important to be clear what the strategic aim is.

■ The legal fragility of individual patents leads companies to build "portfolios" of patents. In theory, more patents means more protection; it also allows "more shots on goal" when it comes to suing a competitor.

■ In sectors where companies have built patent portfolios, it can be disadvantageous to be the company with the smallest portfolio.

■ Although investors perceive patents as adding value, in general patents remain poorly understood by those in the investment world.

3 Trademarks

Points to note

■ Trademarks identify an organisation as a source of products or services; they are a critical part of its overall branding.

■ Words, logos, distinctive product and packaging configurations and other identifiers may be protected under trademark law, which protects broadly against wrongfully trading off the reputation and goodwill of a business.

■ Generally, trademark rights will not be granted for anything anyone operating in a market needs to be able to use. For example, it is not possible to trademark a word such as "car", "book" or "chocolate" that simply describes a product.

■ The more "arbitrary" or unusual the trademark, the easier it is to register and protect.

■ Trademark law differs significantly between common law countries (those that have followed English common law), where trademark rights may arise through first use of the mark, and civil law countries (continental Europe and its former colonies), where rights generally depend on first registration.

■ Trademarks are applied for and registered in "classes" of similar goods or services, but these classifications have in many cases failed to keep pace with the digital world.

■ Trademark rights are national, but treaties can be used to register such rights in many countries when a new application is filed.

■ The legal strength of a trademark, if lawyers have done their job properly, generally reflects its business strength; with patents there is much more uncertainty.

■ Trademarks are protected against uses that are likely to confuse the public.

■ Famous marks are protected more broadly than just against use on similar goods or services.

■ So long as a trademark is still in use owners retain their rights, provided that registrations are renewed and fees paid.

- A trademark owner may obtain an injunction and damages against an infringer and may have imported products seized at the border by customs.

- Speed is often important in trademark actions, especially if an injunction is sought.

- The validity of trademarks may be lost through failure to use the trademark, failure to police infringement, or by assignments and licences that do not comply with legal requirements, especially control of the quality of products or services bearing the trademark.

- Trademark rights may be lost if efficient administrative systems are not put in place to monitor trademark and domain name renewals and to ensure that registrations continue to cover the trademarks of a business, as these may be changed over time.

Strategic considerations

- Trademark laws may protect many aspects of overall branding – the mark itself, and distinctive colours and formats.

- Non-traditional trademarks such as those protecting the distinctive shape of products and packaging or even retail or webpage configurations can be part of protecting the overall brand. These aspects may also be protected by copyright and design rights. A meticulous and consistent approach using available forms of IP can garner strong protection as well as consumer recognition.

- When launching a new international brand, it is crucial to check well in advance that the proposed trademark is available in the relevant classes in all major markets and to formulate a trademark and domain name filing strategy that provides international protection.

- Trademark searching is simpler than patent searching; searches can be made that reveal not only registrations but also other business uses. Bear in mind that in common law countries unregistered users of a trademark may have rights.

- New brands are hard to find. To save money, quick "knockout" searches for registered marks should be carried out online.

- Separate searches are needed with company and domain name registrars to check that corporate and domain names are available.

- For a business with an international presence, an international registration programme is almost unavoidable.

- There are no time limits on registering a trademark, but delay leaves the door open for a third party to register a blocking mark.

- Brand owners should monitor applications to register trademarks that conflict with their brand and search services are available to do this; difficult cost-benefit analyses can occur where a trademark is not a material problem but may become one in the future.

- A focus on quality of products and consistency of trademark use, as well as policing of infringing or inaccurate trademark use, is the key to a strong trademark.

- Counterfeit and knock-off products require a multi-pronged strategy including not only selective litigation to send a message to the market, but also use of customs and criminal procedures, consumer education, policing of suppliers, work with reputable online markets, obtaining rights in countries of manufacture and often collaboration with other industry members.

4 Copyright

Points to note

- Copyright is the most easily obtained of the IP rights. It arises automatically and without cost when a work is created and written down or recorded.

- Copyright protects authors against their works being copied without permission and other unauthorised dealings with copyright works, but it is subject to principles of "fair use", which vary in different parts of the world.

■ Authors also have "moral rights" protecting their right of attribution and the integrity of their works; these rights are strong in civil law countries across Europe.

■ Copyright is enforceable in most countries without any registration procedure. In the US, there are significant advantages to registration.

■ Copyright protection is limited to the copying of creative expression and does not extend to facts, ideas, methods or purely utilitarian objects. For example, how a computer program is written is protected by copyright, but at a higher level the program's structure is simply an unprotected idea or method, protectable only under a patent or as a trade secret.

■ Copyright lasts for long periods that depend on the law of each country, the type of work in question, and when it was first published.

■ Databases are protected in the EU by special laws and more generally if they are sufficiently original.

■ In a work of music or entertainment, there will be a variety of different copyright interests.

■ The value of a copyright depends on the revenues it generates and could generate over its remaining life.

■ Because of the long duration of copyright, new technology and changed circumstances can make it difficult to establish who controls what rights under old contracts.

■ Open-source software is freely available, but the terms and conditions under which some types of open-source software are licensed require that when combined with proprietary software and redistributed, the source code of the proprietary software has to be made public.

Strategic considerations

■ Copyright provides strong protections against direct copying of written materials and artistic works; it is generally inapplicable to protecting ideas and inventions.

■ Despite its limitations, the boundaries of copyright protection are unclear. Obtaining copyright ownership in all materials used by a business is a worthwhile investment of time and resources, and should be built into management procedures for works created by employees and contractors.

■ Copyright, patent and trade secret protections may be cumulative. For example, the detailed code of software may be both kept secret and subject to copyright, and the function of software that has an inventive technological application may also, but rarely, be protected by patent.

■ Technology developments have impinged on the rights of copyright owners, and in practice copyright owners' main remedy against internet-enabled piracy is to reduce the incentives to provide or buy pirated content.

■ Legitimate new business models exploiting third-party copyrights such as Google Books may be protected by fair use, but these types of new businesses are often challenged and the outcome will depend on litigation. This uncertainty may lead to businesses deciding to collaborate rather than litigate.

■ Commercial software companies that make use of open-source software need sophisticated policies and procedures on such use.

■ Purchasers of copyrights need to understand both what rights they are acquiring and what other rights owned by third parties may need to be purchased or licensed so they can use the copyrights they have bought.

5 Design rights

Points to note

■ Design rights (in the US, design patents) protect the shape and design of useful products from being copied and fill a gap left under copyright law (although the rights may overlap in some countries). They are often complemented by trademark rights protecting distinctive product shapes and designs recognised by consumers.

- The US will soon be integrated into the international design rights system.

- Near costless unregistered rights are available in the EU as well as registered rights offering greater protection. Similar rights are available on a national basis.

- Registered design rights are cheap to obtain as compared to patents covering inventions.

Strategic considerations

- There is a new focus on design rights/patents following the "phone wars", where Apple succeeded in enforcing design patents that were the basis of large damages awards.

- Design rights are increasingly being used successfully in the fashion world.

- Design rights are a comparatively low-cost form of protection and may be integrated into a set of IP protections.

- Protection for the shape of things will become more important with an increase in 3D printing.

6 Trade secrets

Points to note

- Trade secret law protects secret information of all types and gives protection against the unauthorised taking and misuse of that information. Injunctions and damages may be obtained.

- Trade secrets (knowledge exclusive to an organisation) retain their value only while they remain secret. They depend on their owners taking diligent and thorough steps to keep them secret.

- Keeping secrets secret has become much harder as a result of the internet and developments in communications technology and social media, as well as hacking.

- There is no protection against the independent creation of the same idea and some risk that a third party may patent it.

- Concern over industrial espionage has resulted in moves to strengthen trade secret laws.

- Personal information about individuals is subject to its own set of laws and liabilities, and there are important compliance issues for a business (see Chapter 7).

- In the EU, databases of information (which need not be confidential) are subject to their own special protection.

- The submission of new product ideas to a business is problematic for all involved because the business may already have had the idea, but may be wrongly accused of stealing it.

Strategic considerations

- Trade secret protection depends on setting up and maintaining rigorous security systems that embrace people, technology and premises. However, at least some of that work may be unavoidable because it is required for regulatory compliance, especially where a company retains personal information of customers or website users.

- If secrecy is maintained, unlike with other forms of IP, there is no legal cost of enforcement because the trade secret is simply not available for copying or use.

- It may be preferable to treat an invention as a trade secret rather than disclose it by making a patent application; for example, a manufacturing process may be kept secret and competitors may never learn it, whereas a patent will tip them off. Factors to consider include whether any patent likely to be obtained will be weak; whether the invention can be kept secret and not reverse engineered; the speed at which the invention will be superseded in the marketplace.

- Chapter 8 emphasises the importance of contracts with employees and outside contractors in establishing ownership of IP. These contracts should always include clauses that guard against the disclosure of trade secrets and confidential information.

- Contracts and procedures are also required if a business is to receive from a third party trade secret information of a type that it may already have, so as to avoid "contamination" by the third-party information.

■ Non-compete provisions are useful ways of protecting trade secrets, but if unreasonable they are subject to enforceability challenges.

■ The fast-moving informal collaborations common in start-ups can be hard to square with protecting trade secrets, but the trade-offs should at least be considered.

7 IP and the internet

Points to note

■ The internet continues to have a huge impact on intellectual property, making it more likely that IP rights will be infringed. The burden of policing IP rights is on the IP owner. Given the rampant copying of copyright content and the enablement of IP piracy of all types, including sale of counterfeits, it is a heavy burden.

■ Legal challenges to legitimate internet service providers have generally not had success. However, internet service providers are voluntarily doing more to counter piracy, no doubt influenced by calls from owners of IP for changes in intellectual property laws and the laws protecting internet service providers from claims resulting from infringement of IP by their customers.

■ For companies doing business over the internet, operating a website brings with it regulation and potential liability.

■ Establishing a website that sells goods or services or collects personal information requires a significant amount of co-ordination between business, legal and technical functions to avoid self-inflicted mistakes over what levels of privacy and security are promised or whether enforceable contracts are entered into with customers.

■ The handling and retention of personal information about website users must comply with applicable laws, with controlled access to and use of it. Security is crucial. There are reputational issues as well as financial and legal consequences when personal information is lost or misused.

- The internet practices of employees may cause security risks and damage to IP rights.

- Internet business practices involving copying or linking websites that damage another company may result in infringement claims being made.

Strategic considerations

- Initial investments in website legal and technical infrastructure and data privacy compliance can avoid the reputational issues that have affected a number of start-up companies.

- Branding strategies should take into account that the internet may make a local business international, and that domain names are not segmented by type of product or service. Equally, a local business may need international rights to protect it against piracy from foreign sources. Searches for new trademarks should be international in scope and not limited by product type.

- Companies, especially those selling to consumers, need to have a coherent international IP strategy to reduce internet-enabled piracy. Rights against infringers depend on ownership of, for example, copyright in content and trademarks needed to stop wrongful use of domain names or the sale of pirated or knock-off products.

- Piracy may be better tackled by a holistic strategy including pricing products and making them available conveniently at a level that reduces the incentive for piracy; working with internet companies that provide authorised alternatives to piracy to users (such as legal music streaming); working as an industry with internet service providers to eliminate practices that enable piracy, such as reducing search rankings for known pirate sites; in the case of branded products, policing the supply chain and consumer education on quality and other problems with fakes; working with law-enforcement agencies; and lobbying for policy and legal changes that redress the balance in favour of IP owners.

8 Who owns IP?

Points to note

- Many IP disputes concern the question of the ownership of IP because the default rules on ownership of IP are often contrary to business assumptions or expectations. For example, a patent invented by an employee may be owned by the employee not the employer.

- Ownership of IP of all types developed by a contractor for a business usually remains with the contractor notwithstanding that the business paid for the development of the IP.

- A collaboration between two businesses can result in joint ownership, which is often not what has been assumed or expected. What joint ownership means for the rights of each owner varies by form of IP and by applicable country and legal system.

- Registered IP typically has a form of ownership registry in each country. Updating title records in many countries can be expensive and time-consuming. However, enforcement of the IP may depend on the title record being up to date, and failure to record may mean that a seller can sell the same IP to a third party.

- IP may be mortgaged so obtaining a clear title to IP is important, as it is in buying other forms of property.

- In many groups of companies, IP ownership is established in IP holding companies for tax purposes, but such financially oriented IP ownership structures can give rise to operational complications.

Strategic considerations

- Rules relating to IP ownership are complex. The one simple, overriding rule is to set out IP ownership in a contract at the start of any business or employment relationship.

- Filing for patents or other forms of registered IP owned by a business in an organised manner and updating title as needed will establish the correct record of ownership, which is important for the exploitation and enforcement of IP.

■ IP ownership in an international group of companies may be allocated for tax and other reasons. Co-ordination between corporate financial and IP functions is important to avoid mistakes that damage the value and utility of the IP.

■ Because of tax structuring, when dealing with an international group it is important to know which corporate entity actually owns the IP involved in any deal.

9 What IP costs to obtain, maintain and enforce

Points to note

■ Patents are expensive. There are fees to patent lawyers and agents for drafting and obtaining patents throughout the world, multiple and recurring fees to patent offices, costs for drawings, costs for translations and other international expenses, as well as substantial costs to enforce the patent or defend challenges to it.

■ Trademarks are less expensive than patents. There are similar types of costs and fees, but these are generally an order of magnitude below those for obtaining patents.

■ Copyright may have a purchase price if acquired from the creator, but otherwise costs little unless action has to be taken for infringement. Expenses are associated with registration in the US, but these are small.

■ Design right costs vary. In many countries a choice may be made between registered and unregistered (which are virtually costless) rights for designs. However, registered rights provide greater protection. Costs are more in the range of trademark costs than utility (invention) patent costs.

■ The costs associated with trade secrets are the administrative costs of the system designed to keep them secret, which will involve written confidentiality agreements, maintaining secure premises and networks, and policies that prevent disclosures.

Strategic considerations

■ Detailed budgets should be prepared before embarking on a patenting programme. Starting and then abandoning a patent process may result in loss of trade secret or other protection.

■ Although patents provide unique protection to inventions, the protection offered by a suite of other forms of IP, such as trade secrets, copyright, design rights and trademarks, may be more appropriate or cost-effective.

■ Copyright is largely free of cost (with the exception of any purchase price) and so what is or can be protected should be investigated. Ownership should always be established. Notices of copyright can be used to claim rights. Similar considerations apply to design rights in countries providing unregistered protection.

■ Significant expenses associated with registering trademarks are unavoidable because in many countries registration is the basis of rights and delay may enable third parties to step in. Trademark registrations also provide protection for internet domain names.

■ Expenses associated with protecting trade secrets may also be largely unavoidable, especially where a company holds personal information about employees and customers and is under regulatory requirements to keep that information secure.

10 IP's role in protecting product sales

Points to note

■ IP is a barrier to entry to competing products, but the FRAND (fair, reasonable and non-discriminatory) system is designed to stop patent owners excluding competitors from markets based on technology standards.

■ The ownership of a patent, design or copyright may be used to take legal action to prevent competitors from using an invention or copying a work without permission. This works well in the case of an identifiable business located in a country with a strong legal system wrongly copying an entire product.

■ The internet and activities by businesses in countries with weak legal systems have made it much more difficult to enforce IP rights against piracy and counterfeiting.

■ A trade secret is a barrier to entry simply because the secret is not known to competitors.

■ A well-known brand may be a barrier to entry as a result of customer loyalty or the perception of higher quality.

■ Copyright protection depends on how much independent creative work a competitor has done – in other words, you can take an unprotectable idea and create a new detailed implementation, but if you copy more than the concepts, you may be in trouble.

■ The laws governing IP rights (or rather the interpretation of them) are beset by uncertainty, but the courts are gradually establishing the rules on, for example, fair use of copyright in the context of the internet or when the copying of a patented feature on a multi-feature device should warrant an injunction.

■ IP rights should not be looked at in isolation. A product may have many forms of protection – potentially all or some of trademark, design, patent, copyright and trade secret.

■ A single product may be covered by many patents: the number involved in, for example, mobile communications is staggering. This has led to fierce patent wars as businesses have sought to hobble their competitors by building up huge portfolios of patents and taking legal action to enforce their IP rights.

Strategic considerations

■ The suite of available IP rights should be reviewed and used in a co-ordinated and complementary fashion to create the most cost-effective and broadest protection against competitors.

■ Patent ownership brings with it the risk of time-consuming and expensive litigation, as the phone wars have shown.

■ The FRAND system has meant that standard essential patents are worth less than has sometimes been imagined.

- In a FRAND world where competition is at the level of features, branding and design are increasingly important.

- As well as being a barrier to entry, patents may enable product sales through their use as currency for cross-licences with competitors owning needed patents that are blocking market entry.

- Strong brands foster customer loyalty beyond the scope of IP rights, and may thus increase sales; brand creation and protection should be central to consumer strategies.

- When new technologies use copyright material in new ways, whether that use is protected as fair use depends on, for example, how new and different the use is, but courts are less willing to tolerate directly competing activities.

- Suing a competitor can lead to a tit-for-tat infringement claim by the competitor. Before litigation is started, there needs to be careful analysis of the weaknesses of the strategic position as well as strengths.

- Use of IP against piracy should be part of a holistic strategy as discussed in Chapter 7.

11 IP as a revenue generator

Points to note

- IP may make money for its owner in three ways: the granting of licences in return for payments; damages awards in litigation (or settlement payments prior to trial); or sale of the IP itself.

- "Offensive" patent licensing and litigation has become a sophisticated business with the rise of patent assertion entities (PAEs), especially in the US. Criticism of PAEs is based on the belief that they exploit the US patent system's inefficiencies and costs rather than assert meritorious claims.

- Although windfall awards of large damages may be rarer in future, changes in the litigation system are unlikely to eliminate purchase of patents for licensing and enforcement.

■ The value of a patent as a litigation asset can be estimated based on its past history, legal quality, projected future infringing sales, actual or comparable licence royalty rates, and remaining life.

■ Trademark licensing has become a major business with the growth of lifestyle brands.

■ Virtually all trademark licensing is a result of business negotiations because some trust and business relationship is needed between licensor and licensee.

■ Copyright revenue has historically been based on licensing models, and the software, music, film and publishing industries are all based on this. Disputes and litigation arise when new technologies disrupt distribution models until new norms are established.

Strategic considerations

■ Often a decision to license IP that covers products sold by the IP owner is based on a conclusion that revenues may be maximised by having a non-exclusive model, or that licensing will permit revenues to be obtained from a market that the licensor is unable to exploit itself.

■ A company's patent portfolio can be divided into groups of patents with different intended purposes:
   - barriers to entry;
   - patents to be asserted against competitors or others who may infringe;
   - patents to use against a competitor if that competitor sues the patent owner;
   - patents to license out to non-competitors for fields of use other than the core business of the IP owner;
   - patents to license out as the basis for developing new technologies;
   - patents to be divested, possibly to a PAE.

■ Even a small business with a few patents can use these types of goals to inform the scope and purpose of the patents it tries to obtain.

■ Trademark licensing may be the basis of a business and increase brand awareness, but the crucial touchstones are: rigorous selection of licensees; the maintenance of product quality; proper and consistent use of the licensed trademarks.

■ The challenge with copyright licensing in an era of new distribution models is to satisfy consumer demand (thus limiting piracy) while arriving at equitable splits of revenue with rights holders and distributors.

12 Licensing transactions

Points to note

■ A licence is a permission to use IP from the owner; licensees may be permitted in turn to grant sublicences – this is similar to the concept of a lease and sublease of property. Just as a sublessee may lose its rights if the lease terminates, so may a sublicensee.

■ Licences can slice the IP "pie" by territory, product, field of use and duration, while reserving certain segments to the licensor.

■ Licence rights can be exclusive or non-exclusive in any of the above segments, but it is important to consider whether true exclusivity is possible as a result of free-trade areas, grey markets or internet sales.

■ The most important limitations on the permissible terms of licences are imposed under the antitrust and competition laws of individual countries or wider groupings such as the EU, which is committed to free movement of goods across member states.

■ With trademarks, an agreement may fall within regulations governing franchise businesses.

■ There is freedom to structure the financial terms of licences – that is, to allocate both the value of the licensed IP and the risk of commercial success or failure of the licensed product between the licensor and licensee. The financial terms in favour of the licensor can include:

- an initial upfront fixed fee;

- annual fixed fees;
- milestone payments to a licensor when the licensed product has achieved various stages of development or levels of sales;
- periodic royalty payments based on a percentage of the invoice price (less deductions) or list price of the licensee, where the percentage rate may change if certain events happen (such as hitting a sales threshold or unexpected competition);
- reimbursement of the licensor's expenses under the licence, such as for providing technical assistance or maintenance of licensed software;
- offsets against royalties for expenses of the licensee, possibly including royalties to third parties (stacking royalties);
- allocation of tax withholding costs.

■ Licences can also allocate risks between the licensor and licensee, such as claims for personal injuries or IP infringement and business losses caused by reliance on the licensed technology.

■ Export controls can prohibit transactions with certain countries or the export of sensitive technologies.

Strategic considerations

■ "Slice and dice" licensing arrangements with both the IP owner and licensees exploiting the IP in specific ways or territories can be a good way to maximise revenues.

■ "Own goals" licensors should be careful to avoid include:
- failure to take competition law into account, which leads to cannibalisation of the licensor's sales (for example, where restrictions on exports by a licensee cannot be enforced because the licence restriction breaches local competition law);
- exclusive licences with no get-out clause should the licensee fail to commercialise the technology;
- clauses that could result in the financial claims from a licensee exceeding the (usually fixed) revenue from a licence;

- failure to model all the royalty terms (for example, agreed offsets against royalties for licensee expenses significantly reduce the income of the licensor).

■ Licensees, especially exclusive licensees, should take care to get what they need from the licensor to maintain the rights they have paid for, such as payment of maintenance fees and assistance with infringers.

■ Termination provisions of licences are important because the possible events of termination affect the bargaining power of the parties during the contract. For example, the threat of termination will have an impact on a licensee who has invested heavily in developing a licensed technology.

■ Assignment provisions of licences affect their value. Freely assignable licences are more valuable than non-assignable ones but create the risk for the licensor that they find themselves stuck with an undesirable licensee.

■ Planning for counterparty risks such as bankruptcy may mitigate future problems, for example termination of a needed licence.

13 The market for IP: how IP rights are bought and sold

Points to note

■ There is a growing market in IP, with some large transactions in recent years and more intermediaries who can facilitate transactions.

■ It is common for technology and software patents to be sold separately from any underlying business, often with intermediaries facilitating those transactions.

■ Outsourcing of manufacturing and other functions means that brands can be bought and sold more easily.

■ Libraries of copyrights are regarded as attractive investment assets.

■ Assignments of extensive international IP portfolios are substantial and expensive undertakings. To be confident of ownership of what has been paid for, title registration should be updated promptly.

Strategic considerations

- Portfolios of patents, especially in the technology world, are regarded as not limited by what may be "home grown", but subject to acquisitions and divestitures to meet strategic goals, such as providing a base for innovation, matching the patent arsenals of competitors, avoiding potentially threatening patents falling into hostile hands, or, in the case of divestitures, gaining some revenue and reducing unnecessary costs over time.

- With the exception of well-maintained brands, often with IP what you see is not what you get. In other words, due diligence is needed to establish not only the quality of the IP assets but also basics such as whether the IP is actually owned by the purported seller – remarkably often it is not.

- Due diligence of IP being sold should focus on: the scope of rights and apparent value; future duration; the history of the IP and how it may affect current value (commercialisation, past licences and royalty rates, FRAND obligations, litigation and validity challenges); ownership of the IP (especially in the case of large software programs); potential legal challenges and legal quality; and risk of third-party claims of infringement.

- Avoid overreliance on boilerplates and old forms when transferring IP; the specific technical details of the deal are crucial to ensuring the buyer actually gets what is paid for.

14 Valuing IP

Points to note

- The valuation and accounting treatment of intellectual property has lagged behind its real value. This is largely due to the individual nature of most IP rights and the lack of comparable transactions that can establish value.

- Patent values vary hugely. Average values gleaned from other patent sales may make sense when buying a large portfolio, but when buying an individual patent, averages are often only a moderately useful point of reference.

■ Patent values vary depending on the state of the law. For example, a change in the law reducing the eligibility of software for patents may devalue older patents obtained before the change. Similarly, changes in the law may affect how damages are calculated.

■ The value of copyright libraries such as music catalogues may be affected by legal issues such as piracy of music over the internet.

■ Brands are less subject to legal issues, but in valuation the difficulty lies in separating the value of the brand from the value of the other assets of a business.

■ Valuation of IP is multidimensional because it depends on the volume of sales of products using the IP. In the case of a patent it may require analysis of:
  - size, growth and profitability of the underlying product market covered by the patent;
  - contribution of the patented technology to that profitability;
  - how much of the market has already been licensed and at what royalty rates;
  - duration of the IP;
  - susceptibility of the IP to legal challenge (which may affect duration).

■ Current accounting standards do not require identification and valuation of all IP – usually only in the case of acquisition of IP from a third party.

■ Where IP is valued for tax or other purposes, various valuation models are used. These include the cost approach, the market approach and the income approach.

■ Cost-based theories are based on the actual cost to create, or the estimated cost to recreate or substitute for the IP in question.

■ Market approaches attempt to determine value based on comparable transactions.

■ Income approaches attempt to calculate the value of the future income stream attributable to the IP in question.

Strategic considerations

- Most financial statements do not reflect the value of the underlying IP of a business. Only acquired IP may be stated as a line item, hence understanding the IP value of a business requires detailed analysis.

- There can be wide differences in opinion as to the value of IP that is put up for sale or where valuation is needed for tax purposes. A well-reasoned valuation needs deep legal and market analysis.

15 Using IP to raise finance

Points to note

- IP is often part of the assets used by a lender to secure a loan to a business (collateral).

- IP standing alone has not historically been viewed as valuable collateral. Reasons for this include:
  - lack of expertise among lenders in valuing IP, especially whether it is desirable to other businesses;
  - accounting rules which do not identify and value IP;
  - the lack of a liquid market for IP.

- Markets in technology patents now support use of such patents as collateral by specialist lenders. In addition, IP is used as collateral in specific structures in other industries.

- While using IP as collateral is comparatively simple technically, complexities arise when lenders try to capture the value of a package of IP and associated in-licences and out-licences.

- What may happen to IP and IP licences in the event of insolvency or bankruptcy is often crucial to a lender's assessment of the value of IP collateral.

- Lenders focus on making sure that there are no issues affecting the ownership of the IP being used as collateral and want to make sure that after a loan is made the borrower does not take steps that reduce the value of the collateral.

Strategic considerations

- Raising finance based on IP alone is still relatively unusual. Finance providers may be interested in fields such as technology where there is an established market in patents; pharmaceutical patents covering marketed products where there are predictable cash flows associated with patents; and brands and copyright libraries where multiple streams of revenue may be the basis for securitisation.

- A business seeking finance based on patents in other areas should be prepared to undertake detailed due diligence, to demonstrate why the patents are valuable beyond the business of the borrower, and to identify transactions where similar patents have been sold.

- Loans will be made on terms that protect the lender and limit the freedom of the borrower to deal with the IP pledged to the lender.

- Specialist lenders may also fund IP litigation.

16 Developing an IP strategy

Points to note

- Many businesses do not have a coherent approach to IP. Often they:
  - do not actually own the IP they think they own;
  - file for registered IP on a haphazard basis and allow other IP to fall into the public domain;
  - have registered IP that does not cover the current products and brands of the business and costs money to maintain;
  - have not considered their IP risks or how to mitigate them;
  - have not looked at whether they use the most cost-effective methods of protecting their business from copying or piracy.

- In many businesses, IP is regarded negatively as being costly and risky – for example, the risks of infringing third-party rights, or failures to prevent copying – rather than as a valuable asset.

- However, basic risk mitigation can be achieved through a simple programme of obtaining ownership of IP developed by or for a business, protecting against loss of IP and registering IP assets.

- The importance of documenting ownership of IP in business relationships should drive contractual practices that result in ownership of unregistered IP developed by or for a business and allow the opportunity to obtain registered IP.

- Many businesses hold personal information on customers or website users and are under regulatory obligations to keep that information private and secure. All businesses are subject to the risk of hacking. These risks should give rise to confidentiality, privacy and security policies that will help prevent loss of confidential business or technical information.

- Brands are often a business's most important IP asset and the different elements of a brand should therefore be registered and otherwise protected.

- Although patents are expensive and not applicable to all businesses, the full suite of other IP protections (design, copyright, trademark and trade secret) can be used in a holistic and consistent manner to develop a cost-effective approach to IP protection.

Strategic considerations

- The goals of an IP strategy should include:
  - identification of the IP used and generated by a business, including third-party IP used under licence;
  - ensuring that the business owns all the IP it develops and hires others to develop, especially copyright;
  - mitigating risks of loss of IP, such as loss of trade secrets;
  - mitigating the loss of needed third-party licences through long-term arrangements, availability of alternative technology and/or protection against insolvency of the licensor;
  - ensuring that the registered IP that is obtained supports and protects the present and future products, services, brands and strategies of the business, with a particular focus on protecting brands;

- determining how IP and related issues such as protection of personal data of customers and security of systems from cyber-attacks should be managed, and what obligations are incumbent on the board of directors;
- as part of that management function, ensuring co-ordination among the groups responsible for different types of IP protection and that the overall IP function is co-ordinated with other management groups, including marketing and strategy;
- at an operational level, ensuring efficient administration of applications and renewals for registered IP rights, domain names and licences.

■ Further strategic goals may include:

- mitigating risks of third-party infringement claims through establishing ownership of the business's own technology by a registration and patenting programme, IP clearance and freedom to operate searches followed by actions to address risks uncovered, monitoring and benchmarking of competitor IP strategies and implementing appropriate defensive actions, and indemnities and insurance where available;
- ensuring that the enforcement strategies of the business against competitors and pirates are as cost-effective as possible;
- given the IP that the business owns and may develop, determining how that IP will be protected (for example, patents versus trade secrets) and how the suite of IP protection will be used;
- determining how the IP owned by the business will be exploited (for example, as barriers to entry, as currency for cross-licences, for defensive purposes when sued by a competitor, or for raising revenue by licensing or divestiture) and whether those decisions will change over time;
- determining when and for what purposes IP should be acquired from third parties (innovation, defensive, etc), or whether IP should be disposed of for reasons of cost and lack of applicability;

- determining how IP strategies may support the business's commercial strategies (for example, setting industry or regulatory standards, innovation, brand creation).

Glossary

Cross-references are in **bold**.

Agreement on Trade-Related Aspects of Intellectual Property Rights (TRIPS)	The most recent comprehensive international treaty setting minimum standards for IP protection for members of the World Trade Organisation
assertion	Making or pursuing a claim of IP **infringement**
assignment	The name of the document that transfers ownership of IP
attribution or paternity right	One of the two **moral rights**: the right of a creator to be acknowledged as the author of their work (the other one is the right of integrity that allows an author to prevent certain distortions or modifications of their works)
claim (of a patent)	The part of a patent that sets out the **scope** of rights granted – a series of usually short paragraphs that identify each feature of a product or process that must generally be present to **infringe** the rights of the patent owner
collateral or security	The property that a lender is able to take or sell if a borrower fails to pay back a loan or pay interest

cover (of a patent)	The **scope** of products or services that **infringe** the patent – these are defined in the **claims** of the patent
cross-licensing	An agreement under which two or more owners of IP each license their IP to the other; a reciprocal **licence**
defensive patent aggregator	A business that provides a service to its clients (often software or technology companies) by acquiring patents that may fall into the hands of or are already owned by hostile **patent assertion entities** (PAEs) and licensing those patents to its clients
design-around	A new or revised product designed with the intention of avoiding **infringement** of a patent
droit de suite	The right of an artist to be compensated upon a subsequent sale of one of their works
filing	Another word for applying to a patent or trademark office for a patent or trademark
foreclose, foreclosure	The action of a lender who has a mortgage on a borrower's property in taking possession of the property when the borrower has defaulted on the loan
goodwill	In accounting: the value of an acquired business that is not attributed to other identified assets
	In IP: the assets of a business that are responsible for the reputation and quality of a business's products and services

holdup or lock-in value	The value beyond the true economic value of a patent that a patent owner can extract because an alleged **infringer** is locked in to a particular technology; for example, because it is required to conform to a technical standard, or because it has invested heavily in the technology before becoming aware of the patent
infringe, infringer	Violating the rights of an IP owner – using IP in a manner that is unlawful without the permission of the IP owner An individual or organisation that does this
infringement	Wrongfully using IP rights without the permission of the IP owner; for example, selling an invention that has been patented
International Trade Commission	A court in Washington, DC, that can issue orders enforced at the borders excluding infringing products from the US
internet service provider (ISP)	A business that provides access to the internet or services over the internet such as hosting websites or search services
inter-partes review	A US patent office procedure under the America Invents Act 2011 which allows a patent to be challenged and possibly invalidated on the basis that the invention claimed is not patentable. It has become a game changer in allowing an effective way to challenge patents outside litigation in court
knock-off	A derogatory term for copies of a branded product; for example, copies of a Chanel or Hermès brand handbag

licence	An agreement providing permission to use IP
lock-in	See **holdup**
moral rights	Rights granted to an author or artist to receive **attribution** and preserve the integrity of their works
naked licence	A **licence** under a trademark where the trademark owner does not control the quality of the goods or services sold under the trademark.
non-practising entity (NPE)	Another name for a **patent assertion entity**
ordre public	Principles of public policy
orphan work	A usually older copyright work where the owner of the copyright cannot be found
paid-up licence	A **licence** under which no future payments are required from the licensee to the licensor
passing off	Creating a product that so resembles the product of a third party that the public would assume that the product originates from the third party
patent assertion entity (PAE)	A business that purchases patents to make money by licensing the patents to third parties, often after suing, or threatening to sue, the third parties for **infringement** of the patents. Derogatorily called patent trolls and sometimes NPEs (non-practising entities)
Patent Cooperation Treaty (PCT)	An international treaty that makes the process of applying for patents in multiple countries simpler by enabling an initial single filing of a patent application to be pursued in all those countries

patentee	The owner of a patent
patent troll	A derogatory term for a **patent assertion entity**
paternity right	See **attribution**
petty patent or utility model	A form of patent often used for a mechanical device usually providing protection that is easier to obtain but shorter and weaker than that provided by a typical patent. Of great importance in China.
prior art	Pre-existing relevant patents and other publications in the field
priority date	The date on which the original patent application was filed from which a patent has descended. This is important, because to be valid a patent must be novel and not obvious when looking at a technical field before the priority date, but not after it
prosecution	The technical term for the process of obtaining a patent or registered trademark from a patent or trademark office
razor-blade company	A company that mostly makes its money not from the sale of a particular product, such as a razor, but from the sale of products used with that product; for example, print cartridges used with printers and coffee capsules used with coffee machines
remediate	A term used with respect to open-source software. Where a piece of open-source software is used in a problematic manner in a proprietary program, the situation may be remediated by removing the open-source component and replacing it with a proprietary component

scope	The range of products or services that **infringe** a patent. The scope can be narrow and specific or broad and covering a class of products or services
security	See **collateral**
security interest	Another word for a mortgage
shop right	The right of an employer in the US to use an invention made by an employee where there is no **assignment** agreement transferring ownership to the employer
standard essential patent (SEP)	A patent that is required to be used to make a product that complies with an industry standard; for example, a patent on a communications protocol necessary for a mobile phone to interact with mobile phone networks
trade dress	The distinctive appearance of a product which is protectable under trademark law
Trans-Pacific Partnership (TPP)	A trade treaty under negotiation during 2014 among the US, Canada, Mexico, Australia, New Zealand, Brunei, Chile, Peru, Japan, Malaysia, Singapore and Vietnam, which among other provisions requires minimum standards of IP protection
tying	Requiring the purchase of a product or service as a condition of access to another product or service – for example the sale of a patented salt dispenser on condition that the purchaser also purchase salt from the manufacturer
utility model	See **petty patent**

Abbreviations

CBP	Customs and Border Protection
CTM	Community Trade Mark
FRAND	fair reasonable and non-discriminatory
FTC	Federal Trade Commission
GPL	General Public License
gTLD	generic top-level domain name
IP	intellectual property
ISP	internet service provider
ITC	International Trade Commission
NPE	non-practising entity
OHIM	Office for Harmonization in the Internal Market
PAE	patent assertion entity
PCT	Patent Cooperation Treaty
RAND	reasonable and non-discriminatory
SEC	Securities and Exchange Commission
SEP	standard essential patent
TLD	top-level domain name
TPP	Trans-Pacific Partnership
TRIPS	Agreement on Trade-Related Aspects of Intellectual Property Rights
TTBE	Technology Transfer Block Exemption
UDRP	Uniform Domain Name Dispute Resolution Policy
USPTO	United States Patent and Trademark Office
WTO	World Trade Organisation

Notes

1 An introduction to intellectual property

1 Ocean Tomo, *Annual Study of Intangible Asset Market Value*, 2010: www. oceantomo.com
2 BrandZ, *Top 100 Most Valuable Global Brands* 2014: www.millwardbrown. com
3 Vranica, S. and Hansegrad, J., "IKEA discloses an $11 billion secret", *Wall Street Journal*, August 9th 2012.
4 Lex Machina, 2013 *Patent Litigation Year in Review; Patent Litigation Damages Report*, 2014: www.lexmachina.com
5 *Patent Assertion and US Innovation*, Executive Office of the President, June 2013: www.whitehouse.gov/sites/default/files/docs/patent_report.pdf
6 Khan, B.Z., *Trolls and Other Patent Inventions: Economic History and the Patent Controversy in the Twenty-First Century*, Hoover IP 2 Working Paper Series, Working Paper No. 13001, October 24th 2013: www.hoover.org
7 "Untouchable intangibles", *The Economist*, August 30th 2014.
8 Beattie, A., "Intellectual property: a new world of royalties", *Financial Times*, September 23rd 2012.
9 Bajaj, V. and Pollack, A., "India's Supreme Court to hear dispute on drug patents", *New York Times*, March 6th 2012 (print article published March 7th 2012 with the headline "Patent v. Patient").
10 Kazmin, A., "Indian pharmaceutical groups shed copycat image", *Financial Times*, July 22nd 2013.
11 www.wipo.int/about-ip/en/
12 Kroes, N., "From Crisis of Trust to Open Governing", Bratislava, March 5th 2012: http://europa.eu/rapid/press-release_SPEECH-12-149_en.htm

2 Patents

1 Carley, M., Hegde, D. and Marco, A., "What is the Probability of Receiving a US Patent?", *Yale Journal of Law and Technology* 16, 2014: ssrn.com/ abstract=2367149

2 Magliocca, G.N., "Blackberries and Barnyards: Patent Trolls and the Perils of Innovation", 82 *Notre Dame Law Review* 1809, 2007.
3 Beattie, B., "The battleground of choice in patent wars", *Financial Times*, October 2nd 2012.
4 Allison, J.R., Lemley, M.A. and Schwartz, D.L., "Understanding the Realities of Modern Patent Litigation", 92 *Texas Law Review* 1769, 2014.
5 See, for example, Schankerman, M. and Pakes, A., "Estimates of the Value of Patent Rights in European Countries During the Post-1950 Period", 96 *Economic Journal* 1052, 1986; Schankerman, M., "How Valuable is Patent Protection? Estimates by Technology Field", 29 *Rand Journal of Economics* 77, 1998; Gambardella, A., Herhoff, D. and Verspagen, B., "The Value of European Patents", *European Management Review*, Vol. 5, Issue 2, 2008, p. 69; Crouch, D., *Patent Maintenance Fees*, Patently-O, September 26th 2012: http://patentlyo.com

3 Trademarks

1 Phillips, E.E., "Customs chase knockoffs", *Wall Street Journal*, November 29–30th 2014.
2 Twitter, Inc., Annual Report (Form 10-k), at 29 (2013).
3 Various trademarks are used in the text of this book which are the property of their respective owners. These include: Apple, Bass, BP, Cadbury, Cadbury's Dairy Milk, Chanel, Coca-Cola, Dell, Ford, Google, Google Books, Heinz, Hermès, Hershey, IKEA, Kit-Kat, Lenovo, Louboutin, Mercedes, Microsoft, Nestlé, Pink, Ritz, Shell, Sky, Sony, Thomas Pink, Trump, Tweet, Virgin, Washington Redskins.

4 Copyright

1 *The Register's Call for Updates to U.S. Copyright Law: Hearing Before the Subcommittee on Courts, Intellectual Property, and the Internet Community on the Judiciary*, 113th Cong. 1, May 20th 2013 (statement of Maria A. Pallante, Register of Copyrights, US Copyright Office): http:// copyright. gov/regstat/2013/regstat03202013.html

7 IP and the internet

1 *Uniform Rapid Suspension System (URS)*, ICANN: http://newgtlds.icann. org/en/applicants/urs
2 See www.emdgroup.com

8 Who owns IP?

1   Norris, F., "One Response to Apple Tax Strategy May Be To Copy It", *New York Times*, May 21st 2013.

9 What IP costs to obtain, maintain and enforce

1   Quinn, G., "The cost of obtaining a patent in the US", IPWatchdog blog, January 28th 2011 (updated April 30th 2013): www.ipwatchdog.com

10 IP's role in protecting product sales

1   Chien, C., "Race to the bottom", *Intellectual Asset Management Magazine* 51, pp. 10–17, January 2012.
2   Isaacson, W., *Steve Jobs*, Simon & Schuster, 2013.

11 IP as a revenue generator

1   Rivette, K. and Kline, D., *Rembrandts in the Attic: Unlocking the Hidden Value of Patents*, Harvard Business School Press, 2000.
2   Moore, K.A., "Xenophobia in American Courts", 97 *Northwestern University Law Review* 1497, 2003. See also Allison, Lemley and Schwartz, op. cit. (Chapter 2).
3   Decker, S. and Robertson, D., "Apple told by jury to pay $532.9 million in patent trial", *Bloomberg News*, February 25th 2015.
4   Helmers, C. and McDonagh, L., *Trolls at the High Court?*, LSE Legal Studies Working Paper No. 13, 2012: http://ssrn.com/abstract=2154958; Love, B., Helmers, C. and McDonagh, L., *Is there a Patent troll problem in the UK?*, 2014: http://digitalcommons.law.scu.edu/facpubs/863

13 The market for IP: how IP rights are bought and sold

1   *Facts about Google's Acquisition of Motorola*, Google Inc.: www.google.com
2   Press release, Google Inc., *Lenovo to Acquire Motorola Mobility from Google*, January 29th 2014: www.google.com
3   Press release, ARM, *ARM Announces Participation in a Consortium to Acquire Rights to MIPS Technologies' (MIPS) Portfolio of Patents*, November 6th 2012: www.arm.com

14 Valuing IP

1   *In re Innovatio IP Ventures, LLC Patent Litigation*, MDL 2303, 11-C-9308 (N.D. Illinois, October 3rd 2013) citing Schankerman, M., "How Valuable

is Patent Protection? Estimates By Technology Field", 29 *Rand Journal of Economics* 77, 1998.

15 Using IP to raise finance

1   www.alcatel-lucent.com

As well as the references contained in these notes, further references may be found at www.profilebooks.com/stephen-johnson

Useful resources

There are numerous resources for those wishing to keep up with IP law. The difficulty is that many are aimed at lawyers rather than business people. A generally free service that distributes legal updates provided by law firms to their clients and that can be customised by country and subject matter can be found at www.lexology.com. However, as noted in the Preface, the legal implications of a particular situation depend on the specific facts and a lawyer should always be consulted.

Blogs

There are many blogs devoted to IP, including the following which the author finds informative:

Essential Patent Blog (www.essentialpatentblog.com). Focuses on FRAND and standard essential patents.

Foss Patents (www.fosspatents.com). Informative and entertaining, giving the personal views of the author, Florian Mueller. It is apparently winding down but over the past few years has been a prominent source of news and analysis on the phone wars.

Intellectual Asset Management (www.iam-magazine.com/blog). See below.

IP Finance (http://ipfinance.blogspot.com). "Where money issues meet IP rights."

The IPKat (http://ipkitten.blogspot.com). Informative and entertaining, it manages to combine humour with IP and the academic with the practical.

IPWatchdog (www.ipwatchdog.com). Mainly US patent law.

PATENTLY-O (http://patentlyo.com). Mainly US patent law.

PharmaPatents (www.pharmapatentsblog.com). Pharmaceutical and biotechnology patent isses.

Newsletters and magazines

IP Law 360 subscription service (www.law360.com) provides a daily e-mail newsletter on breaking IP developments, usually with a link to applicable court documents, as well as analysis of legal issues.

Intellectual Asset Management (IAM) magazine focuses on commercialisation, management and monetisation of IP, with useful articles on such topics as brands, patent strategy, IP valuation, the IP marketplace and IP as collateral.

Les Nouvelles is the journal of the Licensing Executives Society and addresses licensing, valuation and other issues.

National and international IP offices

These have much useful information on their websites. The UK and EU trademark and design offices and the US Copyright Office are particularly good for non-lawyers; the US and EU patent offices are more technical.

UK Intellectual Property Office (www.gov.uk/government/ organisations/intellectual-property-office)

EU Office for Harmonization in the Internal Market (https:// oami. europa.eu/ohimportal/en)

European Patent Office (www.epo.org)

US Patent and Trademark Office (www.uspto.gov)

US Copyright Office (www.copyright.gov) provides much information on US copyright law:
- *Copyright Basics*, 2012, available at www.copyright.gov/circs/ circ01.pdf
- *Compendium of US Copyright Office Practices* (3rd edition, 2014) available at http://copyright.gov/comp3/

STOPfakes (www.stopfakes.gov) is a US government website that provides information to businesses suffering piracy.

ROMARIN (International Trademark Information Database), World Intellectual Property Organisation (www.wipo.int/madrid/en/romarin) is a database of trademarks.

The International Trademark Association is a private association of trademark owners and professionals, but it provides useful information on trademarks under "Global Trademark Resources" in the public section of its website (www.inta.org – subject to terms and conditions).

Copyright duration

The duration of copyright protection for a work depends on the nature of the author, the country in question, the type of work, whether it has been published or not, and if so, the date of first publication. It is therefore highly specific to each work. The following websites provide some useful information:

US law:
- www.copyright.gov/circs/circ15a.pdf
- https://copyright.cornell.edu

UK law:
- www.gov.uk/copyright/how-long-copyright-lasts
- www.nationalarchives.gov.uk/documents/informationmanagement/copyright-related-rights.pdf

Statutes

US patent law: *Laws, Regulations, Policies & Procedures*, US Patent and Trademark Office (www.uspto.gov/patents/law)

US trademark law: *US Trademark Law: Rules of Practice and Federal Statutes*, US Patent and Trademark Office, 2014 (www.uspto.gov/trademarks/law/tmlaw.pdf)

US copyright law: *Copyright Law of the United States*, US Copyright Office (www.copyright.gov/title17)

UK law:
- www.gov.uk/intellectual-property/law-practice
- www.gov.uk/intellectual-property/patents
- www.gov.uk/intellectual-property/trade-marks

- www.gov.uk/intellectual-property/copyright
- www.gov.uk/intellectual-property/designs

EU law:

- www.wipo.int/wipolex/en/profile.jsp?code=EU
- http://europa.eu/legislation_summaries/internal_market/ businesses/intellectual_property/index_en.htm
- http://eur-lex.europa.eu/browse/summaries.html

Books

The seminal treatises on US law, which are regularly updated, are as follows:

Nimmer on Copyright, LexisNexis
Chisum on Patents, LexisNexis
McCarthy on Trademarks, Thomson Reuters
Milgrim on Trade Secrets, LexisNexis

UK books on patents and copyrights:

CIPA *Guide to the Patent Acts*, Sweet & Maxwell, 2014
Copinger and Skone James on Copyright, Sweet & Maxwell, 2013

EU IP law:

Cook, T., *EU Intellectual Property Law*, Oxford University Press, 2010

Index

PublicAffairs is a publishing house founded in 1997. It is a tribute to the standards, values, and flair of three persons who have served as mentors to countless reporters, writers, editors, and book people of all kinds, including me.

I. F. STONE, proprietor of *I. F. Stone's Weekly*, combined a commitment to the First Amendment with entrepreneurial zeal and reporting skill and became one of the great independent journalists in American history. At the age of eighty, Izzy published *The Trial of Socrates*, which was a national bestseller. He wrote the book after he taught himself ancient Greek.

BENJAMIN C. BRADLEE was for nearly thirty years the charismatic editorial leader of *The Washington Post*. It was Ben who gave the *Post* the range and courage to pursue such historic issues as Watergate. He supported his reporters with a tenacity that made them fearless and it is no accident that so many became authors of influential, best-selling books.

ROBERT L. BERNSTEIN, the chief executive of Random House for more than a quarter century, guided one of the nation's premier publishing houses. Bob was personally responsible for many books of political dissent and argument that challenged tyranny around the globe. He is also the founder and longtime chair of Human Rights Watch, one of the most respected human rights organizations in the world.

·   ·   ·

For fifty years, the banner of Public Affairs Press was carried by its owner Morris B. Schnapper, who published Gandhi, Nasser, Toynbee, Truman, and about 1,500 other authors. In 1983, Schnapper was described by *The Washington Post* as "a redoubtable gadfly." His legacy will endure in the books to come.

Peter Osnos, *Founder and Editor-at-Large*